CW01666610

Devil's Guard

Devil's Guard

George Robert Elford

NEW ENGLISH LIBRARY
TIMES MIRROR

First published in the United States of America by Delacorte Press, New York
© 1971 by Robert Elford
First published in 1972 by New English Library

*

FIRST NEL PAPERBACK EDITION MAY 1973
Reprinted May 1973
This new edition February 1978

*

Conditions of Sale: This book is sold subject to the condition that it shall not, by way of trade or otherwise, be lent, re-sold, hired out, or otherwise circulated without the publisher's prior consent in any form of binding or cover other than that in which it is published and without a similar condition including this condition being imposed on the subsequent purchaser.

NEL Books are published by The New English Library Limited from Barnard's Inn, Holborn, London EC1N 2JR. Made and printed in Great Britain by C. Nicholls & Company Ltd.

45003754 1

Publisher's Note

This book is being published to provide the reading public with a new and clearer insight into the mentality and personality of an unregenerate and unrepentant Nazi. It is a story that shows the total dehumanization of men in war and it illustrates the hypocrisies and lengths of degradation to which men are driven in order to defend their actions.

It must be stressed most strongly by the Publishers that the production of this book in no way indicates that they in any part agree with or condone any of the actions or points of view described in it.

To my second family:

Süleiman, Hüsnie,
Ibrahim, Djafer,
Sümer, and my little
Yüksel Yalc̄in,
in
Kamil-Oba
Turkey

South, cruel south,
Dreary nights and days,
Green, rolling green,
Where Death rides on the trails.
You're weary? Carry on!
Until the bitter end,
You are Devil's Guard,
The Battalion of the Damned.

A LEGION MARCHING SONG

Contents

Introduction 11
Foreword 15
1 UNCONDITIONAL SURRENDER 21
2 THE TARNISHED FATHERLAND 55
3 THE BATTALION OF THE DAMNED 67
4 "THE CONVOY MUST GET THROUGH!" 82
5 OPERATION "TRIANGLE" 100
6 HUMANE AND INHUMANE INTERLUDES 112
7 THE MAN-HAO INCIDENT 134
8 RAID INTO CHINA 158
9 THE END OF A GARRISON 177
10 WITH BAYONETS AND ARSENIC 195
11 AMBUSHED 208
12 DIALOGUE WITH AN AGITATOR 232
13 THOSE INNOCENT NONCOMBATANTS 247
14 ACTION AND VENGEANCE 274
15 MOVE QUIETLY – KILL QUICKLY! 298
16 THE LITTLE TRAITORS 311
17 THE RED HIGHWAY (OPERATION "DELUGE") 323
18 THE LAST BATTLE (OPERATION "FIREFLY") 342

Introduction

WORKING in the Far East as a zoologist I met many interesting people and, occasionally, a few truly extraordinary individuals. One of them was the real author of this manuscript: Hans Josef Wagemueller, the one time SS *Partisanjaeger* – guerrilla hunter – who later became an officer of the French Foreign Legion in Indochina, now known as Vietnam. We met in a bar in the capital city of a small Asian nation of which he is now a citizen. He was interested in my anaesthetic rifle equipment, which I was using to immobilize wild animals for scientific research.

"I used to be a hunter myself," he said to me with a smile I will never forget. "I was a *Kopfjaeger* – a 'headhunter' as you would say in English. You hunt elephants, rhinos, tigers. I hunted the most agile of all beasts – man! You see, my adversaries were by no means any less ferocious than their counterparts in the animal world. My game could think, reason, and shoot back. The majority of them were what we now call the Vietcong. They posed as gallant freedom fighters, the redeemers of poor people. We used to call them 'the mechanized hordes of a space-age Genghis Khan.' If there was a spark of truth in the Hitlerian credo about the existence of superior and inferior races, we met the real subhumans in Indochina. They tortured and killed for the sheer pleasure of causing pain and seeing blood. They fought like a pack of rabid rats, and we treated them accordingly. We negotiated with none of them, and accepted no surrender by those who were guilty of the most horrible crimes that man or devil can conceive. We spoke to them in the only language they understood – the machine gun."

The life story of Hans Josef Wagemueller is a long and unbroken record of perpetual fighting. He fought against the partisans in Russia during World War II; he spent over five years in French Indochina, fighting against what he described as "the same enemy wearing a different uniform." When that was over, he moved into a small Asian country to train its token, archaic army in the intricacies of modern warfare and the use of modern weapons. "I have managed to turn a horde of primitive, superstitious, and undisciplined warriors into a crack division of daring soldiers," he stated with pride. "You could incorporate them in any European army without further drilling."

The head of state where he now lives has granted him citizenship. The local university has bestowed upon him the title Honorary Professor of Military Sciences. He is now Hindu by religion and has a local name. At the age of sixty-four, he is still going strong. His day begins with rigorous physical exercises. Target shooting is still his favorite pastime, and his steely blue eyes are still deadly accurate when looking through the gunsight.

When the United States became entangled in the Vietnam conflict, Hans Josef Wagemueller offered his experience to the American High Command in a long letter that remained unanswered.

"I probably made a mistake by having written a somewhat haughty and in a way maybe a bit lecturing letter," he said. "But our own long and unbroken record of victories against the same enemy in the same land was still fresh in my memory, and the unnecessary death of every American soldier, every debacle that could have been avoided, hurt me deeply. I could not think of the Vietnam war in any way except that it was my own war. Those GIs scouted the same jungle trails where we had trekked for many years. Many of them had to die where we survived. Somehow it was an inner compulsion to regard them as comrades-in-arms. And you know what? I am not surprised that young

Americans are tearing up their draft cards and refusing to go to Vietnam. To take young college boys out of their supercivilized surroundings and cast them into the primitive jungles of Asia is nothing but murder. Sheer murder. Only experts, highly skilled and experienced antiguerrilla fighters, can survive in the jungles of Asia. It takes at least a year of constant fighting before a recruit turns into an expert."

After that evening together – which left me shaken and sleepless for the rest of the night – I asked Wagemueller if he would tell me his entire story. He obliged by talking into the microphone of a tape recorder for eighteen consecutive days. I have merely altered some of his technical military phraseology for the sake of better understanding. This is a true document with nothing essentially changed except the names. Wagemueller obliged me to keep his true identity, as well as that of all the others, undisclosed.

"I am requesting this not because of my being a war criminal, I have told you the true story. I can give you my word of honor on it. I still consider myself a German officer and a German officer will keep his word of honor no matter what. But I have an eighty-seven-year-old mother whom I would never expose to endless inquiries by the authorities and by the press. And there are certain people mentioned in my story who are still living in my hometown near the Swiss frontier and who helped many other fugitive German officers to avoid prison and prosecution after the war. I do not know who the other fugitives may have been, but what I do know is that there were close to two thousand comrades in distress who left Germany the way I did in 1945. The escape route was extremely well organized and it is quite possible that some important Nazis used it too.

"Another important consideration is that I should not embarrass certain high officials of my adopted country who have been helping me ever since my arrival here. Besides," he added with a smile, "I was not very popular with the Chinese People's Army – and China is not very far from here."

He wants his share of the author's royalty to go to the widows and orphans of those Americans who fell in Vietnam. "I have all I need for the rest of my life. I want no money, only justice to German officers and soldiers who were correct to the core, yet had to share the disgrace of a few. And I want to show the enemy stripped of its mask of gallantry and heroic myth."

I have refrained from adding any comment of my own. It is up to the reader to form his own judgment, as it is up to history to pass the final mandate upon him, his companions, and their deeds.

GEORGE ROBERT ELFORD

Foreword

I HAVE seen many deadly landscapes, from the Pripet swamps in Russia to the jungles of Vietnam. Unfortunately most of what I saw was seen only through a gunsight, with no time to enjoy the scenery. I was a *Kopfjaeger* – "headhunter", as our comrades of the Wehrmacht used to call us. We were a special task force of the *Waffen* SS – the "fighting SS" – which had nothing to do with concentration camps, deportations, or the extermination of European Jewry. Personally I never believed that the Jews could or ever would become a menace to Germany and I hated no people, not even the enemy. I never believed in German domination of the world but I did believe that Germany needed *Lebensraum*. It was also my conviction that Communism should be destroyed while still in its cradle. If my beliefs should be called "Nazism", then I was indeed a Nazi and I still am.

During the Second World War my task was to frustrate guerrilla attacks and suppress insurgency in our vital rear areas and around communication centers, seldom farther than fifty miles from the front lines. Regardless of age or sex, captured guerrillas were, as a rule, executed. I was never interested in their race or religion and tolerated no outrage against prisoners. My orders were to hang them, but I permitted the brave ones to die a soldier's death, facing the firing squad. During five long years we executed over one thousand guerrillas. If there were Jews among them, we shot them too – but without any religious prejudice.

I have not stayed away from Germany because of my crimes but because I have no desire to behold what they call Germany today – a land of bowing *Jawohl Johanns* who can only repeat "yes, sir" or "*da, tovarich*" in either American or Russian servitude. The present German Army is only a shadowy midget of its former self. The old Wehrmacht needed neither foreign advisers nor protectors. It is a fact that we have lost two offensive wars, fighting alone against the world. But I doubt that the Wehrmacht would have lost a defensive war had the frontiers of the Fatherland been invaded from the outside.

Once our German engineers built the best fighting aircraft in the world, and I believe that we can still build the best if given a chance. Instead we must use Starfighters in which the young German airmen are obliged to fly *kamikaze* missions. About eighty of them have already crashed without having been shot at. Germany is obliged to purchase foreign rubbish; tanks, for instance, many of which are probably inferior to our wartime Tigers and Panthers. Our formidable NATO allies will not permit German industry to produce equipment for the army. Our best brains are siphoned away by foreign countries because our government will not pay them the wages they deserve. Should another war come, Germany will be expected to stand by her allies, who are, nevertheless, still scared of the Teutons, and any proposal for a German rearmament remains anathema for them. Our Western allies have yet to realize that the map of the world has changed. Now the nations of all continents may choose between only two camps. Any thought of neutrality between those two camps is nothing but self-delusion that will crumble under the first serious pressure from the outside.

Fortunately the East German régime fares no better. The Russians, too, would think twice before giving the People's Army any sophisticated weapon. But the *Volksarmee* has an ideology to follow and it certainly does not have draft dodgers.

I spent five years in Indochina, fighting the same enemy that I had fought in Russia, wearing another uniform. I know well the marauders of Ho Chi Minh. We fought them and routed them a hundred times, in the mountains, in the jungles, in the swamps. We beat them at their own game. We never regarded the terrorists as demigods or specters who could not be destroyed. After our years in Russia we could put up with hardship and misery. When we arrived in Indochina we were not beginners. When we moved into Communist-dominated territories, there was soon peace. Sometimes it was the peace of the bayonet, sometimes the peace of a cemetery. But it was peace. Not even a lizard would dare to move. If history records any French victory in Indochina, it was won either by the French paratroops, who were magnificent fighters, or by us Germans.

The war in Indochina was not lost on the battlefield but in Paris. The Americans are losing the same war in Paris – right now. Paris and Geneva . . . the only battlefields where the Western world has suffered debacles, and where the Western world will always lose.

It is, of course, nonsense to say that the American Army cannot defeat the guerrillas in Vietnam by force of arms. After all the American fighting men defeated Japan. The jungles and swamps of Guadalcanal or Okinawa offered no easier going than, for instance, the Mekong delta. Besides, what army in military history was more effective in jungle fighting than the Imperial Japanese Army?

But now American generals are compelled to fight world opinion instead of the Vietcong. History will only repeat itself. At the beginning of the Second World War the German generals were free to plan and conduct their own battles and they won every battle on every front. Then Hitler took command and everything was lost. When General MacArthur was permitted to act to the best of his abilities, the world saw a marvelous landing at Inchon and the North Korean rout. But when he had to obey orders coming from ten thousand miles away, American soldiers had to sacrifice their lives for no gains whatever.

C'est la guerre!

HANS JOSEF WAGEMUELLER

Devil's Guard

1

Unconditional Surrender

THE news of the German capitulation reached us by radio deep in the Czechoslovakian mountains, east of Liberec. We had been up there for almost a month, holding an important pass, waiting for the Russians to come. But as the days went by, nothing disturbed our positions and even the local partisans refrained from engaging us in a major skirmish. Unusual stillness blanketed the peaks and the valleys – the sort of sullen tranquility that, instead of relaxing the mind, only charges it with tension. Strange as it may be, after five years of war and hundreds of engagements with the enemy, both regulars and insurgents, we were in no condition to bear the quiet of peace. Of all the natural human functions which we had once possessed we seemed to have retained only those that were important for our immediate survival: to eat, to sleep, to watch the woods – and to pull the trigger.

None of us doubted that the end was near. Berlin had fallen and Hitler was dead. Military communications had long since broken down, but we could still listen to the foreign broadcasts, including those of the victorious Allies. And we knew that our saga would not end with the capitulation of the Wehrmacht; that there would be no going home for the tired warriors of the vanquished army. We would not be demobilized, but outlawed. The Allies had not fought only to win a military victory. Their man objective was revenge.

The last dispatch which we had received from Prague eight days before had ordered us to hold our positions until further orders – orders that never came. Small groups of haggard German soldiers came instead. Unshaven and hollow-eyed troops who had once belonged to every imaginable service in the Wehrmacht – the SS, the *Luftwaffe*, and the SD (Security Service). Among them were the surviving members of a decimated motorized infantry brigade, a *Luftwaffe* service group, a *Panzer* squadron left with only two serviceable tanks; there were also five trucks of a one-time supply battalion and a platoon of field gendarmery. The remnants of an *Alpenjaeger* battalion had survived the retreat all the way from the Caucasus to end up with us, near Liberec. We were all waiting for a last sensible order, the order to evacuate Czechoslovakia and return into Germany. The order to cease hostilities came instead.

For us, deep in hostile territory, the news of the armistice sounded like a sentence of death. We had no one to surrender to except the Czech guerrillas or the militia, neither of which recognized military conventions or honor. Up to the very end we expected to be ordered back to Germany before the weapons were laid down. We could expect no quarter from the partisans – we had killed too many of them. As a matter of fact we could expect no prisoner-of-war treatment from the Red Army either. The truck drivers of the supply battalion might be pardoned but not the *Waffen* SS, the archenemy. In a sense we felt betrayed. Had we know in advance that we were to be abandoned to our fate, we would have withdrawn despite our orders to stay. We had taken more than a soldier's share of the war and no one could have accused us of cowardice.

For five long years we had given up everything: our homes, our families, our work, our future. We thought of nothing but the Fatherland. Now the Fatherland was nothing but a cemetery. It was time to think of our own future and whether our beloved ones had survived the holocaust wrought by the Superfortresses during the last two years of the war.

Our headquarters had ordered us: "Stay where you are and hold the pass." Then our headquarters returned to Germany. Like the Roman sentry who had stood his guard while Vesuvius buried Pompeii, we too remained soldiers to the bitter end.

We had survived the greatest war in history, but if were to survive peace, the most bloodthirsty peace in history, we had to reach the American lines two hundred miles away. Not because we thought much of American chivalry but at least Americans were Anglo-Saxons, civilized and Christian in their own way. Around us in the valley were only the Mongolian hordes, the Tartars of a mechanized Genghis Khan – Stalin. I had the notion that it was only a choice between being clubbed to death by cavemen or submitting to a more civilized way of execution.

To reach Bavaria and the American lines we had to cross the Soviet-controlled Elbe. We were still confident of our own strength. We had survived more hell than could possibly wait for us on the way home. German soldiers do not succumb easily. We could be defeated but never crushed.

All day long Captain Ruell of the artillery had been trying to reach the headquarters of Field Marshal Schoerner. No one acknowledged his signals but finally he did manage to contact General Headquarters at Flensburg. I was standing close to him and saw his face turn ashen. When he lowered his earphones he was shaking in every limb and could barely form his words as he spoke: "It's the end. . . . The Wehrmacht is surrendering on all fronts. . . . Keitel has already signed the armistice. . . . Unconditional surrender." He wiped his face and accepted the cigarette which I lighted for him. "The Fatherland is finished," he muttered, staring into the distant valley with vacant eyes. "What now?"

Suddenly it dawned on us why the Russians had refrained from forcing the pass. The Soviet commander had known that the war was about to end, and he did not feel like sacrificing his troops only minutes before twelve o'clock. But he was aware of our presence in the neighborhood. Within six hours after the official announcement of the German capitulation, Soviet PO-2s appeared overhead. Circling our positions the planes dropped a multitude of leaflets announcing the armistice. We were requested to lay down our weapons and descend into the valley under a flag of truce. "German officers and soldiers," the leaflets read, "if you obey the instructions of the Red Army commander you shall be well treated, you will receive food and medical care due to prisoners of war, according to the articles of the Geneva Convention. Destruction of war material and equipment is strictly prohibited. The local German Commander shall be responsible for the orderly surrender of his troops."

Had our plight not been so bitterly serious we could have sneered at the Russians quoting the Geneva Convention, something the Kremlin had neither signed nor acknowledged. The Red Army could indeed promise us anything under the articles of the Convention; it was not bound by its clauses.

The following morning our sentries spotted a Soviet scout car as it labored uphill on the winding road to our positions. From its mudguard fluttered a large white flag of truce. I ordered my troopers to hold their fire, and called a platoon for lineup. Everyone was shaved and properly dressed. I wanted to receive the Soviet officers with due respect. I was astonished to see the car stop three hundred yards short of our first roadblock, and, instead of sending forward parliamentaries, the enemy began to deliver a message through loudspeakers.

"Officers and soldiers of the German Wehrmacht. . . . The Soviet High Command knows that there are Nazi fanatics and war criminals among you who might try to prevent your accepting the terms of armistice and consequently your return home. Disarm the SS and SD criminals and hand them over to the Soviet authority. Officers and soldiers of the Wehrmacht. . . . Disarm the SS and SD criminals. You will be generously rewarded and allowed to return home to your families."

"The filthy liars!" *Untersturmführer* Eisner sneered, watching the Russian group through his binoculars. "They will be allowed to return home! That is a good joke."

It was amusing to note how little the enemy knew the German soldier. After having fought us for so many years, the Soviet High Command should have known better. Cowardice or treason was never the trade of the German soldier. Nor was naïveté. They had called us "Fascist criminals" or "Nazi dogs" ever since "Operation Barbarossa." In the past they had made no distinction between the various services. Wehrmacht, SS, or *Luftwaffe* had always been the same to Stalin, yet now he was endeavoring to turn the Wehrmacht against the SS and vice versa.

The loudspeakers blared again. Eisner pulled himself to attention. "*Herr Obersturmführer*, I request permission to open warning fire."

"No! Nothing of the sort, gentlemen," Colonel Steinmetz, the commanding officer of the small motorized infantry group protested. "We shouldn't fire at parliamentaries."

"Parliamentaries, *Herr Oberst?*" Eisner exclaimed with a bitter smile. "They are sheltering behind the flag of truce to deliver Communist propaganda."

"Even so," the colonel insisted. "We may request them to withdraw but we should not open fire."

Being an officer of the Wehrmacht, Colonel Steinmetz had no authority over the SS. He was, however, a meticulously pedantic officer and much our senior both in rank and age. I did not feel like entering into futile arguments, especially in front of the ranks. Trying to avoid the slightest offensive quality in my voice I reminded him that I was in charge of the pass and all the troops therein. Even so the colonel stiffened at my remark and said, "I am aware of your command, *Herr Obersturmführer*, and I hope you will handle the situation with the responsibility of a commander."

The Russian loudspeakers kept blaring. Eisner shrugged and began to observe the enemy again. I exchanged glances with Erich Schulze and saw defiance in his eyes. Both men had been my comrades for many years. Bernard Eisner had been my right hand since 1942. He was a cool and hard fighter. Having been well-to-do landowners, Eisner's father and elder brother had been beaten to death by a Communist mob during the short-lived "proletarian revolution" after the First World War. It was Bernard's conviction that no Communist on earth should be left alive. Schulze, who had joined my battalion in 1943, was rather hotheaded but always polite and considerate.

A few steps from where we stood two young troopers sat behind a heavy machine gun, which they kept trained on the Soviet scout car. Their faces were tense but lacking emotion, as though they were statues or a part of the gun. Both were young, only nineteen years old. Drafted in 1944 they had not experienced the real trials of the war.

I asked for a loudspeaker and addressed the Russians:

"This is the German commander speaking. We have not

received an official confirmation of the armistice and we will hold our positions until such confirmation can be obtained. I request the Soviet commander to furnish an authentic document related to the question of armistice. I also request that, in the meantime, the Soviet propaganda unit refrain from using the flag of truce for communicating subversive propaganda. I request that the Soviet propaganda unit withdraw from our positions within five minutes. After five minutes I shall no longer consider them immune to hostilities."

"German officers and soldiers. . . . Disarm the SS and SD criminals and hand them over to the Soviet authority. You shall be generously rewarded and allowed to return home."

"I request that the Soviet propaganda unit refrain from using the flag of truce for communicating subversive propaganda," I repeated. There was a pause; then the loudspeakers blared once more. "German officers and soldiers. . . . Disarm the SS and SD criminals. . . ."

I ordered, "Fire!"

The scout car burst into flames, then exploded. When the smoke and dust settled we saw two Red Army men scurrying down the road. "That should fix them for the time being," Eisner remarked, lighting a cigarette. "Bullets are the only language they understand."

An hour later a squadron of Stormoviks dived out of the clouds with the intention of strafing and bombing our positions. To reach us, however, the planes had to come in level between a cluster of high cliffs, then drop sharply over the small plateau which we occupied. The Russian pilots flew well, but they had bad luck. I had deployed eight 88s and ten heavy MGs to cover that narrow corridor and our gunners were experienced men. Within a few minutes five of the planes had been shot down. Trailing smoke two more had escaped toward the valley and a third one had banked straight into a three-hundred-foot rock and exploded, fuel, bombs, ammunition and all. At that point the four remaining planes had given up and departed without having fired a shot. We spotted two Soviet pilots parachuting downward. One of them hit a cliff, slipped his chute, and tumbled to his death at the bottom of a ravine. The other one, a young lieutenant, landed right on one of our trucks. He was made prisoner.

"*Zdrastvuite, tovarich!*" Captain Ruell, who spoke impeccable Russian, greeted our astonished visitor.

My men searched the pilot. I looked into his identification book but handed it back to him. And when Schulze gave me the officer's Tokarev automatic, I only removed the bullets and returned his gun as well. He was so surprised at my unexpected behavior that his chin dropped. He tried to smile but he could not. He only managed to draw his lips in a paralytic grin.

"The war is over," he muttered. "No more shooting," he added after a moment, imitating the sound of a submachine gun. "No tatatata." His face showed so much terror that we could not help smiling. He must have been told that Germans were maneaters.

"No more tatatata, eh?" Erich Schulze chuckled, mocking the Russian.

The pilot nodded quickly. "*Da, da.* . . . No more war."

Schulze poked him in the belly. "No more war but a minute before you wanted to bomb the daylight out of us here."

"*Ja, ja,*" the Russian repeated, his eyes glued to Schulze's SS lapel.

Erich poked him gently again, and the Russian paled.

"Leave him alone," Captain Ruell interposed. "You are scaring the shit out of him."

"Sure," Eisner added, "and we don't have many extra pants up here, Erich."

The captain spoke to the pilot briefly and his presence seemed to lessen the Russian's fear. "Don't let the SS shoot me, officer," he pleaded. "I have been flying for only eight months, and I want to go home to Mother."

"We have been fighting for five years. Imagine how much we would like to return home," Captain Ruell replied with a bitter smile.

"Don't let the SS shoot me. . . ."

"The SS won't shoot you."

Schulze offered the Russian a cigarette. "Here, smoke! It will do you good."

"Thanks." The pilot grinned, taking the cigarette with shaking fingers.

Erich opened his canteen, gulped some rum, then wiped the

canteen on his sleeve and offered it to the pilot. "Here, *tovarich.* . . . Drink good SS vodka."

Realizing that his life was not in danger the Russian relaxed. "Our commander says that you don't want to surrender," he said, shifting his eyes from face to face as though seeking our approval for what he was saying. "You must surrender. . . . There are two divisions in the valley; forty tanks and heavy artillery are expected to come in a day or two."

"*Tovarich*, you have already told us enough for a court-martial," Schulze exclaimed, slapping the pilot on the back.

"You shouldn't tell the enemy what you have or don't have," Captain Ruell interpreted for him.

"I only said that heavy artillery is on the way."

"Who cares?" Eisner shrugged. "There is a mountain between your artillery and us."

"The mountain will not help you." The Russian shook his head. He turned and pointed toward a ridge five miles to the southeast. "The artillery is going up there."

"Nonsense!" I said. "There is no road."

"There is a road," Captain Ruell interposed, "right up to hill Five-O-Six. We had four Bofors there in early March."

Looking at the map I realized that Captain Ruell was right and what the Russian pilot was saying had a ring of truth. Should the Soviet commander mount some heavy artillery on that hill, he could indeed shell our plateau by direct fire.

We gave the Russian a hearty meal and allowed him to leave. He was immensely happy and promised to do everything for us should we meet again after surrendering. "Food, vodka, cigarettes, *Kamerad.* My name is Fjodr Andrejevich. I will tell our commander that you are good soldiers and should be well treated."

"Sure you will," Eisner growled, watching the Russian leave. "You just tell your commander and you will be shot before the sun is down as a bloody Fascist yourself."

The pilot walked away slowly, turning back every now and then as though still expecting a bullet in the back. Having passed our last roadblock it must have occurred to him that he was still alive and unhurt, and he began to race downhill as I had never seen a man run. Eisner was not very enthusiastic about the Russian's departure.

"He saw everything we have up here," he remarked with barely concealed disapproval in his voice.

"We had no choice but to let him go," Colonel Steinmetz challenged him sharply. "The war is over, *Herr Untersturmführer.*"

"Not for me, *Herr Oberst,*" Eisner replied quietly. "For me the war will be over when I greet my wife and two sons for the first time since August 1943, and it isn't over for the Russian either. He came here flying not the white flag but a fighter bomber."

"I haven't seen my family since June, 1943," the colonel remarked.

I drew Eisner aside. "You should not worry about the Ivan," I told him with an air of confidence. "What can he tell? That we have men, weapons, tanks, and artillery? The more he tells the less eager they will be to come up here." I put an arm around his shoulder. "Bernard, we've killed so many Russians. We can surely afford to let one individual go."

He grinned. "I have read somewhere what the American settlers used to say about the Indians, Hans. The only good Indian is a dead Indian. I think that is also true of the Bolsheviks."

"Maybe the pilot was not a Bolshevik?"

"Maybe he wasn't – yet. But if you ask me, Hans, I can tell you that anyone who is working for Stalin is game for me." He lit a cigarette, offered me one, then went on. "I know that we are defeated and that there will be no Fatherland to speak of for a long time to come. For all we know the Allies might break up the Reich into fifty little principalities, just as it was five hundred years ago. We scare them stiff, even without weapons, even in defeat. But I cannot suffer the thought of having been defeated by a rotten, primitive, lice-ridden Communist mob. I know that no conqueror in history was ever soft on the conquered enemy. We might survive the American and the British but never the Soviet. Stalin won't be satisfied with what he may loot now. He will not only take his booty, but he will try to take our very souls, our thoughts, our national identity. I know them. I've been their prisoner. It was for only five days but even then they tried to turn me into a bloody traitor. The Russians are mind snatchers,

Hans. They will not only rape our women, they will also turn them into Communists afterwards. Stalin knows how to do it and now he will have all the time on earth. He is going to increase the pressure inch by inch. I could gun down anyone who is helping Stalin."

"You would have quite a few people to gun down, Bernard. Starting with the British and finishing with the Americans. They have not only helped Stalin, but also brought him back from his deathbed and made him a giant."

"Stalin will be most obliged to his bourgeois allies," Eisner sneered. "Just wait and see how Stalin will pay for the American convoys. Give him a couple of years. Mister Churchill and Mister Truman are going to enjoy a few sleepless nights for Mister Roosevelt's folly."

"That won't help us much now, Bernard!"

"I guess not," he agreed. After a brief pause he added, "If you decide to surrender, Hans, just let me have a gun and a couple of grenades. I will find my way home."

"You won't be alone." I gave him a reassuring tap. "I don't feel like hanging in the main square of Liberec, either."

"I don't feel like submitting myself to what comes between the surrender and the hanging," he added with a sarcastic chuckle.

Early in the afternoon the PO-2s returned, but we did not fire on the flimsy canvas planes which carried no weapons. The Russians had sent us another load of leaflets, among them newspaper cuttings announcing the armistice, and photocopies of the protocol bearing the signature of General Field Marshal Keitel. Again we were requested to lay down our weapons and evacuate into the valley under the flag of truce.

"This is it!" Colonel Steinmetz spoke quietly as he crumpled the Soviet leaflet between his fingers. "This is it!" And as though providing an example, he unbuckled the belt which supported his holster, swung it once, and tossed the belt on a flat slab of stone. I expected nothing else from Colonel Steinmetz. He was a meticulously correct officer, a cavalier of the old school who would always keep to the letter of the service code. He could see no other solution but to comply with that last order of the German High Command, or what was left of it. Moving like automatons, his three hundred officers and men began to file past our sullen group, the troops casting their rifles and sidearms onto the mounting pile. But the artillery, the small *Panzer* detachment, and the *Alpenjaegers* kept their weapons, and, with a skill born of habit, the SS took over the vacated positions.

"I am sorry," Colonel Steinmetz said quietly, and I noticed that his eyes were filled. "I cannot do anything else."

"There is no longer a high command, *Herr Oberst*, and the Fuehrer is dead. You are no longer bound by your oath of allegiance," I reminded him.

He smiled tiredly. "If we wanted to disobey orders we should have done it a long time ago," he said. "Right after Stalingrad. And not on the front but in Berlin."

"You mean a successful twentieth of July, *Herr Oberst*?"

"No," he shook his head. "I think what Stauffenberg did was the gravest act of cowardice. If he was so sure of doing the right thing, he should have stood up, pulled his gun, shot Hitler, and taken the consequences. But I don't believe in murdering superior officers. The Fuehrer should have been declared unfit to lead the nation and removed. Had Rommel or Guderian taken command of the Reich, we might have won – if not the war, at least an honorable peace."

"It is either too late or still too early to discuss the Fuehrer's leadership, don't you think, Colonel Steinmetz?"

"You are right. Now all we can do is hoist the white flag."

"We have no white flags, *Herr Oberst*," Captain Ruell remarked with sarcasm. "White flags were never standard equipment in the Wehrmacht."

The colonel nodded understandingly. "I know it is painful, *Herr Hauptmann*, but if we refuse to surrender, the Russians may treat us like we treated their guerrillas."

"Are you expecting anything else from the Soviet, *Herr Oberst*?" Eisner asked.

"The war is over. There is no reason for more brutalities," said the colonel. He turned toward me. "What do you intend to do?"

I suggested that we should try to reach Bavaria, two hundred miles away, but the colonel only smiled at my idea. "By now, the Russian divisions are probably streaming toward the line of demarcation," he said. "All the roads and bridges will be occupied by the Russians and precisely opposite the American lines you will find most of their troops. Stalin does not trust either Churchill or Truman. He has exterminated his own general staff. Do you think he would trust Eisenhower or Montgomery? The days of 'our heroic Western Allies' are over for Stalin. In a few weeks' time the Western Allies will be called bourgeois, decadent, imperialist, and Stalin will deploy a million troops on the western frontiers of his conquest. Besides," he added after a pause, "you should not expect much from the Americans, *Herr Obersturmführer*. I have heard many of their broadcasts."

"So have we," Eisner remarked.

"Then you should know about their intentions. A prisoner is always a prisoner. The conqueror is always right and the vanquished is always wrong!"

"We have no intention of surrendering, *Herr Oberst*, neither here nor in Bavaria," I said softly.

"Are you planning to go on fighting?"

"If necessary . . . and until we arrive at some safe place."

"Where, for instance?"

"Spain, South America . . . the devil knows."

"You should not count on Franco. Franco is all alone now and they might put pressure on him soon. With Hitler and Mussolini dead, Stalin will never tolerate the existence of Franco, the last strong leader in western Europe. Stalin knows that he will be able to push around everyone but Franco. He will regard Spain as a potential birthplace, or rather a place of resurrection, for the Nazi phoenix. And to reach South America you will need good papers and plenty of money. But, to speak of more immediate problems, do you have enough food to reach Bavaria? I know you have enough weapons but your trip might take two months over the mountains, and I presume that is the way you intend to go. Man cannot live on bullets."

"We have enough food for two weeks. One can always find something to eat. It is getting on to summer now," I said. "There are villages and farms even in the mountains."

He shook his head disapprovingly. "Are you planning to raid the farms and villages? Will you shoot people if they refuse to accommodate you?"

"If it is a matter of survival, Colonel Steinmetz . . ." Eisner said before I could answer. He left the sentence unfinished for a moment, then added, "Have you ever seen a humane war?"

"It will no longer be an act of war but common banditry," the colonel stated frankly. "Of course you still have the power to do it but you won't be able to do it in silence. The Czechs will know about you. The Russians will know about you and your destination. The news of your coming might reach Bavaria before you do."

"And we might have an American reception committee waiting for us at the frontier. This is what you wanted to say, *Herr Oberst*?" I interposed.

"Precisely!" said he. "And if up till now you haven't committed something the Allies may call a war crime, you had better not furnish them with any evidence now!"

"*Herr Oberst*," I spoke to him softly but firmly, "if we do reach Bavaria, nothing will stop us from getting farther. Neither the Americans, nor the devil himself. We have given up many things a man would never willingly part with, and we are ready to give up more, even our lives. But not our right to return home. On that single item we will never compromise."

"I wish I was as young as you are," Colonel Steinmetz spoke resignedly. "But I am tired, *Herr Obersturmführer* . . . so very tired."

Despite the old soldier's pessimism I felt that somehow we had a fair chance of getting through, saving at least our bare lives. The prospect of being hanged by the guerrillas, or at best carted off to a Siberian death camp, did not appeal to me at all. The colonel might survive. He might even return home one day. The SS could entertain no illusions about the future. No Soviet commander would lift a finger to protect us. Should their Czech allies decide to get even with us, the Russians would quickly forget about their Geneva Convention pledge for humane treatment. For seven years the Czechs had been waiting for this day, and I could not blame them either. In 1944 alone we had killed over three thousand of their guerrillas.

"We should travel high up in the mountains, avoiding contact with the enemy. We have excellent maps of the areas involved, and if necessary we can fight our way through a Soviet brigade."

"With a few hundred men?" the colonel asked sceptically.

"We have at least a hundred light machine guns, Colonel Steinmetz," Eisner interposed. "We can put out so much fire that the Ivans will think a division is coming."

"For how long?"

"Hell, we can play hide-and-seek in the woods until the Day of Judgment, *Herr Oberst*!" Schulze exulted. "We should at least try! To surrender here is sheer suicide. What have we got to lose? One may commit suicide at any time."

Bernard Eisner and Captain Ruell were of the same opinion.

"We have mountains and woods all the way to Bavaria," Ruell said. "I am quite sure that every one of us has been through similar trips a dozen times in the past."

The colonel shook his head slowly. "Hiding in the forest? Sneaking in the night like a pack of wolves . . . stealing or robbing food at gunpoint, shooting people if they resist? No, gentlemen, I have been a soldier all my life and I shall finish it all like a soldier, obeying the orders of those who are entitled to give them."

"The Soviet commander down in the valley, for instance?" Eisner remarked bitterly. The colonel frowned. "I am talking of General Field Marshal Keitel and Grand Admiral Doenitz," he said.

"Keitel and Doenitz have no idea what a *dreck* we are in, *Herr Oberst*."

"I guess not," he agreed. "They have eighty million other Germans to worry about now. We are only a few hundred. We are not so important, gentlemen. We are neither heroes nor martyrs. We are only a part of the statistics. The death of a single individual may be very sad. When a hundred die they call it a tragedy, but when ten million perish, it is only statistics. I still believe in discipline, even in defeat. And we are defeated."

"The only trouble is that I still cannot feel that I am licked," Schulze remarked with a grin, tapping the stock of his machine gun. "Not while I still have this thing. But I would like to see the Ivan who comes to tell me all about it."

"Shut up, Erich!" I snapped curtly and he froze with a brisk "*Jawohl*." "This isn't the right time for wisecracking!"

I turned to the colonel. "*Herr Oberst*, I am convinced that you will have a better chance if you surrender to the Americans."

"I have already advised you not to expect too much from the Americans, *Herr Obersturmführer*. All that is going to happen from now on was agreed upon by the victors a long time ago. But I concede," he added with a smile, "that an American jail might be somewhat more civilized than those of Stalin's. Stalin would kill a million Germans cheerfully. The Americans will meticulously prove that they are doing the just and legal thing. On doomsday morning they will give you a nice breakfast, a shave, a bath, and should it be your last wish, they might give you a perfumed pink rope to hang on. But the end will be the same."

I spoke to the rest of the troopers, telling the men frankly that Colonel Steinmetz's decision was the only correct one, as far as the military code goes. But the German Army had ceased to exist and therefore I no longer considered them my subordinates but only my comrades in peril who had the right to speak for themselves. As for myself, I stated, I would leave for Bavaria!

The artillery platoons, the *Panzer* crew, the *Alpenjaegers* decided to follow the SS rather than surrender. "You might be a bunch of sons of bitches," Captain Ruell said smiling, "but you seldom fail. I am with you!" The motorized infantry and the supply group were for Colonel Steinmetz.

The colonel shook hands with us and I saw anguish in his face as he spoke in a choked voice. "I can understand you. It is going to be hard on the SS. The victors have already decided that you are nothing but killers, including your truck drivers and mess cooks. I wish you a safe arrival, but be prudent and do not make it harder on yourself than it already is, *Herr Obersturmführer*."

With a gently ironic smile he handed me his golden cigarette case, his watch, and a letter. "Take care of these for me," he asked quietly. "Give them to my wife – if she is still alive and if you can ever find her."

"I will do it, *Herr Oberst*."

His officers and the men followed the colonel's example and began to distribute their valuables among those who were to stay. "The Ivans would take everything anyway," some of them remarked with a shrug. In exchange we gave them our spare shirts and underwear, some food, cigarettes, and most of our medical supplies. Then Colonel Steinmetz assembled his troops. We saluted each other and they departed.

We could hear them for a long time as they marched down the winding road singing: the colonel, six officers, and NCOs under an improvised flag of truce, a bedsheet. Behind them two hundred and seventy men. Beaten but not broken. The men were singing.

Two miles down the road, around a lonely farmhouse at watch were the Russians and a battalion of militia with six tanks and a dozen howitzers. In the valley near the village we could observe more Red Army troops.

The beloved old tunes began to fade in the distant valley where the road turned into the woods as it followed the course of a small creek. The singing was abruptly drowned in the sharp staccato of a dozen machine guns. Explosions in rapid succession shook the cliffs, echoing and reechoing between the peaks, and we saw fire and smoke rising beyond the bend. It lasted for less than five minutes. The howitzers and machine guns fell silent. We heard the sporadic reports of rifles, then everything was still.

Standing on a boulder, overlooking the valley, Captain Ruell lowered his field glasses and slowly raised his hand for a salute. Tears were flowing freely from his eyes down his cheeks and onto his Iron Cross. I saw Schulze bowing his head, covering his face in his hands. Only Eisner stood erect, staring into the valley, his face like that of a bronze statue. My own vision blurred. My stomach knotted. I turned toward my men wanting to say something but my words would not form. I felt an attack of nausea. But Eisner spoke for me.

"There is the Soviet truce for you, men. I know easier ways to commit harakiri!"

Three PO-2s rose from the fields and came droning over the hills. We dispersed, taking cover, and resolved not to reveal ourselves no matter what the enemy might do. Flying a slow merry-go-round, the flimsy planes began to circle the pass and came in low over the trees. Working the dials of our wireless, Captain Ruell quickly tuned in on the Russian wavelength. He translated for us the amusing conversation between the squadron leader and a command post somewhere in the valley.

"Igor, Igor . . . Here's Znamia . . . *ponemaies*? There are no more Germans up here," the pilot reported. "You got them all!"

"Znamia, Znamia! None of the ones here belonged to the SS. We examined all the bodies. Fjodr Andrejevich says the SS

Commander and his two officers are not among the dead! Znamia Znamia! . . . Take another look!"

Fjodr Andrejevich, the Russian pilot whom we permitted to leave. Cigarettes, food, vodka. Eisner must have read my thoughts, for he remarked quietly. "What did I tell you, Hans?"

"The positions are empty!" the pilot reported. "I can see the gun emplacements and two tanks. Znamia, Znamia! If there were more troops here they must have withdrawn into the woods."

"Igor! Igor! Try to locate them. . . . *Ponemaies*?"

Fifteen minutes later the PO-2s left and soon afterwards we spotted Soviet infantry moving up the road, two companies with three tanks to lead the way. Their progress was slow, for a dozen yards ahead of the tanks a group of demolition men moved on foot searching for mines. We allowed them to proceed up to the fifth bend below the pass where the road narrowed to traverse a small bridge between the rising cliffs. The demolition squad spent over an hour looking for mines or hidden electric wires around the place but neither the bridge nor the road around it had been mined. Our engineers had had a better idea. They had enlarged a natural cave on the precipitous slope and stuffed nearly two tons of high explosives in the crevasse.

Observing the enemy through his binoculars, Bernard Eisner slowly raised his hand. A few yards from where he stood a young trooper sat, his hand gripping the plunger of the electric detonator, his eyes fixed on Eisner's hand. From down below came coarse Russian yells. The leading tank lurched forward. The enemy was moving across the bridge.

Eisner's hand came down.

"*Los!*"

There was an instant of total silence, as though the charge had misfired, then earth began to rumble. The rocks seemed to rise; stone and wood exploded from a billowing mass of flames and grey smoke. The tanks stopped. The infantry scattered, taking shelter – or what they thought was shelter. High above the road a cluster of cliffs tilted, hung at a crazy angle for a second, then began to tumble down. A cascade of earth, stone, and shredded pine roared from above to carry tanks, cars, and troops into the abyss below. One car and some fifty Red Army men escaped the landslide and now clung to a short stretch of road that had turned into a flat, coverless platform, a jutting precipice with no way to escape except by parachutes. We waited until the smoke and the dust settled, then opened up on the survivors with two 88s. Direct fire with fragmentation shells, at three hundred yards. Only eight shells were fired. There were no survivors.

"I guess this is the end of World War Two," Erich Schulze remarked when our guns fell silent.

"Sure!" said Eisner pointing toward the debris down below. "Down there are the first casualties of World War Three!"

We stripped off our rank badges, army insignias and emblems; tore up our identity papers and pay books; burned everything including our letters from home. The Panther tanks and the guns went over the precipice. They were faithful companions and they had served us well. None of them should fall into enemy hands.

Ammunition for the rifles, machine guns, and submachine guns had been distributed equally among the men. We had more than enough bullets and grenades. Each man could carry five spare mags and a hundred loose bullets along with six grenades. Our supply of cheese, bacon, margarine, and other food stores had been likewise distributed. Water was no problem. There were plenty of creeks and streams in the mountains.

We were about three miles away when the Stormoviks came buzzing over the plateau. This time they could fly the corridor unpunished. The planes bombed and gunned our vacant positions for an hour without a break. When some of them departed, others came, and their uncontested attack was delivered with true Communist zeal and determination. The action would surely be remembered by Soviet war historians as a great Russian victory.

Seven weeks of hard trekking followed. We kept in the mountains, moving mainly at night, resting in remote ravines or in caves when we came upon some large enough to accommodate us. Only in the caves could we light small fires to boil coffee or to warm up our canned meat and vegetables. There was no need to warn the men about eating sparingly. Our self-imposed ration was one meal per day.

Every day we spotted swarms of PO-2s as they flew reconnaissance over the woods, sometimes passing overhead at treetop level. Fortunately we could always hear them coming from miles away and had time to scatter and camouflage. We strapped green twigs around ourselves and onto our helmets and we looked more like moving bushes than men. When a trooper froze, no one could spot him from twenty yards.

After about a week the planes stopped worrying us. The Russians had given up the futile idea of detecting us from the air. Instead they endeavored to block every bridge and every pass in our way, compelling us to choose the most impossible trails for our grueling journey. When we could cover five miles in one night, we considered it good going. It was a trying cat-and-mouse game. Death was away only in time but never in measurable distance.

The enemy had never really known where we were and with the element of surprise preserved, we were strong enough to challenge a battalion of Russians. We could have pierced their roadblocks but the action would have given away our presence in a specific area and also our direction. By avoiding contact we kept the Russian commander in suspense. He could only guess which part of the map we were heading for. We wanted to preserve the element of surprise for the most perilous part of our trip: the crossing of the Elbe. Therefore I decided to bypass the enemy roadblocks and stick to the paths of the mountain goats. Erich Schulze, who was born and had grown up in the Alps, and some Austrian Alpine Rangers were of immense help to us.

In a small clearing, not very far from our trail, we came upon a dilapidated hunting lodge. Eisner spotted two Red Army trucks parked under the trees – a most unwelcome sight. A pair of GMCs could transport eighty men, and there was no way of bypassing the place except by making a twenty-mile detour. I decided to wait and see whether it was only a coincidence or a trap in the making. Then suddenly we heard the thud of axes and trees falling. The enemy was only cutting wood!

We wanted to lie low until the Russians departed but fate decided otherwise. Escorted by a dozen Red Army men, a small group of German prisoners emerged from the woods. Pushing and pulling at the heavy logs, the men tried to lift their burden onto the trucks. As the prisoners strained the Russians amused themselves with filthy oaths and laughter. Some of them were kicking the men as they struggled past their grinning guards.

Schulze suddenly swore. "*Gott verdammte noch mal* . . . look over there!" He exclaimed and handed me his binoculars. "They are officers!"

I could distinguish two officers among the working prisoners. They were the ones the Russians seemed to abuse the most. "The taller one is a captain," Eisner announced. "The other one I can't tell."

"What shall we do about the poor devils?" Schulze queried. "We cannot sit here and look on."

I glanced at my men, deployed along the forest's edge. Filthy, unshaven, and worn as they were, I could see on their faces that they would have resented inactivity. "I am all for freeing them," I said briskly, answering their silent question. "But if we still want to reach Bavaria, we should stage a pretty good diversion afterwards."

For some days we had been moving northwest, making a beeline for a small German town, Sebnitz, where we hoped our people could help us in our trip across the Elbe. We could not liberate the prisoners without killing the Russians and consequently revealing our presence to the enemy, the very thing I was trying to avoid all the way. A line drawn on the map between the pass which we had evacuated and the small clearing down below would inevitably point at the border near Sebnitz. I turned the problem over and over in my mind but it seemed more hopeless at every new angle.

Captain Ruell found the only feasible solution.

"We wanted to move toward Sebnitz," he began excitedly, motioning us to have a look at the map. "Having hit the Russians here, we will probably have all night before the enemy sends someone up to investigate. We are about . . . here!" He placed his finger on the map, then looked up. "After liberating the prisoners we should turn south. Away from Sebnitz and the German frontier. Here is a small village. We could make it by midnight. We need some civilian clothes anyway. I don't think our folks at home will have many clothes left. A quick raid on the village might confuse the Russians especially if we grab every Czech identity paper we come across."

"Czech papers!" Schulze exclaimed. "What for?"

Ruell grinned. "The Russians might conclude that we are heading inland, toward Austria. Otherwise why should we collect Czech papers?"

"I think it is a good idea, *Herr Hauptmann*," a young lieutenant of the Austrian *Alpenjaegers* remarked cheerfully. "Austria is precisely the place we would like to go. After the raid we might as well keep going south."

"And run into a Soviet blocking party," Eisner grunted. "You had better stick with us, taking the longer way but arriving safely."

"After the raid on the village we should double back toward the north and cross the border at Sebnitz," Captain Ruell concluded.

"So be it!" Eisner stated and I agreed. Captain Ruell's plan seemed as feasible as any we might conceive.

By five o'clock in the afternoon both trucks were loaded and the prisoners had been lined up for head count. There were twenty-three of them, escorted by twelve Russians. Schulze deployed three sharpshooters for each Red Army man. "Drop them with a single bullet, otherwise some of the prisoners may get hurt."

"Don't worry," one of the troopers remarked. "At two hundred yards we could hit a field mouse between the eyes."

Schulze waited until the prisoners had climbed aboard the trucks. Standing in a small group the Russians watched them with their submachine guns ready.

"Fire!" said Schulze.

Thirty-six rifles fired a single volley. The bewildered prisoners threw themselves flat thinking that they were about to be killed. But our sharpshooters had aimed well. There was no return fire.

Our liberated comrades, as we soon learned, had been captured five days before the capitulation. The majority were officers. The captain, whose rank Eisner had recognized, was the former commanding officer of a signal battalion. He had naïvely believed that the Soviet commander would react chivalrously to his protest against compelling captive officers to remove roadblocks, fill anti-tank ditches, and perform other manual labor. The Soviet officer in charge, whose name Captain Waller never learned, had been quite drunk at the time, and having booted the "Fascist dogs" from his presence, he had ordered his troops to strip the "Germanski" officers of their rank badges and insignias. Then roaring with drunken laughter he yelled: "Now you are no longer officers but ordinary ranks, . . . *tvoy maty!*" Captain Waller and Lieutenant Mayer were, however, permitted to retain their badges "to serve as an example" of what happens to complaining Fascist officers. "Now you go and cut wood, we need telephone poles." The Soviet Officer swore. "You destroyed all the telephone poles. . . . Now you are going to make new ones from here to Moscow."

"You are lucky, *Herr Hauptmann*, that we came by here," I said after our mutual introduction.

"You were more lucky that you could come by here at all," he replied with a smile. "There's no prisoner-of-war treatment for the SS, *Herr Obersturmführer*. I saw with my own eyes how the Russkis lined up and machine-gunned four hundred of your men into the Vistula."

"They did that, eh?" Eisner grunted.

"Not the officers, mind you," the captain added. "The officers are to be tried and hanged. It was all agreed upon between the Americans and Stalin." He uttered a short sardonical snort. "And that will be about the only Soviet-American agreement Stalin will keep! You had better watch out."

"They won't get us, *Herr Hauptmann* . . . at least not alive," I stated, more resolved than ever to reach Bavaria. "Not me, that's sure!"

Schulze nodded, lifting his gun. "First they'll have to take my toy away."

"I expected nothing else," Eisner fumed. "Now comes the great carnage . . . the revenge, gentlemen. There is going to be such a bloodbath in the Fatherland that all the SS ever did will look like a solemn church ceremony in comparison. . . ."

"You may thank Himmler," Waller said. "To kill the Jews was a great folly, my friends. He could have gotten away with anything but the Jews. . . . The Jews are a world power, but not those wretched bastards whom Himmler was busy exterminating around the clock. These had done nothing and would never have done anything against the Reich. Nevertheless their ghosts are returning now, many of them wearing the conqueror's uniform or the judge's stola."

"But what have we got to do with the whole bloody affair?"

Schulze cried. "I was hunting partisans in the *Gott verdammte* Russian swamps and in the forests of Belgorod. They should hang the '*Einsatzkommandos*' or the Gestapo. It was their lousy job to kill Jews, not mine. Are we responsible for what those loafers did?"

"Don't ask me, ask Stalin!"

"What does Stalin care about the Jews? He always regarded them as rotten capitalists. Most of the Ukrainian Jews were rounded up and executed by the Ukraine Militia."

"What the hell are you arguing about!" Eisner snapped. "Himmler did kill the Jews, didn't he? Now the world needs a scapegoat and it is the SS. Whether we pulled the trigger or just threw a ring about a village while the militia or the Gestapo rounded them up, it is one and the same thing for them. It was all because of the SS. We murdered everybody in sight, looted the corpses, and are now returning home loaded with stolen Jewish gold. We are the Scourge of God, the Devil Incarnate, the Teutons. They are murdering right now a million German prisoners in Siberia, maybe not by shooting – Stalin simply starves them to death. But is there any difference? All right . . . we gunned down a hundred hostages. They take a group of army officers from a prison camp, give them a mock trial, then hang them. It is one and the same treatment as far as I am concerned. I know that the SS destroyed Lidice. I have not been there, but if they did it – they had a reason. Why did the SS level that particular place? Why not the other ten thousand? Maybe it was because of the assassination of Heydrich, maybe it wasn't, but there must have been a reason for it. They say the killers of Heydrich were Czech commandos from England, who dropped by chutes. Why did they go hide in Lidice? They should have stood up, fought, and gone down fighting – the brave paratroopers. No one would have associated them with the Czechs in Lidice. And what if the SS destroyed Lidice? Was it an overkill? How about Hamburg which the Allied bombers demolished, killing eighty thousand civilians in a couple of hours? How about Dresden and the hundred thousand civilian dead there? Just before the war's end. . . . Because their execution was done by bombs and not by machine guns should we call the Allies saints? Goddamit all," he swore, wiping the sweat from his forehead, "all that kept us alive was the thought of surviving and returning home. If we still have homes to return to," he went on. "Now everyone is telling us that we are going to hang. It is enough to drive you mad."

"I am sorry," Captain Waller said apologetically. "I did not want to upset you. Especially not after what you did for us. But I thought you had better know the truth instead of falling into a trap at home."

"Just let them come and try to trap me," Eisner fumed. "I haven't killed an American yet but I don't think they are tougher than the Ivans – and I sure as hell killed a lot of the Ivans."

"That's enough for now!" I interposed authoritatively. "We have more urgent things to do than talk about postwar politics. How about moving on?"

"A good idea," Captain Ruell agreed. "But before we leave let me booby-trap those GMCs. It may help the Ivans to get downhill the shorter way." The troops laughed.

I knew their nerves were strained to the breaking point and each individual was a potential time bomb that might explode at any moment. My men were not killers at large, yet they already felt hunted, outlawed. They were brave soldiers bled white defending the Fatherland. The majority of them had been called up to the SS just like others had been called up to the various other services and put into uniforms. We were Nazis to be sure, but who was not a Nazi in Hitler's Third Reich? No one could hold any position in the Reich without becoming a Nazi. And if someone held any position in the Reich, his son volunteered for the SS – the "Elite Guard." Others volunteered because it was known to be an honor to serve in the SS. Besides, the uniforms were better, the food, the pay, and the treatment were better, leaves were more frequent. But no one had volunteered because he was told, "Join the SS and you may kill Jews, or guard concentration camps." I would never deny that the SS was probably the most brutal fighting force ever conceived in the history of warfare. We were tough, maybe even fanatics. We were scared of nothing and no one. We were brought up to be brave. Our brutality was only iron discipline and an uncompromising belief in the Fatherland.

We had been taught and drilled to execute orders and had I been given the order to shoot Jews, gypsies, or prisoners of war, I would have executed that order just as I would have shot deer if ordered to do so. If that is a crime, they should hang every soldier in the world who wouldn't pull his gun and shoot his superior officer through the head whenever he feels like disobeying an order. But my orders were to insure the safety of supply trains, to keep a forest around a vital bridge free from enemy infiltrators, or to track down partisans after an attack against a garrison. And that is exactly what I did! When I was ordered to take hostages, I took hostages, ten of whom were to be shot for every German soldier murdered by the guerrillas. When the guerrillas stabbed a German sentry in the back or threw a grenade into a staff car, a given number of hostages were executed. Their names had been made known to the population in advance. The partisans had always known that if they committed murder, we would retaliate.

The partisans would never tell a German soldier in advance that he was going to be killed. We did tell the guerrillas that if they killed a German soldier, Pjotr or Andrei would die! We gave them a chance, but they gave us none. Who was then the more guilty? Who did actually kill those hostages? Were the partisans innocent? They were as innocent as the lever of a guillotine. The lever does not kill. It only releases the blade!

As soon as darkness fell, we moved on to execute Captain Ruell's plan. We found a fairly wide dirt road that ran through the forest and, following a small advance guard, made good progress. Having arrived at the village about midnight we quickly deployed along the forest line, and I sent out a reconnaissance party with Schulze in charge. Schulze reported that there were no Soviet troops in the vicinity, only a group of Czech militia billeting in the ancient stone mansion of the local fire service. A captured Wehrmacht troop carrier stood in the archway but he saw no sentries and the place looked ripe for the taking. I selected ninety men to form three groups with Schultze, Eisner, and myself in command. The rest of the troops were to stay behind under the command of Captain Ruell. I told him that should any trouble develop he was not to interfere but should move northward according to our original plan.

Skirting the fields we moved into the village with so many dogs barking that they should have wakened the dead. "Don't shoot except in the utmost emergency," I told my men. "If you have to kill, use your bayonets. And if you must use your bayonets, don't miss!"

"And if you see a window lit up, occupy the house!" Eisner added. "Seize everyone you find awake."

To my great relief I discovered that the battle of Stalingrad would not have disturbed the militiamen whom we found all boozed up and sleeping it off happily on a dozen bare mattresses strewn about the wooden floor. "They haven't got a worry on earth," a young trooper beside me remarked as we quietly removed the militia's weapons. "I sure wouldn't mind being one of them. Boy, to be able to sleep like that."

With the militiamen disarmed, the occupation of the village was only a matter of routine. My troops did not wait for instructions. They knew how to go about their business swiftly and with the skill of veterans. One detachment cut the telephone wires; two platoons left to cover the roads with MG's; four men seized the belfry – an important precautionary measure for a church bell can be a very effective instrument if someone wants to raise the country for miles around. The wires of the air-raid sirens in front of the church were also cut.

Breaking up into groups of five men each we searched every house, confiscated civilian clothes, food, and personal papers and caused great consternation among the people. Some of them spoke German and were told we were Austrians on the way home, terribly sorry for the inconvenience but we needed their papers to survive the trip across Czechoslovakia. I knew that the nearest Soviet commander would be informed before dawn.

At last on German soil – at the Elbe but still on the wrong side. A battered old farmhouse stood on the edge of the woods with the burned shell of a Tiger visible among the ruins of a barn. Children were playing around the dead tank and smoke rose from the chimney. We kept the place under observation for several hours but spotted no Russians. Schulze decided to visit the farm at dusk. He returned with the farmer, Hans Schroll, a war cripple; a short, lean, embittered man in his early fifties hobbling on a pair of crutches.

"I shall try to help you," he said, his face showing great concern. "But keep in the woods, for heaven's sake. The Russkis are visiting us every day and one never knows when they might show up."

"Life must be hard on you people," Captain Ruell remarked sympathetically.

"Hard?" Schroll exclaimed with a short laugh. "Life here is nothing but assault, robbery, rape, and murder. I am the only man here for miles around. A half of a man," he added bitterly.

"No, Herr Schroll," Schulze shook his head, placing a hand gently on the man's stump. "I think you are more than a man."

"The Russkis herded away the entire male population," Schroll went on. "They wouldn't take me because of my leg. Nowadays you may call yourself lucky for having lost a leg and a female is safe only if she is seven months pregnant or seven years old."

He sat with us for a while and from his embittered words we could form our first impression of our tarnished Fatherland. A Wehrmacht battalion was still fighting on a ridge half a mile away when the invaders had raped Schroll's wife for the first time.

"One of them held a gun to my head," the farmer said. "He threatened to shoot me if I moved. I couldn't have moved much even without a gun at my head, could I? They were the front-line mob. Finally a major came yelling, trying to send the bastards out to fight. Do you know what happened to the major? They just grabbed him, took his pistol, and kicked him in the ass . . . kicked him right through the door. . . ."

"How is it now?" I asked wearily.

"*Na ja.*" He smiled resignedly. "The occupation troops are more polite. They are taking me and the children out of the room when they come to visit my wife."

"Don't say –"

"*Jawohl, Kameraden.* The German homes have become Red army whorehouses. But we should not condemn our wives and daughters. It is all our fault. We should have fought better. Fought like the Japanese with their suicide pilots and human torpedoes. We did not kill enough Russians."

Schroll told us about the pontoon bridge at Pirna. Four T-34s and several machine gun emplacements covered its approaches.

"No Germans are allowed to cross the bridge without a special pass," Schroll said. "You will never make it across there, but I can give you a boat."

The boat was a leaky one and could carry only eight men at the most. We had to wait in the forest until the farmer had managed to patch it up. He left it at a prearranged place, driven ashore and camouflaged under the riverside shrubs. In it we found five loaves of dark bread, a sack of homemade biscuits, and two bottles of schnapps. There was also a note: *Glueck auf!* – Good Luck!

Only a thin slice of bread and a small gulp of brandy for each man but it had been our first slice of bread for weeks and the brandy felt good. So did the small note of Hans Schroll – a great man in a great desert.

Only the clothes and the weapons were ferried across the river. The men had to swim as it would have taken too long, making it very risky. Nine of them never made it.

We pushed on toward the American zone. Four times we ran into Soviet patrols or Czech militia. We had to kill them in order to survive. The enemy troops were getting thicker every day, but the closer we came to Bavaria the more resolved we became to arrive there. We no longer cared to bypass the roadblocks or the enemy camps but attacked them, pouring lead as if we had an inexhaustible supply of ammunition. We were only forty-two men when we finally reached Bavaria at Wunsiedel. Three hundred and seventeen of our comrades had fallen so that we might arrive home.

Three miles from the border we encountered our first American patrol: a jeepload of young men led by a lieutenant. Clean, neatly dressed, and obviously well fed, they were sitting around the jeep with a mounted MG having dinner. Dinner with a record player in the grass blaring the "Stuka Lied," the lively march of the German dive bombers.

We had the Americans like sitting ducks, but I saw no reason for killing them the way we had killed every Russian who blocked our way. I decided to pay them a visit, alone and unarmed.

Leaving Eisner, Schulze, and an NCO to watch the development, I left the shrubbery and walked up to the group. The soldiers stared at me with astonishment and reached for their guns. The lieutenant turned off the record player. He was a handsome young man of about thirty, tall and blond, just like some of us Teutons. He wore sunglasses which he removed to have a better look at me.

"I see you are having quite a picnic here, lieutenant," I spoke to him nonchalantly, gesturing toward their rifles that almost poked me in the belly. "You don't want to shoot me, do you? The war is over."

"Who the hell are you?" he blurted out glancing at his men, then back toward me. "What are you doing here?" I thought *God bless my mother who had always insisted that I should learn English.*

"What could a German do in his own country?" I asked him in return. "I am on my way home."

"Who are you?"

"Only a German officer. Coming home from far away."

"How come you speak English so well?"

"We are quite civilized people, lieutenant. As you see, some of us can even speak English."

I noticed that they were completely taken aback by my sudden appearance and for some time the officer seemed at loss as to what to say or do.

"Are you carrying any weapon?" he asked finally.

"Only a pocketknife."

"Hand it over!" he ordered me briskly. I knew he said that only to say something. I handed him my knife and he motioned his men to frisk me. The result set him at ease. He offered me a cigarette, lighted one for himself, then taking a notebook from the jeep he began to rattle off a number of questions.

"Your name, rank, and unit?"

"Hans Josef Wagemueller," I obliged. "*Obersturmführer*, twenty-first special *partisanjaeger* commando."

"What's that?" a freckled, lanky soldier interposed.

"Guerrilla hunter," the lieutenant explained and I bowed slightly. "That's right."

"Your last combat station?"

"Liberec, Czechoslovakia."

"Have you killed any Americans?" a squat little corporal cut in.

I smiled. "If there were any American troops serving in the Red Army, then I sure as hell did."

The lieutenant made a quick, impatient gesture. "He said he was in Czechoslovakia," he said to the corporal.

"Wehrmacht or the SS?" he now demanded to know. I could barely conceal my amusement. Only the SS had *Obersturmführers*. The Wehrmacht had lieutenants. I shrugged.

"Wehrmacht, SS, *Luftwaffe* – what's the difference?"

"There's a helluva difference, buddy," he snapped. "The Wehrmacht and the *Luftwaffe* go home but we hang them SS cut-throats good and high." He extended his hand. "Show me your pay book."

"I haven't got any."

"How come?"

"Well, I just figured that our paymaster's office might be closed for a while, so I threw my pay book away."

He frowned. "You like jokes, don't you?" he remarked curtly and turned to the squat little corporal who wore a pair of horn-rimmed glasses. "Joe, you had better call headquarters."

"I wouldn't do that if I were you, lieutenant," I suggested mildly and lifted a protesting hand toward their guns, which were coming up once more. "Please do not threaten me. At this very moment there are at least a dozen rifles pointing at you. My men are expert marksmen and they are a bit nervous. I don't want to see you killed – unless in self-defense."

The soldiers paled visibly. The lieutenant ran his tongue over his lips but his confusion did not last long. My troops began to emerge from the woods with their guns providing the necessary dramatic undertone. Their chins dropped, then their weapons. The lieutenant began to unbuckle his holster but I stopped him.

"Oh, never mind your gun, lieutenant. We don't want to shoot at each other. The war is over."

We took them, jeep, guns, and record player back into the woods. "*Nicht schiessen, Kamerad,*" squat little Joe muttered in broken German. "Don't shoot."

Somewhat bitterly I acknowledged that even the SS cut-throats could quickly turn into comrades when the business end of the sub-machine gun had turned the other way. The face of the lieutenant revealed sheer agony. He must have thought that we were going to kill them right then and there. I motioned the Americans to sit down on a fallen log and told them briefly about the surrender of Colonel Steinmetz and our odyssey across Czechoslovakia. They seemed impressed.

"Are you telling me that the Russians just gunned them down under a flag of truce?" the lieutenant asked. "It is a helluva way of treating prisoners of war."

"Indeed, lieutenant?" I queried him sharply. "Do you consider hanging more sophisticated?"

"We aren't going to hang anyone without a fair trial," he protested.

"Can you call a trial of the vanquished by his victors a fair trial, lieutenant? I presume you will be holding your fair trials in some neutral country to ensure their fairness... in Geneva, for instance. We had been listening to your broadcasts and know your intentions about the so-called war criminals. A new class of the doomed; everyone who served in the SS now belongs.... If you speak of the Jew-haters or those who preferred to guard concentration camps instead of fighting the Red Army, you might make a point. But do you know that on Hitler's order every German soldier serving in the rear was free to choose front-line duty. And if a man demanded to be sent forward, his commanding officer had no right to turn him down. Do you think we front-line soldiers did not sneer at the swine who wanted to survive the war by flaying Jews a thousand miles from the trenches? I was an officer of the SS, lieutenant, and I was fighting terrorists whose mere shadows would have sent you screaming into the nearest mental institution. They were not concentration camp inmates but armed insurgents who spat on all the game rules. Now just tell me, you immaculate American lieutenant, what will you do to guerrillas captured in your rear, wearing civilian clothes, guerrillas who blow up bridges, derail trains, stab your buddies in the back, or toss hand grenades into your officers' mess? Won't you hang them, lieutenant?"

"But the SS... during the Ardennes offensive...."

"I've heard of them, lieutenant," I cut him short. "Some bastards murdered a group of American prisoners at Malmédy.

If it is true, then hunt them down. Hang *them* for all I care. But then go and hang some of your fellow Americans who gunned down German prisoners with their hands in the air. Just look around a bit and you will find them too. You shouldn't play the holy man here. You had your Chicago and Al Capone long before the SS was born. In the meantime, you had better remember that among us were thousands of enlisted men, ordinary people who had been drafted and put into SS uniforms. Or do you think they should have protested against their uniforms? How about the SS tank drivers, the signal men, the artillerists? Would you consider them war criminals? Would you hang them *all*, American lieutenant?"

"They will be examined . . . each individual," the lieutenant stated feebly.

"Sure, lieutenant, every one of them. A half a million individuals or more."

A long pause followed. I knew that my violent outburst would be of little use but it made me feel better to have set the record straight for at least five American servicemen. Again they appeared ill at ease.

"What are you . . . up to now?" the lieutenant finally asked. He spoke hesitantly, as though fearing to hear my answer. I knew what he was thinking.

"We are up to – home, I hope," I told him.

"You will never make it. We have roadblocks at every village. Every bridge is guarded by the MPs and Germans need passes to travel from one place to another."

"The Russians had roadblocks too, lieutenant," I answered firmly. "They couldn't stop us."

He stepped to the jeep and withdrew a carton of Camels, trying to smile. "Do you want some cigarettes?"

"You don't have to bribe us, lieutenant."

"We have plenty."

"So I have heard. You Americans seem to have plenty of nearly everything – except common sense and political wisdom. You keep your cigarettes. We have come a long way without smoking."

His face clouded. My refusal sent him back to his former worries about their immediate future. "What do you intend to do with us?" he asked hesitantly.

"It depends. I hope you understand that you could be of great peril to us with your jeep and radio. Having come this far, we wouldn't like the idea of ending up in one of your jails, waiting for the rope."

"We won't give you away!" he said quickly. "Honestly we won't!" The others nodded in consent.

"That, lieutenant, we will have to make pretty sure of!"

He paled again and ran a nervous hand over his face. "You aren't going to shoot us, are you?"

Then squat little Joe said in a shaky voice, "You have just disassociated yourself from the war criminals. You want to go home, you said. Hell, man, so do I."

I took Schulze and Eisner aside to discuss our next move. We agreed that it was about time to break up. A couple of men together might have a better chance to get some papers and make it home. If we stuck together sooner or later it would have come to fighting the Americans too, which I wanted to avoid.

Our low-keyed conversation only increased the consternation among the Americans and they could not stand our whispering for long.

"Listen, officer!" the lieutenant exclaimed, stepping forward. "We will not hinder you in getting home. You have taken our weapons and having been a soldier you surely know that I cannot return to base and report to my commanding officer that we were disarmed by a group of stray Germans. I could lose my rank for that."

"You may have a point there, lieutenant," I conceded.

He seemed relieved. "Why shouldn't we call it quits?" he insisted. "You let us go and we saw nothing of you."

We stood for a while facing one another, then on a sudden impulse I motioned him to follow me. I walked to the edge of the woods. Pointing inward to the forest line about two miles away, I handed him my binoculars. "There is a wooden tower there," I said. "A shooting stand for deer hunters."

"I can see it," said he.

"We shall leave your weapons in that tower, so that you won't lose your shoulder bars, lieutenant. Is it a deal?"

"It's a deal!"

I ordered my men to remove the jeep's distributor cap and

some wires of their radio set. "I am afraid that you will have to walk all the way there and back, Lieutenant. We will leave the parts with your guns. And don't walk too fast."

I gave them a brief salute and we began to move. I was a dozen paces from the jeep when the lieutenant suddenly called.

"Officer!"

I turned.

"Keep away from the highways and don't go toward Bayreuth," he yelled. "The commander of counterintelligence there is a Jewish major whose entire family was killed by the SS in Poland."

2

The Tarnished Fatherland

WE ate our last supper together in an abandoned stone quarry near Cham, in the Bavarian forest. Some of the men were talking in low subdued voices, discussing the pros and cons of their long trip home to the various parts of the battered Fatherland. Men who had lived in Bavaria or in the Schwaben could be more optimistic than those who were to traverse the entire country if they wanted to rejoin their families in Hamburg or in Aachen. None of us could anticipate what might come on the way or what to expect at home. Whether there was a home at all or a family to embrace.

The thought that we were dispersing lay heavily on everyone's mind. Together we had come a long way and together we felt strong. Now with our weapons at the bottom of a pond, wearing civilian clothes after so many years, we felt defenseless and exposed.

I gave them my last advice. No more than two men together, I told them, and remember that you are supposed to be Czech refugees looking for brothers, sisters, and friends in Germany. Should someone shout an unexpected command at you in German, do not freeze but keep on going. Or just look around confused. Forget that you understand German. Not many

Americans will speak Czech. You will have a fair chance of getting away with it. Behave innocently and submerge among the people, I told them. The peasants will always help you but you should beware of the cities where the occupation troops are probably quartered. There might be many turncoats who would betray you for a tin of beef or a loaf of bread.

Whenever you see a chance disguise yourselves by pretending to be engaged in some peaceful activity. Carry a shovel or a log on your shoulder and cut across the fields. The enemy will think that you belong to the next farm. Get hold of a wheelbarrow, load it with hay or manure, and never mind if it stinks to high heavens. The more it stinks the less eager the Americans will be to embrace you. They are clean boys. You should never try to get hold of a vehicle but you may thumb a ride on an American army truck. A genuine Czech refugee would do it. And should you find life impossible, come to Konstanz, my hometown. It is on the Swiss frontier. We shall have people there to help you. I gave them my address.

I was the only one among them who could be sure of still having a home. Konstanz had never been bombed and its lucky inhabitants had suffered less hardship throughout the war. It was located only a few dozen yards from the Swiss town of Kreuzlingen, and the frontier actually ran across the center of a built-up area which, from the air, appeared a single, undivided unit. Konstanz was one of the very few German communities which never experienced blackouts. Throughout the war the city had been kept fully illuminated just like the nearby Swiss towns and villages, to confuse the enemy bombers.

The sun had dipped beyond the horizon. Our farewell was a brief one. We shook hands and those who had known each other for years embraced. "*Glueck auf!* . . . Good luck!" When dusk set in, the men began to leave singly or in twos and threes; one after another they melted into the woods, the darkness. I embraced Eisner and Erich Schulze. They had a long way to go to Frankfurt and to Münster. "You have my address," I reminded them. "My people can always tell you where to look for me." I knew they were still carrying their parabellums, and cautioned them to be careful.

"Don't worry, Hans." Eisner gave me a quick, reassuring

squeeze. "We will arrive home, if only for an hour. We will get through."

A few minutes later I was alone, a fugitive in my own country.

I sat on a tree stump for a long time studying the map of the route I was to take and tried to memorize it as best I could. Then I tore up the map for it bore many markings related to our trip across Czechoslovakia. I decided to follow roughly the course of the Naab river, cross the Danube at Regensburg if possible, then continue toward Augsburg where I had some relatives – provided, of course, that they were still alive and around.

Such "ifs" had become constant companions of every home-coming German soldier. If I can cross the river. . . . If I can take that road. . . . If I arrive home. . . . If they are still alive. . . . If . . . If . . . If. . . .

The man sat on a small boulder overhanging the water's edge. He was a tall dark man maybe in his late twenties but his bushy moustache and beard prevented me from guessing his age exactly. He wore Tyrolean *lederhosen* and a high-necked pullover; an old hat was pushed high on his forehead. Puffing away at a curved clay pipe, he seemed to concentrate on a floating cork that supported the line of his improvised fishing rod, a long cane. Beside him rested a wicker basket with six small *Karpfen*, some of them still wiggling. He was perfectly hidden in the riverside meadow and had I not decided to have a quick wash up, I would have bypassed the place where he sat without ever noticing him.

"I see you are having luck," I spoke to him. He glanced up. His eyes measured me for a while, then he gestured me to sit down.

"Pfirstenhammer's the name." He gave me a casual hand.

"Hans Wagemueller," said I, "Just call me Hans."

"Likewise," he nodded, "just call me Karl. Are you coming from far?"

"Quite far."

"You hungry?"

"I wouldn't mind having some fried fish for a change, Karl."

"You may have all you want. I am sick of it. Do you have any bread?"

"Only some biscuits. But I have some margarine."

"Splendid!" he exclaimed, taking the small container from me.

He tossed it into the air and caught it with one hand, playfully. "Where are you coming from, Hans?"

"Past Liberec, Czechoslovakia . . . some two hundred and fifty miles from here."

"Fighting all the way?"

"On and off. It took us almost eight weeks to get here."

He nodded. "I reckon the Munich-Prague express isn't running yet. Where are you going from here?"

"To Konstanz, on the Boden See. Say, you aren't from the Gestapo, are you?"

"Not lucky me." He laughed, tugging at his fishing rod. "But you had better watch *your* step, Hans. The Americans are hunting for the SS all over the place."

"Who told you that I was with the SS?"

"Who else would have come back all the way from Liberec? Only a bloody SS or a paratrooper. I have been walking since March."

"From where?"

"From Poznan, Poland."

"I know the place, been through there twice."

"Filthy, isn't it? I was already on the POW train. Headed for the Ukraine."

"And?"

"I had seen the Ukraine before and wasn't particularly keen to visit Stalin's paradise again. I did what a good paratrooper is expected to do. I jumped. Right off the moving train, and not only myself but the whole bunch of us."

"Wait!" he exclaimed suddenly, jerking at the cane. "I think we've got one more." He flung the fish ashore, coiled the line onto a bit of wood, then tucked it into his pocket. "We have enough for two. Let's collect some twigs."

"Do you have a pot or something?"

"What for? We'll just rub the fish in your margarine and fry them over the fire. It will do."

"It will do for me, Karl. I haven't eaten anything warm for weeks, except for an occasional soup."

The fish was quite tasty. Satisfied, I stretched out in the soft grass. Karl handed me the cask.

"Go ahead," he said, lighting his pipe. "I can always get more. Do you smoke?"

"Cigarettes – but I haven't got any."

"Too bad," said he, "we can take turns with my pipe."

Once again silence prevailed for a while, then I asked, "What's the nearest town here?"

"Ingolstadt," he replied pointing a thumb upstream. "Or what is left of it. We should cross the Danube there."

"I tried it at Regensburg but there was a barrier with the MP checking everyone."

Karl nodded. "I know. I tried it myself five days ago. They seem to collect everyone who might be a soldier in disguise."

"Are papers of any help?"

"It all depends on the papers," Karl said with a shrug. "The MPs have the habit of carting off people and doing the questioning inside a camp. It might take a couple of months to have your turn at explaining but they have time. They are here to stay."

"They cannot stay forever."

"I didn't say they would. Eventually they'll mock up some sort of anti-Nazi, democratic government whose only obligation will be to say 'yessir' to the Allies and '*Schweinhund*' to their German brothers. Besides, Stalin will never give up an inch of what he has gained. That is certain. The Fatherland is *kaput* . . . finished." He paused for a moment, then added. "What papers do you have?"

"Czech papers."

"You might get away with it, provided you can speak Czech."

"I can speak about fifty and a half words in Czech."

"Tough on you, Hans. The MPs carry little books with the most important words of a dozen languages listed in them. You are lucky to have come as far as this."

"How about you?"

"I am from Breslau, Silesia, and I can speak Polish like the vicar at a Warsaw sermon. Besides I have a Polish DP card."

"What's that?"

"Refugee card which the Allies are giving to all genuine Nazi victims and refugees in Germany."

That was something new to me. "How did you get one?"

"I hit a Pole over the head for it," Karl said flatly. "*Na ja*, life is difficult, Hans. The Pole can always get himself another one."

"I was born in Dresden."

"Now it's a town on the map only. But it's the same in Hamburg, Düsseldorf, Mannheim, and scores of other cities. We have had it good and proper, but at least the Americans and the British have some discipline. The Tartars of Stalin have none. In the Soviet Zone the Black Plague is at large, Hans. The Ivans are free to do as they please. And I can tell you they are worse than the Gestapo. Life is an endless nightmare over there."

"Do you still have a family in Breslau?"

"I had," he replied and his face darkened. "My mother and elder sister are dead and the younger one is now with relatives in Hannover. My father was a captain in the infantry. The Russians caught him near Orsha. He was forced to climb a tree at minus twenty centigrade and shout 'Heil Hitler' until he froze to death."

I was sorry for having reminded him of something so tragic. Placing my hand on his shoulder, I muttered something awkward about the war and its victims but Karl only shook his head slowly and said with a bitter smile: "My mother and sister did not die because of the war, Hans. The Russians raped them, then shot them. My younger sister was only thirteen and her escape was nothing but a miracle."

"I am sorry, Karl –"

"Never mind, Hans. It is something I should remember as long as there are Communists on earth. I don't think we have finished with them yet. When another round comes, we will be wiser."

"Where are you heading now?"

Karl shrugged. "Who knows? Only one thing is sure, that we cannot stay in Germany. It would be like being a deer during the hunting season. But *this* hunting season will last for years. There's going to be lots of hangings around here, Hans."

"That might concern me but not you," I exclaimed. "No one is going to hang paratroopers as war criminals."

"Don't be so naïve." Pfirstenhammer uttered a short laugh. "*Everybody* is going to hang. The SS is only on the top of the list of the guests. The generals are going to hang because they won victories but were imprudent enough to lose the war. The *Luftwaffe* will hang because it bombed Coventry to smithereens – a war crime; the *Kriegsmarine* for having torpedoed ships, the Medical Corps because they nursed vicious Nazis back to life, and Hitler's cook will hang because he did not poison the Fuehrer in 1939. Everyone contributed to Hitler's crimes, Hans. We are like a big manufacturing company where the board of directors are holding the stocks. Joint responsibility and no bankruptcy court."

"They cannot hang or jail two-thirds of Germany."

"They won't have to." Karl glanced at me, rubbing his hands. "In a year's time they will have lots of loyal German patriots to do the dirty work for them, Hans. Every country has her traitors. Why should we be an exception? Some Nazis will surely slip through the great sieve and they are going to be the real screamers who demand justice, denazification, and democracy. Wait until the shock waves abate. You will see twenty million anti-Nazis and ten million devoted resistance fighters chanting 'yessir' whenever an American corporal snaps his fingers. They are going to be more anti-Nazi than the chief rabbi of Jerusalem."

"You no longer believe in our country, do you, Karl?" I asked him slowly, accepting his pipe.

"Our country?" He repeated my question, pursing his lips. He let the sentence hang.

"Karl," I spoke after a while, "would you care to come along with me?"

"To Konstanz?" he said. "It is in the French Zone."

"Is it an advantage or a disadvantage?"

"I guess it is good enough there. The French are probably too lazy to hunt. Besides when they do hunt they prefer to hunt for girls."

"Are you coming along?" I urged him.

"Konstanz is on my way."

We swam the Danube that evening and walked halfway to Augsburg. We walked during the nights and slept through the days. Abandoned bunkers, ruins, tanks, burned-out trucks, and remote farmhouses gave us shelter. By luck, prudence, but mostly due to our people's goodwill, we managed to evade occasional pursuers and avoid controls. Sometimes the peasants, many of them women and children, would lead us from farm to farm and from forest to forest. One young farmer, an army veteran both of whose arms had been amputated, escorted us safely past Landsberg, where the U.S. Army was maintaining a huge prison for arrested Nazis. As a result the whole area was especially heavily guarded and patrolled.

"I am celebrating tonight," he said before we parted. "You were my number two hundred!" He had escorted two hundred German fugitives safely past Landsberg. A twelve-kilometer trip for no payment whatsoever, except for thanks.

Peasants told us that the Americans were raiding the villages too, but they could always see them coming and had time to usher the fugitives into the fields or the woods. In the cities it was different, for the hunters could come without warning. They would seal off a street, then comb the area house by house, room after room, from the cellar to the attic. Using trained dogs, the MPs would even search the ruins. Many traitors were helping them. "In the village we have no traitors," a farmer said proudly. "We would know about them right away." It was a comforting thought that the victors had not yet succeeded in corrupting our rural folk.

I decided not to look for my relatives in Augsburg. "We are making good progress in the woods. Why risk everything by entering a town?" Karl said and I agreed with him. We continued across the fields and into the forests. We beheld many scenes of utter debacle but met no one who condemned the Fuehrer.

"You cannot stay here, son," my father sobbed into my ear as he embraced me, still unable to believe that I had returned. "We have two officers living in your room, and they usually come in before midnight. One of them is quite friendly, but his companion, a captain, is full of hatred. He would arrest you the moment he saw you."

"You will be safer in Switzerland and you will be close to us," my mother said, wiping away her tears. "You should go to see Josef Weber. He will help you across."

"The old U-boat skipper? I am glad to hear that he is back."

"He has been asking about you ever since he returned."

We stayed only long enough to shave and wash up. My mother brought in two of my old suits, one of them for Karl.

"It might be a little short for him," she excused herself, "but it is still better than the one he has on." She packed a small suitcase with clothes and some sandwiches. "I know it is not much, Hans, but food is so difficult to get."

"You shouldn't worry about us, Mother."

She slipped a small leather pouch into my hand which felt hard and heavy for its size. "I am giving you some of my jewelry and your father's gold coins," she said.

"There is no need – "

"Yes, there is," she cut me short. "We don't need them, Hans. It's going to be a long time before German women wear jewels again."

I knew how my father loved to collect coins but now he insisted on my taking them. "I knew they'd come in handy one day, Hans – this seems to be the day." I handed him the colonel's gold watch, the cigarette case, and the letter, and asked my father to try to locate Steinmetz's wife later on, when life became more consolidated.

A short embrace, a last kiss, a quick "take care of yourself," and we left as quietly as we had come.

"I am glad your folks are all right," Karl remarked as we skirted the town along the lake. "Where are we going now?"

I had known Josef Weber since my childhood, when he used to be the skipper of a ferryboat between Friedrichshafen and Romanshorn on the Swiss side. In 1941 he was commissioned in the navy and when I met him during a leave in 1943, he was a U-boat commander. Weber was a short, powerfully built man with an aggressive chin, steely blue eyes, and a small reddish beard.

"Welcome aboard," he beamed as he embraced me after such a long time. "Glad to see you back and all in one piece." He shook hands with Karl. "You want to jump the lake. A wise decision. Especially on your part, Hans," he said, stressing his words significantly.

"That's what I've been hearing all the way home."

"It is the truth!"

"Dammit, skipper – I wasn't out to shoot Jews!"

"I believe you but it might take a long time to convince the

Allies, *Junge*." He went to the other room and returned with some jackets and ties. From a drawer he took a small camera.

"Change your ties and jackets," he commanded briskly. "I am going to take your pictures for your new papers and we wouldn't want them to look too recent." We changed and he took our pictures.

"Make yourselves comfortable," Weber spoke, putting on his hat. "You will find some drinks and glasses in that cabinet. I shall return in about an hour. The windows are properly shaded but should anyone come, do not open the door, just put out the candles and wait. If the visitors seem to insist on entering, they are the French. Now come with me."

He led us into a small chamber and showed us a trapdoor that matched the flooring perfectly and could not be spotted unless pointed out. "In case of any trouble, you go down there and wait for my call."

"Are you expecting any trouble, Herr Weber?" Karl asked.

"I am expecting trouble twenty-four hours a day," Weber replied casually. "It goes with the job. Down in the cellar you will find another exit. It is concealed behind an old cabinet and it leads to the lake."

"You've got a private *Fuehrerbunker* here, Captain?" Karl remarked jokingly when we had returned to the living room.

"And a better one than the *Fuehrer* had," Weber conceded. "My bunker has safety valves." From his desk he lifted up a small model of a powerful speedboat. "At the end of that corridor behind the cabinet there is the lake and a grown-up sister of this baby here. She can do seventy kilometers per hour."

It was past midnight when the one time U-boat commander returned. He was not alone. The stern-looking, middle-aged, silver-haired man who accompanied him shook hands with us but did not introduce himself. After a few words of mutual courtesy, he took a small green notebook from his pocket and spoke to us crisply and without preliminaries.

"State your rank, serial number, division, and last station, please." We told him and he made some notes. He questioned us for some time, then exchanged glances with Weber and nodded. "It will do!"

He handed us two long yellow envelopes. They contained Swiss birth certificates, identity cards, and other related documents. "You will also find there five hundred Swiss francs, along with an address. Herr Weber will take you across the lake and you will report at the given address as soon as possible. Good luck!"

He left immediately afterwards.

"I guess you are all set up," Weber remarked with a grin as we examined our new papers. They were perfect. "Skipper," I told him, "if you weren't here and I didn't know you, I would think we had just passed a Gestapo interview. Who was that gentleman?"

"You should not be inquisitive, Hans," was his only answer.

The given address turned out to be a small Renaissance villa near Zurich. On the polished oak door was a brass plate: H.M. Dipl. Engineer. A little white-haired old lady opened the door for us. "The Herr Engineer isn't home yet but please come in. We are expecting him at any moment now." She did not even ask who we were or why we were coming. Nor did Herr Engineer later. He merely drove us to a magnificent mansion overlooking the lake. "Pension Particulaire" an inscription read.

"You will be staying here for a while," he informed us. "Room and board are all paid for but you may give small tips."

"Who is paying for all this?" Karl blurted out.

"Why should you care?" our host snapped. We had noticed the moment he spoke to us that he was a born Swiss.

The madam of the establishment, a tall, energetic woman in her mid-fifties, was no more talkative than the Herr Engineer had been. She wore a long pearl necklace with a golden butterfly glinting above her small breasts. Playing with the necklace she said, "You will find many other gentlemen here, some of them coming, others leaving. None of them staying for very long and none of them paying much attention to names and stories. You have had a difficult time, so now relax. Walk in the city, play tennis in our park or chess in the library, but ask no questions. And something else," she added as the maid came in to take us upstairs, "if you have cameras, please deposit them with our clerk. You are not allowed to take pictures within our establishment. I hope you understand." We understood.

Three weeks later, Eisner and Schulze arrived. They had gone through the same routine. "My kids are dead. A bomb hit their school last April," Bernard stated. "My wife is the whore of an American sergeant."

"There is a two-hundred-foot pond where my home used to be," Erich said. "My family is listed as 'missing' since December forty-five. They seem to be missing all right." He glanced about the magnificent reception hall. "What about this joint here, Hans?"

"It's the Prinz Albert Strasse turned into a chess club," Karl remarked before I could answer. His reference to the former Gestapo center in Berlin made us smile. "You enjoy life and ask no questions," he went on. "Be glad that you were accepted in the family. You'll meet many dignified, middle-aged gentlemen at the breakfast table. We don't know who they are but they weren't sergeants in the Wehrmacht, that is sure."

"I see," Schulze nodded. "We'll try to abide by the rules."

"I am afraid that you will have to leave Switzerland," the police officer in civilian dress informed us. "We are under strong diplomatic pressure. Our authorities might be willing to overlook transit passengers from Germany but they are not happy about your documentary arrangements." I had already noticed that many of the "guests" had departed during the past ten days.

"When are we supposed to leave and to where?" Eisner wanted to know.

"There is no need for you to panic," the officer replied with quiet benevolence. "Let us say . . . in twenty days?" Then he added reassuringly, "Your papers are still good for any country except Switzerland. The world is large."

"You know what?" said Eisner after the police officer departed. "I have the notion that someone somewhere is holding this entire Swiss outfit at bayonet point. And hang me if it isn't the Gestapo!"

"The Gestapo is dead as a doornail," Schulze snorted.

"Dead, my aunt Josephine. You won't see any of those guys hanged. I wonder if the boss of your Josef Weber back in Konstanz was one of them. His face seemed familiar enough to me but I can't put my finger on him."

"Who cares?" I asked.

3

The Battalion of the Damned

THE old vaulted gate with the Tricolor fluttering overhead was open and inviting. At last, at the end of an odyssey across half of war-torn Europe, we were safely hidden – or so we thought. In a way we were indeed safe, but far from being hidden. Our bogus passports, identity cards, and birth certificates would not fool the French for long. Our meticulously prepared cover stories had been accepted, but only in the spirit of the Foreign Legion's ancient tradition: Ask no questions about a man's background, one is always fit enough to die. The short farewell speech of Major Jacques Barbier had made that quite clear.

"Your papers say that you are coming from Holland, Poland, Switzerland, and only God knows from where else. You should not think that we have swallowed all this German sauerkraut. You are nothing but Nazi canaille – all of you. Professional killers who just cannot stop shooting or who prefer a bullet to the rope. In Indochina you may do some more killing and receive all the bullets you want. Whether you perish or survive is of little importance to us. You belong to this army. You are wearing its uniform. But remember, we have no illusions about your allegiance to the Tricolor. All you've wanted was to cheat the hangman and you've succeeded, at least for the time being. But you should not be too overjoyed, for death is going to be your constant companion in Indochina."

The departure of the Japanese from Indochina had created a dangerous vacuum there which the postwar French Army could not readily fill. The British forces were about to quit, and the veteran troops of General de Gaulle were needed at home to prevent anarchy and a threatening Communist takeover in Paris. The prewar colonial army had been much humiliated by the Japanese and its survivors had but one desire left: to return home as fast as possible. If the colonial empire was to be preserved, France urgently needed a large number of skilled fighting men. The Foreign Legion had welcomed everyone willing to serve under the Tricolor – including the one-time "Nazi canaille."

Life was hard for the escaped German veterans. Soldiers of a defeated army seldom fare well, especially when they have no homes to return to. Relentless persecution and prolonged confinement was the share of those who had thrown themselves at the mercy of the victors. Interrogations, degradations, denazification trials . . . *Vae victis!* . . . "Woe to the vanquished!" The victors had even coined a new definition to outlaw the former nuclei of the German military might: "War Criminals." No victor in history had ever hanged defeated enemy generals, not even Attila the Hun or the Visigoths. The Allied revenge resembled the medieval *auto-da-fé* of the Holy Inquisition, brought forward into the twentieth century. Every general or staff officer, every functionary automatically fell under this damning definition. Every officer who had served in the SS, whether in the Dachau death camp or in the "Viking SS Panzer" division, had been judged en masse and denounced as a criminal. In the Allied occupation zones a hunt was on to put the SS behind bars or on the gallows. The French had better ideas. They would offer an arrested SS officer a choice: Join the Foreign Legion or be hanged!

France could not afford to ignore a rich well from which experienced veterans had been flowing ever since the day of the armistice. They required little training and even less explanation about their coming jobs. They could learn soon enough the few dozen French words of military importance.

Guns speak only one language.

After a few months in our new uniforms we no longer cared what the French may or may not have known about our past. It was becoming difficult to pretend military ignorance and play the stupid recruit, when we could have given a real *Kriegspiel* to our sergeants and corporals and shown them how to properly handle army hardware. We were seasoned veterans of countless battles and whatever the French were trying to teach us seemed utterly ridiculous to me. Erich Schulze, for instance, had won the Iron Cross twice in four years for his sharpshooting in Russia. He had enlisted in the Legion with the bogus papers of a Swiss clerk from the city electric board of Zurich. At the beginning of our new careers we were still careful to avoid any conflict between our filed background stories and our practical military behavior and always feigned the awkwardness that a greenhorn should display. "For God's sake don't try to perform here," we warned Schulze on our first shooting exercise. "You are supposed to be a Swiss clerk and not Wilhelm Tell."

"Oh, damn it all," Erich snapped, grabbing his rifle. "Few people are playing more army games than the Swiss. Every month they are probably shooting more bullets than the Sixth Army ever fired in the battle of Stalingrad. How long are we going to play the amateur? Do you think the French will kick you out because you hit the mark? At three hundred yards I could not miss that blasted board, not even if I wanted to." And without batting an eye he proceeded to put his bullets through the bull's-eye.

"What did you do in civilian life?" Sergeant Maurier queried Schulze.

"In the civilian life, Sergeant? I was in the army too!"

"Which army?" (As if he did not know.)

"The wrong one!" Erich grunted.

Maurier grinned. "I hate your guts, you German bastards," he commented. It was Maurier's pet expression while talking to us. He seemed to use that term even when he wanted to say "well done" or something similar. He must have found immense pleasure in showering us with insulting remarks and acid comments but I cannot really recall his ever having been deliberately mean or unjust. He just hated Germans, and made sure that we always kept that in mind. We were not in love with the French either. Our union was not even a marriage of convenience. It was a shotgun marriage.

Christmas was only five days away when we were sent to practice with heavy machine guns. Firing from eight hundred yards, Bernard Eisner shot his moving target, a mock-up troop carrier, to bits. Watching the display through his binoculars, Sergeant Maurier only grunted a quiet "I hate your guts, you German bastards." He spat and spoke to Eisner. "What were *you* doing before signing up?"

"Poultry farming!" Bernard replied, snapping home a fresh magazine.

"I hate your guts," Maurier complimented him again, "but you can shoot. It is no wonder that the Allies could not kill you all. I would like to see you shooting it out with the Viet Minh . . . the man-eaters." He chuckled. "Do you know what those yellow apes are shooting with? Poisoned arrows! You get it and the Holy Ghost cannot save you. You are dead in fifteen minutes. For you it might take a bit longer for you are tough. You should have bitten the dust a long time ago but you are still around . . . *merde!*" He spat again. "How I hate your guts, you goddamned German bastards. . . . *Rompez!*"

He walked away toward a small mound where he had been directing the target practice. As the sergeant moved, Eisner's machine gun slowly arched after him. Bernard's lips were set in a thin line and I saw murder in his eyes.

"Don't shoot, you idiot!" Schulze yelled jumping forward. "Bernard is going to blast Maurier" flashed through my mind. The next instant the fifty-caliber gun was blazing away, spitting a hail of tracers, mercifully past the mound but barely twenty inches from the slightly protruding belly of Sergeant Maurier. The edges of his tunic flipped violently under the tremendous pressure of air as the heavy slugs tore past him. Let it be said to his credit the sergeant did not duck, only paled and stood petrified. The bullets hit a small pine far out in the field, cutting it neatly in half. Eisner rose. He walked to the broken pine, brought it back, and stuck it into the soft earth in front of Maurier.

"Christmas is coming, Sergeant Maurier. The day of *love*. I know you have a large family to support on a small income. Here is a Christmas tree for your kids. . . . You don't have to buy one!"

Never again would Sergeant Maurier call us German bastards.

Oran, Colomb-Béchar in the African desert . . . one can't say that the soldiers of the Foreign Legion have not received the most grueling training that army recruits could ever experience. The combat readiness of the legionnaires surely matched the standard of any front-line German troops during the war. But one should remember that the majority of the recruits were already experienced veterans when they signed up.

For months we did nothing but train eight to ten hours every day. In a way it was quite understandable. In the desert there was nothing else to do and our corporals and sergeants would rather conduct field exercises than bore themselves to death sweating in the hot oppressive barracks. It never occurred to any staff officer that training in the desert would do little good to troops destined to serve in Madagascar, the Congo, or Indochina. I have to admit that the French were not entirely prejudiced, for even the most hardened German-hater in the High Command would probably agree that a former German officer should know a great deal more about warfare than, for instance, a North African corporal. Promotion of German veterans on merit was not entirely out of the question and before long we were sub-officers ourselves.

We were quite enthusiastic about leaving Africa for Indochina. For most of us the Far East meant only a wonderful pleasure trip at the state's expense: golden pagodas, exotic girls, ample shade against the ever-blazing sun, and maybe diamonds scattered about jungle ravines ready to be collected. Fighting? What could a few thousand wretched rebels do against the cream of the army? We might be compelled to fight a few rapid police actions but no one expected real fights. Besides, who was scared of real fights? We had survived a hundred of them. A couple of forays into the hills, and the rest would be only sightseeing. The sarcastic remark of

Major Barbier, "Death will be your constant companion in Indochina," scared no one. The good major obviously hated Germans so immensely that he found pleasure in trying to intimidate us. As for Sergeant Maurier and his "savages with their poisoned arrows," Maurier was an old windbag who considered himself a veteran although the only peril he had ever faced, as Eisner put it, was probably chronic indigestion due to lack of exercise. We knew that he had sat for seven months in the Maginot Line near Strasbourg, fifty feet underground, and then spent the rest of the war in a prison camp in Saxony.

The French have never been famous "housekeepers," but their Indochina household was indeed the most confused political, military, economic, and social mess a colonial power could possibly get itself into. Communism had little to do with the situation. It was a pure, twentyfour-carat French mess! In all my years there I could never really figure out what the French wanted or did not want to do and how they were planning to handle any of the alternatives. In the North it was different. For all his faults, Ho Chi Minh was keeping order, the sort of order the Soviet GPU maintained after the Russian Revolution. Nevertheless it *was* order. Dead men have no complaints, and when someone is being gently tickled with a bayonet and told to cheer, one cheers! The population of the South was divided among a dozen political parties, religious sects, chiefs, and chieftains. Every one of them had a different view on every issue – different aims and *modus operandi* – but all were corrupt to the core. Each party had its private army composed of common bandits, smugglers, and similar ruffians, often numbering as many as twenty thousand men. They would fight with or against one another or against the French authority. In reality these political groups were nothing but an Oriental version of the Sicilian Mafia, the overlords of city, vice, prostitution, and dope trade. It often happened that a private army would team up with the French for a couple of months to fight the guerrillas or a group of rival rebels. Then they would switch sides and assist the Viet Minh in exterminating a French garrison. They were not driven by any political consideration and fought only to share the spoils. The supreme leader of such an army often sat in a Saigon nightclub and exchanged merry toasts with a French general whose troops were being slaughtered at that very moment only fifty miles away. A few weeks later the same outfit might rejoin the French and be welcomed instead of disarmed, tried, and hanged. It was a total chaos which no orderly German mind could ever hope to comprehend, let alone consent to.

Germans can suffer much hardship but never chaos. Sometimes we felt like grabbing a couple of machine guns to clean out the city, moving from bar to bar, from villa to villa, and from whorehouse to whorehouse, starting with the local police chief, then continuing with such exalted party leaders as Diem and his cabinet – the whole rotten system that turned the country into a quagmire which swallowed up money, material, and men. It was a relief when we were sent out to fight in the jungle. The foul stink of corruption and utter impotence that hung over Saigon was choking us. We celebrated the invasion of the North as the first real action the French had undertaken in Indochina. But unfortunately (and once again) the easy victory was not followed up by the political and social measures that were essential and could have consolidated the French conquest. Instead of cleaning house the French only added a few more garbage dumps to the already existing ones.

Viet Tri, a small village north of Hanoi, had become the headquarters of the Legion. The only benefit that we received from the invasion of the North was that Hanoi seemed less infested with the red ants that pestered our lives in the South. We were still intermixed with troops of every race and creed, the majority of whom were entirely at a loss in the kind of war we were obliged to fight.

The guerrilla movement expanded. Engagements became more frequent and we suffered heavy losses. Mixed troops can never fight well. Men with different experience, stamina, and temperament can only hinder each other. Once we were deployed around a small settlement west of Hanoi, where, according to intelligence reports, a guerrilla attack was expected within a few hours. Bernard Eisner had sent three African legionnaires by jeep a few miles uproad. Their assignment was to keep a trail under observation. Suddenly we saw the jeep racing back, burning its tires in a cloud of dust. If its crew had fired they would have overtaken their own bullets.

"They are coming!" the men shouted as the vehicle skidded to a screaming halt. "We have to move into the woods."

"How many are they?" Eisner wanted to know.

"A thousand!" the North African corporal cried.

Bernard only lit a cigarette and asked for a cup of coffee, remarking, "If there are only a *hundred*, we will chew them up for breakfast."

"I said a *thousand!*" The corporal corrected what he thought was a misunderstanding.

"I heard you," Eisner reassured him. "But if *you* saw a thousand, there are only a hundred or even less."

Eisner was right. We deployed along the road and wiped out the Viet Minh detachment of seventy men. Had we not been there, the North Africans would have evacuated the important road junction and a convoy coming along the road an hour later would have been shot up.

We spent most of our time trying to prop up the faltering platoons or rescuing those whose positions were overrun by the guerrillas. "The eternal German duty," Eisner called it. Steadying a faltering ally, the Rumanians and Hungarians in Russia, the Italians in Africa, the French in Indochina. It was always the same story.

The Viet Minh soon realized on which section to concentrate an attack. They would seldom attack where we deployed. The effectiveness of the opposing fire alone had provided them the essential information as to where the hated Germans were. The enemy avoided us and concentrated on the Africans. But once they managed to break through a wavering flank we could do little about stemming the tide.

In the spring of 1948 we received a new commander. He was a short stocky man with a narrow Clark Gable moustache, dark hair and eyes; a tough, realistic officer who was willing to listen to the advice of experts, even if those experts happened to be ex-Nazi officers. To Colonel Simon Houssong, military service and political issues were two different things. Four days after he took charge of the brigade he called Eisner and me into his office.

"Sit down, gentlemen," he addressed us in a stern but friendly manner. "My name is Colonel Simon Houssong. I am in charge here. I have examined some reports on a few of your achievements in Indochina and I think we will get along together. I am not particularly fond of Nazis but I'm a soldier who fought you in fair combat during the war and I can appreciate soldierly valor. As you probably know by now, you were accepted by the Legion and brought to Indochina to die. You refused to succumb where hundreds of others had perished. I know that you have been sent to accomplish nearly impossible tasks, yet you have survived and returned. From now on we will plan and work within reason and as a team. What you were and what you may have done before joining the Legion is of no importance to me. Now we are only Europeans trying to stem an eastern tidal wave which threatens to bury my country and your country alike. Should the Communists win here, they will spread death and destruction elsewhere, even in Europe. We are in the same boat now and we will have to forget about the past."

We had a long informal talk about the general situation. The colonel seemed impressed by some of our suggestions. Soon our meeting looked more like a conference of general staff officers, rather than one of subordinates listening to their superior officer. The colonel ordered sandwiches and drinks. He addressed us as "Gentlemen" all the time. It was truly refreshing. After the first hour together we began to regard Houssong as shipwrecked sailors might regard a faraway lighthouse.

"I have not much sympathy for Nazis and particularly none for the SS," he repeated. "But I have seen the SS in action – military action I mean," he added with a smile. "Fight with the same zeal and we will get along fine," He went on. "What you have told me makes sense. The Viet Minh do follow Soviet and Chinese guerrilla strategy and tactics. From what you have told me I gather that you could counter them more effectively if given a chance. After all you have known them for a long time." From his desk he took a folder and handed me a thin, typewritten manuscript. "It is a translation of some of Mao Tse-tung's concepts on guerrilla warfare. I am sure you will find most of it familiar from your experience in Russia, but adapted to local conditions. Study the material and bring it back when you are through with it. In the meantime I shall endeavor to concentrate you in a single fighting unit composed only of Germans. Should I succeed, I will see to it that you regain your former ranks."

He shook hands with us, the first French officer to do so. We were not only overwhelmed but almost cried like children. "You do that, *mon colonel*, and we will see that you are the most decorated officer in Indochina," I said with enthusiasm before he dismissed us.

"I am not doing it either for decoration or for your benefit," Colonel Houssong answered quietly but firmly, "I am doing it for France. France should not suffer another defeat – especially not from the hands of Stone-Age savages. Were it for the good of France, I would ally myself with the Devil himself. I don't want to see Red flags flying either in Indochina or from the Eiffel Tower in Paris.

The Viet Minh was not a newcomer in Indochina. They were not a postwar phenomenon as many people may think. The movement was born in the Chinese town of Tienshui, in 1941, with the aim of fighting the Japanese invaders in order to earn the right to self-determination after the war. The leader of the movement was a hardened professional Communist, Ho Chi Minh, who enjoyed the full support of the Allies. American weapons, advisers, and even commando troops had been placed at Ho's disposal during the war, and the Viet Minh had fought the Japanese with resolution and bravery. After Japan's defeat British forces occupied the southern half of the country but soon ceded power and administration to the former French colonial overlords. Ho Chi Minh felt betrayed, and rightly so. His Viet Minh had not fought the Japanese so that the French could return. When he realized that the Allies were not even willing to talk with him about independence, he dissolved the Communist party and called every Indochinese patriot to gather under the flag of liberation. "Come to us, regardless of your political beliefs or social status," Ho Chi Minh proclaimed. And the people came.

The French reinstituted the corrupt and morally weak emperor Bao Dai, and this move widened the breach between the French and the Indochinese people. Yet there was still a chance to prevent a general war. In August 1945, the unpopular emperor resigned, handing over his powers to Ho Chi Minh, who then established a popular government in the North, composed not only of Communists but incorporating the leaders of various political factions and religious sects. A hundred thousand people gathered on Hanoi's main square to celebrate the birth of the Vietnam Democratic Republic. Strange as it may be now, Ho's guests of honor were not Soviet commissars but United States officers who appeared entirely satisfied with the state of affairs in the North.

Ho Chi Minh had to overcome immense difficulties. The Potsdam conference had partitioned Indochina into two occupation areas and Ho could harbor little hope for uniting the South with the North. After the first general elections in 1946, the Vietnamese parliament still included some of the openly anti-Communist political parties, but the Communists had already taken control of every key position. Elected as the first President of the Republic, Ho Chi Minh assumed dictatorial powers and was free to manage the nation's affairs the way he deemed fit. As a rule, no Communist government tolerates any opposition for long and Ho, too, chose the path of all Communist dictators. He began to liquidate his former non-Communist allies. He still wanted to preserve peace, especially with France, and was even ready to make concessions, promising that he would keep the independent Indochina within the French Commonwealth. But General de Gaulle, the hero of France and head of the government, was fully resolved to restore France to her former glory. The abandonment of an inch of French territory was out of the question. When the Fontainebleau conference ended in failure, Ho's guerrillas began to attack remote French garrisons. General Valluy decided to deliver a lasting lesson to the Communists and (certainly with the consent of the French Government) ordered a massive bombardment of Haiphong. The strike resulted in over 4,000 civilian casualties. Nguyen Giap needed only a few weeks to assemble his guerrillas and retaliate in kind by exterminating a dozen garrisons in the South. The Foreign Legion invaded the North. Ho Chi Minh withdrew into China and the Viet Minh moved into the hills, their former and familiar battlegrounds.

The Indochina war never really had a start and one has to admit that the Viet Minh were not the only ones to be blamed for the general conflagration. British and American political ignorance and senile strategy, along with French arrogance, were even more responsible for the outbreak of the "war without an end," as we used to call it. But it *was* the usual Communist sadism and inhumane brutality that turned the war into massacre and Indochina into a giant slaughterhouse where the opposing forces did not fight so much as butcher each other, with no mercy given or expected.

I was there at the beginning and I know that it was *not* the French who started the atrocities and what one may rightly call genocide. Genocide is a Communist specialty. Even Hitler's extermination camps were modeled after Stalin's death camps in Siberia. The GPU existed long before the Gestapo was conceived by the Nazis; Ho Chi Minh and Nguyen Giap had been attending the Soviet schools of subverison and murder long before the chimneys of Auschwitz began to smoke.

A curious interlude. . . .

Accompanied by Colonel Houssong and his aide, Lieutenant Derosier, two stern-looking civilians drove up to our barracks. Their visit was a short one but when they departed, Karl Stahnke was taken along with all his possessions. Tough for him, we thought. Stahnke had been a Gestapo agent during the war, the only one among us that we knew of. His life had been an enigma, even in the Legion. Stahnke never talked about his past. Except for some vivid descriptions of the various tortures the "Organization" used to employ, he said nothing of himself. "I was with the Gestapo," he stated flatly and that was that.

Stahnke could not have been a very bright agent, for few clever Gestapo agents were ever caught and prosecuted after the war. Maybe a couple of the lower-ranking bullies, but not the sophisticated experts. The Gestapo men had excellent papers and good connections at home and abroad, in many countries, including those of the victorious Allies. They could safely approach any of their wartime "associates", among them many influential people on whom the Gestapo was holding some compromising files. Eisner was convinced that our former Zurich refugee, the Herr Engineer, the madam, and maybe a few of the higher-ranking Canton officials and police officers had been, in one way or the other, under pressure from the German Gestapo. The fingers of the Gestapo had been very long and God knows what files may have been kept on our Swiss "friends". The Swiss were always good businessmen who would seldom do something for nothing. Stahnke must have been quite inept if his only escape route was the French Foreign Legion.

"That's the last we will see of Stahnke," Eisner remarked. "He should never have come along in the first place. The *Deuxième Bureau* has him cold. Why, he even worked in France!"

But Eisner was wrong. We met Karl Stahnke a few months later in, of all places, a Hanoi bar! He was wearing a clean white tropical suit, had plenty of money, and looked quite drunk.

"*Merde alors, kameraden*," he greeted us cordially, shaking hands, slapping shoulders, pulling over some more chairs. "Don't look at me as if I were a ghost.... Sit down. How are you doing?"

"How are *you* doing, Karl?" Schulze countered. "We thought you had had it."

"Had it? What?"

"With the *Deuxième Bureau*."

"Oh, you are talking about *those* boys," he boomed. He rose. Drawing his chest full of air he fingered the lapels of his expensive suit. "What do you say to this, eh?"

"Don't tell me that you have only been discharged," Eisner said.

"Discharged? It is not *that* easy to get out of the Legion." He downed his beer and ordered a round for everyone. "No, fellows. Old Uncle Stahnke is doing his familiar and beloved job. They had a dozen captured terrorists at Hué who seemed to know much but wanted to talk little. The French thought that with my experience I might be of better use."

"Hell, man!" Schulze blurted. "Are you telling us that the French know all about your Gestapo business and let you get away with it?"

"I have no idea what the French may know or may not know," Stahnke exploded. "But they sure as hell *know* something, otherwise they would never have taken me to Hué. Boys," he chuckled, "they have everything that belongs to the trade at Hué. Only the Fuehrer's picture is missing from the walls."

"How about the Frenchmen you worked over in Calais, Karl?"

Stahnke uttered a short derisive snort. "Frenchmen? For the

guys I am working with, they weren't Frenchmen but bloody Communists."

"Don't say!"

"And don't you be naïve." Stahnke laughed. "*Le Grand Chef* has a complete list of the fellows I used to entertain at Calais. Do you know what was his comment? 'You've saved us a lot of work and plenty of bullets, Stahnke.' That's what *he* said. 'Now you make the Commies talk'."

"Did you make them talk?"

Stahnke laughed drunkenly. "No one has ever refused to talk to good old Uncle Stahnke. I had a very fruitful panel discussion with the Communists the French were holding at Hué. I mean it was fruitful for me. One of the toughs had been at the Agitprop school in Russia. Was he ever stubborn! It took me six hours of convincing to make him sing. But it was entirely his fault. I told him at the very beginning, 'Your game is up so you had better tell Uncle Stahnke everything he wants to know. You will have a quick, painless death. You won't feel a thing. If you keep your mouth shut, your death is going to be a long, endless cry of agony.' Do you think he appreciated my offer? Like hell he did. He made me work all night, but when I was through with him he sang all the same. He sang like a nightingale, even though I was squeezing his bloody balls with a nutcracker. Then all of a sudden he broke free and came at me with a glowing steel rod which he grabbed from the fire. I had to shoot him in the head."

Stahnke emptied his glass and looked around. "Boys, you had better get ready. Soon there'll be plenty trouble here. The *Légion Etrangère* will need every German bastard – otherwise the world may wake up one morning to see the hammer and sickle flying from every damned pole from Hanoi to London and from Stockholm to Rome."

Karl Stahnke was well informed both on the coming trouble and the Legion's need for German bastards. In the summer of 1948, all former German troops were carefully screened (this time properly, with a bespectacled French captain quoting the various details of our real backgrounds, from a bulging pile of green, yellow, and red files) and interrogated again. One-time paratroopers, partisan hunters, Brandenburgers, field gendarmery, mountaineers, commandos, Wehrmacht, and SS, were all regrouped into a new battalion. The battalion consisted of about nine hundred men forming three companies. Its future existence or nonexistence was of little importance to the French High Command. We became a sort of special task force which was to be given minimum support yet expected to accomplish the impossible. The North Africans nicknamed us "The *Kamikaze* Battalion" and the men would greet us with raised fists crying, "*Banzaaai!*" Colonel Houssong succeeded in concentrating us in a single fighting unit and even "recovered" some of our former ranks. More he could not do for us. For Paris and the French High Command we were the battalion of the damned. So we set out to earn their respect.

4

The Convoy "Must Get Through!"

SOME North African and other mixed troops of the Foreign Legion were magnificent soldiers, incredibly brave in the attack and tenacious in the defense. What they lacked was proper food and medical care, ample ammunition, timely reinforcements; but most of all they lacked the knowledge of how to combat insurgents. They had been given comprehensive training in conventional combat strategy and tactics in the North African deserts and the barren, rocky mountains such as the Atlas. Then they had been sent to Indochina to wage an unconventional war in the jungles and swamps of a country that was totally alien to them. They had fought bravely and suffered fifty percent casualties. The survivors were regrouped, attacked again, and once more their ranks were decimated by the Viet Minh. They could man a fort or a distant stronghold purely on the defensive, but in the jungles the North African troops were useless. To them the impenetrable green sea of bamboo and lianas seemed utterly hostile, full of unexpected traps, tigers, scorpions, venomous snakes, diseases, and other invisible enemies – among them human enemies whom they could not see, let alone destroy.

With us it was different. We could and did adapt to our new

environment and I enforced our new "rules of the game" with vigorous discipline. Being on the average far more intelligent, the former German veterans could put up with more misery yet suffer less than the other troops suffered. I have never regarded my men as only subordinates but as my veteran German comrades in peril. Officers and ranks had been calling each other by Christian names but our intimacy never jeopardized common discipline. When it came to military discipline the otherwise casual "Hello, Hans" or "Damn you, Karl" quickly turned into a "*Jawohl, Herr Oberleutnant*" or "Yes, sir!"

We used to talk things over and my men understood the importance of keeping themselves clean, healthy, and fit for action. We boiled or purefied our drinking water, even in the most adverse circumstances. When we could not do so, we suffered from thirst. Except for climbing steep mountains, one can always move on and make another step forward. The capabilities of a healthy human body are virtually unlimited. One can always go without water for two days even in a land of extreme humidity. In my battalion everyone duly consumed his daily ration of vitamin pills that more often than not we had to purchase from private pharmacists at our own expense. On the road our principal nourishment was rice, sometimes curried, sometimes only boiled, and dried fish, or whatever the jungle could provide. We had purchased large quantities of camphor and menthol creams from which excellent mosquito and leech repellents could be prepared. We had learned that in Russia. Every one of us carried a small mosquito net, good enough to cover one's face and hands while resting in a swamp or near rice paddies after dark. In order to keep fit, sufficient rest was of paramount importance in Indochina. Men with swollen eyes and legs covered with festering sores, men devoid of sleep and tormented by belly cramps could not be expected to fight and defeat the Viet Minh. After the day's march and no matter how worn they may have been, my men had to remove their boots, dry them if wet, clean them inside and outside, and grease the leather to keep the footwear watertight. Also all the weapons had to be cleaned and oiled every evening.

Sometime in 1948 or 1949 I got hold of a book written by a British officer named Spencer Chapman, who had spent several years in the jungles of Malaya leading local guerrillas against the

Japanese. His book, *The Jungle Is Neutral*, I regarded as an alphabet on guerrilla warfare or, for all that, antiguerrilla warfare. For the benefit of my men I held regular daily seminars citing important information from Chapman's book. We used many of the British officer's ruses, such as booby traps hidden in hollow sections of bamboo, with outstanding results. From his descriptions we also learned much about the ideology and psychology of the Communist guerrillas. This gallant officer and former foe forged many "German" victories in Indochina and also saved the lives of many of my men. His book became a sort of Holy Writ on jungle war in my battalion, and in my opinion it was superior to Mao Tse-tung's concepts, the Holy Writ of the Viet Minh. With a couple of field commanders like Spencer Chapman the Foreign Legion would have defeated the Viet Minh in a year.

All the same we also studied Mao's writings on guerrilla warfare and managed to turn many of his ruses against his own Indo-chinese henchmen. Old Ho Chi Minh must have had a few sleepless nights because of our activities. We always paid off the guerrillas in kind: bomb for bomb, bullet for bullet, murder for murder.

They did not like it.

We defeated the Communists at their own game but never as regulars versus insurgents, rather as guerrillas against guerrillas. War against guerrillas in the jungle is not a war of airplanes and tanks. It is a war of wits.

We introduced ourselves to the Communist chief of staff, Nguyen Giap, in the North, near the Chinese frontier where one of his rugged battalions besieged a small French garrison thirty-two miles from Cao Bang. The garrison consisted of a stockade with blockhouses defended by about one hundred and twenty Legionnaires. The fort had been built by the Japanese, then modernized by the French to guard the road between Cao Bang and Bac Kan farther to the South.

The guerrillas, about six hundred strong, surrounded the stockade and kept it under constant fire from the neighboring woods and hills. The Viet Minh battalion commander, who learned his trade in Mao's militia, decided to extort a quick victory before reinforcements could move in. He lined up forty French prisoners two hundred yards from the palisade, in plain sight of the fort, then sent a message that he was going to execute one prisoner every five minutes until the commander of the fort, a young French lieutenant, decided to surrender. When the period of grace was over, the Viet Minh proceeded with the executions in a most horrible fashion, obviously with the aim of intimidating the garrison. They chopped off first the right then the left arm of the prisoners, broke their legs with iron bars and finally shot the men in the head one after another – at five-minute intervals.

After the sadistic butchery of ten prisoners the guerrilla commander graciously granted one hour for the French to decide whether they wanted to witness the massacre of ten more prisoners. The mental torment of the lieutenant must have been shattering; he had arrived in Indochina only a few months before, and it was his first real experience with the Viet Minh. As he told us later he had never dreamed that something like this could ever happen in the twentieth century.

The lieutenant's troops were aghast. Several of the legionnaires in the stockade suffered a nervous breakdown and began to sob like children; one man went berserk and had to be locked up – but that was precisely what the Viet Minh commander had hoped to accomplish by his medieval butchery.

I was on a foray in the vicinity with only one hundred men when I received the order to assist the garrison "by all available means." By the time we managed to establish radio contact, fifteen of the prisoners had already been executed by the terrorists, and the lieutenant was on the verge of raising the white flag. When he learned that we were only one hundred, he almost cried in desperation. "There are more than six hundred terrorists in the woods. You will be slaughtered the moment they spot you," he said. I implored him to hold on.

Knowing that a direct assault on the enemy would be futile, I decided to pull a desperate coup. Instead of rushing to the aid of the fort, we descended on the nearest villages, which were almost devoid of male population. We knew where the men were!

The headman was led forward in the first village. There was no time to waste. "Point out the family of the Communist commander and name all those whose menfolk are assaulting the stockade!" Eisner snapped without preliminaries. The man would not tell. Eisner repeated the question with his gun against the man's temple. He waited for a moment then pulled the trigger. "Bring here three of his kids!" he commanded his troopers, and, as the boys were gathered, their mother ran forward screaming, trying to break the ring of steel. "I will tell you!" she cried. "I will tell you!"

Fifteen minutes later we were on the way toward the stockade, herding over a hundred Viet Minh relatives, the wives and children of the terrorists in front of the column. One of the hostages I sent ahead to the guerrilla commander with the demand that unless he surrendered, their relatives would be executed at five-minute intervals.

I was resolved to show the enemy that terror, brutality, and cold-blooded murder were not their monopoly, a Communist privilege, and that at least my battalion was ready to pay them tit for tat. They understood no other language.

Taking position on a dominant hill about three hundred yards from the enemy, we lined up the guerrilla relatives in plain sight on the edge of a precipice. The Viet Minh commander did not seem to care much for his own family, but his companions did. The shooting around the stockade stopped abruptly; there was a frozen silence, then we heard savage yells and arguments; the enemy camp exploded in a bloody mutiny. The terrorists whose families we were holding began to kill their own superiors and commissars, along with everyone else who wanted to fight on. Then they surrendered.

Our action saved the lives of twenty-four French prisoners and relieved the fort. The hostages were allowed to return home, but all the guerrillas who had surrendered to us were executed on the riverside and their bodies were thrown into the water.

Never in the past had the Viet Minh experienced a similar rebuff, not even under the Japanese. Our swift and stiff action had its effect. For weeks afterwards the terrorists lay low and when we moved into a village there was silence. When we asked questions they were answered without hesitation. The guerrillas held back, measuring us, contemplating, trying to determine the best way to oppose us.

They did not appreciate *our* kind of warfare.

We were ordered to escort a convoy of trucks with supplies for a beleaguered North African garrison near Tuyen Quang, a hundred and twenty miles from Hanoi. It was the sort of action which ordinary regulars could call a "*kamikaze* sortie," because in those days to convoy a train of heavy vehicles across Viet Minh-controlled territory could rightly be called a suicide mission. The vehicles had to traverse jungles and valleys with a visibility of fifteen yards on either side; they had to pass a hundred places where a few hidden mines and machine guns could blow everything to smithereens. The French had already tried to rush a convoy through the same route. It had been destroyed by the guerrillas at a jungle section marked in our operational maps as Point 206.

"The convoy must get through," said Colonel Houssong. "Should the guerrillas blast you, we may write off an entire brigade along with a dozen relatively loyal villages."

We had a conference over the maps and aerial photos of the area, but from whichever angle I surveyed the situation, the project appeared grim. I discussed the mission with my officers and we came up with a feasible plan. Since I could not well present our plan to Colonel Houssong, I only stated that I could guarantee the arrival of the convoy only if I was to have a free hand to do the job by whatever means I saw fit.

"Do it, then," Colonel Houssong consented, giving us carte blanche. "The convoy must get through. And not only five trucks but the *whole* convoy."

I said, "We will take the whole convoy through, *mon colonel* – or we will never return."

Forward!

At a steady fifteen miles per hour, sometimes even slower. We sat on the leading tank, Schulze and I, surveying the jungle. Behind us came an armored troop carrier but it transported only four soldiers.

The rest of the passengers were civilians. Following the troop carrier came, under the command of Bernard Eisner, a half-track with four mounted loudspeakers. Behind the half-track a column of sixteen trucks loaded with ammunition, food, and other supplies. On the crates more civilians: the families of the local Viet Minh. Many of them we knew by name. They had not been harmed, and we had tried to comfort them with food and water. Of course they were crying, lamenting, but so were all those women and children whose breadwinner had been executed by the terrorists for no worse offense than a refusal to join them.

"The convoy must get through!" the colonel had said. We were resolved to take it through. We were also resolved to stay alive in the process – two hundred men against more than a thousand enemy in the area. The enemy was holding all the trump cards, save for one strong ace that we were holding – their families!

Ahead of us lay the jungle, and traversing the jungle, a dirt road. On either side dense underbush, a treacherous green sea of weeds that had swallowed up many convoys and many men. When we entered the first Communist-controlled village, we had found only old people, women, and children at home. Every man of military age – husbands, fathers, brothers, and sons – had been absent. We had known where they were – not very far away. A large army convoy represented plenty of booty for the guerrillas. When they saw us coming, they had grabbed their weapons and had withdrawn into the woods.

My earphone crackled. Eisner was reporting: "We shall be at Point 206 in five minutes."

Point 206, where only ten days ago the guerrillas had exterminated another convoy, blowing up twelve trucks and killing ninety men. Afterwards the enemy had withdrawn into the jungle, taking everything that could be removed. The "Paras" went to search the villages but could find no trace of either guerrillas or of the stolen army hardware. Of course the Paras had known only too well where the culprits were; at home in their villages, tending the fields, milking cattle, or carting vegetables to the markets of Hanoi. The stolen goods and the guerrilla weapons had been safely hidden to be used another day.

Searching the villages would never do much good. The Viet Minh had known better than to leave incriminating evidence lying about. The French High Command had been frustrated.

The generals could not order the arrest of the entire male population of a dozen villages and cart them off for investigation.

Point 206, "Massacre Valley," as the Paratroops had called the place. Eisner's loudspeakers came to life, calling the hidden terrorist leaders.

"Commissar Thiu Xhan... Commissar Thiu Xhan. Your wife, Lha, is asking you not to attack the convoy.... Your children, only ten, eight, seven, and five want to live and grow up. Can you hear us, Commissar Thiu Xhan?... Your wife and children are riding on truck number four. They will be released unharmed when we arrive at our destination...."

Forward!

At a steady fifteen miles per hour. The road disappeared around a bend. As though we were riding inside a tunnel of creepers, frontal visibility was fifty yards; to the left or to the right – nil. The turrent hatch of our tank was open with Schulze and I riding astride; our closest companions were three Viet Minh prisoners; two of them former propagandists, the third one a Viet Minh company leader. We had fastened them to the turret. The prisoners belonged to the same terrorist outfit which we expected to encounter on the road to Yen Bay.

We rode in plain sight. It was like a game of poker between professional gamblers on either side of the table. But our table was two hundred square miles of jungle. The stakes: three hundred lives. We were playing out a strong ace which our partners had not taken into consideration.

The loudspeakers blared constantly.

"Manh Ghiu... Manh Ghiu... Think of your wife and children, traveling in the second truck. They are safe as long as you hold your fire."

The convoy must get through!

In those days the guerrilla setup was somewhat different. Viet Minh units which terrorized a district did not come from any other part of the country but operated within a twenty-to-fifty-mile circle around their own villages. We based our plans on that very fact. Entering the first hostile locality we had rounded up all the guerrilla relatives and loaded them on to our vehicles, then we rested for fifteen minutes, giving time for the Viet Minh runners to spread the news.

The convoy rolled and the loudspeakers blared, calling every known or suspected guerrilla by his name.

"Huo Tanh . . . Huo Tanh . . . Your wife and three children, Sue, Tan, and Minh, are begging you not to shoot at the convoy. They are traveling in the number seven truck. . . ."

"Pam Phu from Nguyen . . . Pam Phu from Nguyen . . . At this very moment you may be sighting a machine gun. . . . Shoot well, Pam Phu, for your father Hanh and wife Shiri are with us in the troop carrier!"

The convoy must get through. We will take it through!

"Ming Ghue . . . Ming Ghue . . . we don't know where you are but we do know where your sons are, Ming Ghue. . . . They are riding in truck number six! Are you going to kill them, Ming Ghue? Then fire your gun. . . . Fire your gun and they will all die. Can you hear us, Ming Ghue?"

Forward!

Another bend. Behind the bend a dozen large logs blocked the road – the usual terrorist preparation for ambush. The convoy stopped. It was now or never. With the engines cut, silence fell on the stationary vehicles. I could hear the sharp clicks as my men bolted home cartridges. I could hear my heart throbbing.

We took no cover. One should display confidence in a battle of nerves. No shooting yet. . . . A woman was speaking through the loudspeakers. Her faltering voice was choked with emotion and fear.

"Commissar Thiu . . . Thiu my husband . . . There are eighty women and fifty children in this convoy, among them our own children. . . . We were not harmed and the soldiers gave us food.

They will release us near Yen Bay. . . . If you fire on the convoy, you will shoot us too. . . ."

Five minutes went by, yet no attack came. Our ace was holding good. It was a very mean card, but in a very mean war one cannot play the fair gentleman or one will perish. The convoy *will* arrive. Not only five trucks but the whole convoy. There will be rewards. I could already imagine the headlines of *L'Humanité* in Paris: "SS killers at large in Indochina, slaughtering innocent civilians." The living hostages will be "slaughtered civilians" in Paris and in the leftist press. And, of course, they were innocent. Always innocent, even while blazing away with mortars or machine guns. Those who shot poisoned arrows into the backs of the sentries or the guerrilla wives who had once tried to plant cholera-infected human refuse into the wells of a garrison – they, too, had been innocent. The Communists are always innocent.

The roadblock had to be removed.

"Commissar Thiu . . . Can you hear us Commissar Thiu? We are going to remove your roadblock. . . . Our men will carry no weapons and if you kill them, we shall consider it cold-blooded murder. For every one of them killed, three of your own will pay with their lives. We are not North Africans, Commissar Thiu. We are Germans! You have surely heard of us in the Soviet schools. You have never met us before but you will soon find out that we are not beginners. We were fighting Communist marauders long before you learned how to load a rifle. We shall give you bomb for bomb, bullet for bullet, and murder for murder. . . . Do you hear us, Commissar Thiu? We are removing your roadblock and we are moving on. . . ."

Karl Pfirstenhammer and twenty men began to work on the logs, roping them to the tank one by one. The engine roared and the logs moved. Fifteen minutes later the road was clear. We had won the first round.

Forward!

The valley widened and we came upon the charred skeletons of the vehicles of another convoy. We passed the graves of those who had traveled in them.

More woods – more bends. No one could tell what might be waiting for us beyond a bend. Our tank churned around the bend.

Halt!

A lone guerrilla was standing on the road waving a white flag. For a second time the convoy stopped bumper to bumper. The guerrilla spoke fluent French. "You cannot move on," he said, his face full of hatred. "The road is mined. We had no time to remove the mines."

I glanced at Erich Schulze. He began to laugh, loudly, hysterically. "Wonderful," he mumbled, dropping from the turret. He leaned with his head against the armor shaking with laughter. "Hans, you have pulled *this* one all right. . . . Don't ever tell it in Hanoi or they'll call you the bloodiest liar who ever lived."

I walked up to the guerrilla. He was a young man, maybe thirty years old, wearing a grey canvas overall and a pair of French army boots. His bearing told me that he was of some rank. We stood for a while sizing up each other. I could see no fear in his eyes, only hatred, defiance, fanaticism – the well-known symptoms of the "Red Malady."

They had mined the road but had changed their minds.

"We need thirty minutes to free the road," said he and the muscles in his face twitched. The man was nervous, outplayed, frustrated.

"*Très bien, mon ami,*" I replied quietly. "Do it fast." I jerked a thumb toward our three captive guerrillas prominently roped to the turret of the tank. "Your comrades are not very comfortable up there and we have yet a long way to go."

"It will be your last ride, you swine!" he sneered, his eyes ablaze with savage courage. "We will skin you alive for this!"

"You may swear as much as you like, *mon ami,*" I shrugged. "You are holding a flag of truce."

"Yes!" Schulze interposed, stepping up to the guerrilla. "Would you mind putting it down for a moment? Just long enough for me to smash your face, you little yellow ape, you jungle midget. We have eaten bigger boys than you are for breakfast in Russia."

"Hold it, Erich!"

The guerrilla fixed his eyes on me.

"You are in charge here?"

"It could be. . . ."

"You have my wife and children with you."

"Most unfortunate."

"I want to see them."

"At your beautiful little town of Yen Bay – let us hope."

"I want to see them now!"

"If you wish to surrender," I suggested, lighting a cigarette, "you may even join them in the truck. The ride is free."

He spat contemptuously, barely missing my boots. A tough one!

"I shall never surrender," he hissed, his voice full of malice. "I shall see you all dead and rotting in the jungle."

"The Russians wanted the same and they had a great deal more bullets than what you have, *mon ami*," Schulze sneered. "And they were the masters. You are only little apprentices. That little." He showed it with his open fingers. "If you want to see us dead, you will have to kill us nine times over."

Standing in the bend we could see a dozen camouflaged men working on the road farther down, digging up mines, filling ditches, removing more logs.

"Where is your esteemed Commissar Thiu?" I spoke to the terrorist. "This is a good time for mutual introduction. I would like to see him."

"You will see him soon enough," said he. "Thiu always inspects the enemy corpses!"

A witty one as well.

Schulze stepped right up to him. The frail form of the five-foot Viet Minh seemed to shrink even more against the background of Erich's muscular shoulders and six-foot-two-inch frame.

"Your Thiu spent a long time in Russia, learning the Communist ways of setting the world afire." He spoke slowly but his voice was a long spell of threats. "You will soon learn that we have also attended some classes in Russia. Thiu won't be the first Red commissar whom we have hanged."

"That I can believe," the guerrilla sneered, pursing his lips in contempt. "Using women and children to shield your tanks. Great fighters are you – you Germans! The French must really be hard up to have needed you here to fight their wars."

Schulze smiled. "You don't like our kind of warfare, do you? But you will see more of it, worse than what you are seeing now.

The days of your hide-and-seek games with the Legion are over. You may have played your killing games with the apprentices, my friend, but now the professors are coming, the experts. Do you know what the Russians used to call us? The headhunters! That's right. And we know the rules of all your games. We have played them before a thousand times against those who taught you. You may run into the jungle when you see us coming but beware when you see us leaving, for you may find no village to go back to."

There was a yell, and the guerrillas vanished from the road.

The emissary glanced at his watch. It appeared an expensive one, probably taken from the wrist of a French officer. "You may start in ten minutes," he said. "We shall let you pass here. We have no choice. You leave our people at Yen Bay."

"Don't worry, friend. We always keep our part of a bargain."

He snapped. "Don't call me a friend. It is an insult!"

"I will remind you of that when we meet another day," I replied.

"I hope we will meet."

"So do we."

We drove on and reached the next village without trouble. There we released some of our hostages and took new ones. Knowing the Viet Minh, I doubted if they would care much about a dozen strange civilians from a distant village. I decided to keep our involuntary cargo up-to-date all the way.

It was getting toward noon and the sun began to blaze in earnest. Riding abreast the tank turret, the three Viet Minh chieftains really suffered. Schulze released them during our rest in the village and gave them food and water. One of the guerrillas, the former company leader, had had enough. Having come from the neighborhood, the man appeared increasingly distressed when the time came to get on the road again. While he was being escorted back to the tank, he told his guard that he wanted to speak to Schulze (Erich had comforted him with a few cigarettes during the morning ride). "I want to talk to your commander," he whispered. "I must see him alone."

"So be it," Schulze nodded without demanding an explanation. We had heard similar requests before. When a guerrilla decided to say something it always had to be in private. I walked a few dozen yards into the jungle and Erich brought the man over.

"What's up, Tan Hwan?" I spoke to the man without preliminaries.

He glanced around nervously, making sure that we were well out of sight and hearing; then he said with great urgency in his voice, "You cannot go on this road to Yen Bay. . . ." He broke off abruptly as though still not quite decided how much to tell. "It is . . . it is. . . ."

I offered him a cigarette. "What is wrong with the road, Tan Hwan?"

"Everybody will die. You, the women, the children."

"The others have not been hurt."

I was becoming a bit impatient with his long prologue before getting to the point. "What is it, then?" I snapped. "Say what you want to say."

He said, "Lieutenant . . . I have been studying in France. I am an engineer –"

"To the point, Tan Hwan!" I cut in sharply. "I am not curious about your life story."

"I've decided to quit this senseless war," he went on quickly. "I want to see my country free but not at such a price. Intelligent people do not shoot at each other. They talk. This is becoming more and more senseless, more and more out of hand."

"We did not start it, Tan Hwan," Schulze interposed. "And if you *are* an engineer, you should be intelligent enough to know that if the French really wanted to fight, no Viet Minh could ever defeat them. What do you want to tell us about the road?"

"Will you set me free?"

"Do you want to change sides?" I asked him somewhat sceptically.

"I don't want to change sides. I want to save those women and children, and your lives as well. Then I want to get away from it all."

"Turn around!" I commanded briskly.

He obeyed, turning slowly – a puzzled look, mixed with anxiety, on his face. Taking my knife I cut away the ropes around his wrists.

"Now, suppose you tell us about the road."

"Bamboo bombs!" he exclaimed. "Hundreds of them . . . only ten miles from here. Do you have a map?"

Schulze opened his map case for the former guerrilla leader.

"Here!" Tan Hwan pointed out a section of woods. "Right here, near the streams. You can never pass."

"By now the guerrilla commander knows that we took hostages."

"Kly wouldn't care. He was educated in China and for him only the Party matters. If you blow up on the bombs, he will display the corpses of the women and children as though they were massacred deliberately by you."

"I see. . . ."

So it was to be bamboo bombs, I thought. I had seen a few of those devilish native inventions: a ball of bamboo leaves packed solid under a netting of wire, filled with high explosive or grenades and hundreds of short, sharpened bamboo fragments, stakes with their points frequently poisoned. Fitted with a primer to act on pressure, or by trip wire, the football-sized bombs could easily mow down a platoon. Also, since they were green, it was almost impossible to spot them against the foliage.

"Many of the bombs are suspended from the trees," Tan Hwan explained. "If they fall on the trucks, they will kill everyone."

"How do you know so much about them?"

He paused, wiped his perspiring face, then said, "I designed them, Lieutenant. The whole trap, and many others before."

"You must have killed quite a few Frenchmen, Tan Hwan."

"I know," he admitted. "I saw them dying. They died horribly."

He asked for another cigarette. Schulze gave him a whole pack. The man broke four matches trying to light his cigarette.

"Is there an ambush in the making as well?" Erich asked.

"No, not immediately. The men are farther up in the hills. But they could not remove the bombs anyway. The Viet Minh will attack only after the bombs have exploded. I know a bypass," Tan Hwan added after a pause. "Will you still set me free?"

"You *are* free! I am going to give you a pass to Hanoi."

"I don't want to go to Hanoi. I am going to Saigon. No one knows me there."

"Where is your family?"

"I have no family. The Japanese killed them."

"We will get you to Saigon, Tan Hwan."

We had to cover up his sudden defection, and I knew the best way of doing it. I told Schulze to escort Tan Hwan farther down the road where he could board the tank without being seen by his companions or the civilians. I drew my revolver. "Now yell!" I told him. "Yell as loud as you can . . . Long live Ho Chi Minh . . . Down with the French colonialists." As he yelled, I fired five bullets into the woods. "Now you won't have to be afraid of any Viet Minh revenge, Tan Hwan," I told him as I reloaded my gun. "Cheer up! You have just been executed. Old Ho might even give you a posthumous medal."

"Come!" Erich urged him and the two walked down the road. I returned to the convoy. The two other guerrillas had already been returned to the tank turret. I ordered them removed to truck eleven.

They had seen us marching off with Tan Hwan, had heard the yells and the five shots. Now they saw me returning without their companion. "You shot him!" one of the captives yelled at me. "You killed him in cold blood. . . . Remember this day, officer. . . . Remember this day." The man cursed all the way back along the convoy, lamenting the fate of the "martyred" Tan Hwan.

Mounting the tank, I called Pfirstenhammer in the troop carrier. "Karl, you stay put with the convoy for about five minutes, then follow us."

"O.K., Hans!"

Driving on with the tank we picked up Schulze and Tan Hwan. Similar tricks had worked well in occupied Russia where we used to "execute" a large number of turncoats every day, especially for the benefit of their families still living in the shadow of Stalin and the secret police.

Forward!

Tan Hwan was as good as his word. He showed us the bypass, a cleverly arranged diversion through a dry, shallow ravine. But we could not leave that deadly booby-trapped section of road behind for other tropps to fall into. Tan Hwan had already mentioned that the guerrilla camp was farther up in the hills and that the enemy was waiting for the explosions before attacking the convoy.

It did not take long for us to prepare a counter-trap. Leaving the convoy in the sheltered ravine we hauled ten large gasoline drums and a few ammo cases onto the road. At a safe distance, Riedl parked two trucks at awkward angles, one of them with its front wheels in a ditch, with its doors and windows wide open. The vehicles appeared to be broken down and abandoned. The tank was driven partly off the road, its turret turned around with the gun pointing against a tree barely five feet from the muzzle. Around the tank and the vehicles we planted a few oily rags and dumped some diesel oil on the ground.

Not far from the trap a narrow footpath ran up towards the hills, the path of the terrorists. "They should be coming down on that path," Tan Hwan explained. "When they hear the explosions they won't be long. There is no other way for them to come."

Taking a hundred men from the convoy we proceeded to establish a ring of steel about the place. Schulze and thirty headhunters took care of the path. Pfirstenhammer, with two platoons carrying light machine guns and flamethrowers, went down the road to seal the escape route toward Yen Bay. Eisner and forty men deployed on the far side of the "abandoned" vehicles, between the road and the ravine. Riedl remained in charge of the convoy and I stayed in the tank with Tan Hwan, the driver, and the two gunners.

I called to my companions in German. We never spoke French on the wireless. Everyone was ready.

Eisner fired a short burst into the gasoline drums. They burst into flame and began to explode, setting off the ammo crates; in a matter of seconds the place looked like hell, with thick black smoke rising above the woods. Ten minutes later Schulze radioed: "They are coming, Hans!"

"Let them pass!"

I signaled to Eisner, who thereupon sent a couple of men to set fire to the rags which had been scattered near the vehicles. The scene was indeed very realistic. Everything on the road seemed to be afire. "They are passing now," Schulze reported again. "About two hundred of them."

"Hold your fire, Erich," I warned him.

"It is damned difficult," he replied in a subdued voice. "We could kick them in the ass."

I closed the turret hatch down to a few inches to permit observation and soon saw the first batch of guerrillas spilling from the bushes, swarming onto the road. "*Xung! Phong!*" they screamed. "Forward! Kill!" The "dead" tank suddenly came to life. Backing onto the road, we began to fire point-blank into the terrified mob. Eisner and his machine gunners began to play their own music and from the trail Schulze closed in with guns blazing. We had the enemy in the bag.

On the road a few dozen terrorists had already fallen, others had dropped beside the road, wounded or dying. Realizing that they had run into a trap, the guerrilla commander wanted to withdraw but bumped into Schulze's outfit. Turning toward the ravine, they were beaten back by Eisner's machine gunners. On the road, Pfirstenhammer's platoon was pushing them back with MGs and flamethrowers spitting fifty-foot flames. It was massacre.

The enemy had only one way to flee – through the booby-trapped patch of forest, a bit of real estate which I cheerfully permitted them to have. About seventy of the survivors now began to throw away their weapons. We stopped firing at them but kept the flamethrowers working, pushing the demoralized mob farther back on the road, step by step into their own trap with the bamboo bombs and God knows what else. They would either run or get roasted.

The trap did the rest. A quarter of an hour later we could still hear explosions and death cries coming from the woods.

Climbing from the turret, I heard a sudden blast inside the tank. Dropping back inside I saw Tan Hwan falling from his seat, blood oozing from his head. Somehow he had got hold of our driver's gun and had shot himself in a moment of anguish. He was our only casualty.

The convoy arrived at its destination. Not only a few trucks but the whole convoy. The Viet Minh had begun to know us in the way we wanted them to know our battalion.

Bomb for bomb! Bullet for bullet! Murder for murder!

They had enjoyed many years of unpunished rampaging. We were resolved to put an end to it. We were determined to make their lives a prolonged cry of agony.

We succeeded.

5

Operation "Triangle"

COLONEL Simon Houssong was a calm and considerate officer who seldom lost his temper. But the extermination of a battalion under the command of Captain Arnold Lorilleaux must have hurt him deeply. Apart from having been a much-decorated officer of the Second World War, the unfortunate captain had also been a brother-in-law of the colonel.

It was well after midnight when he sent a corporal to request my immediate attendance. "The colonel is in his office," the corporal informed me. "He hasn't left his desk tonight, except to get another bottle. He's been drinking all evening."

I was already in bed but dressed quickly and hurried over to our headquarters. In the corridor I ran into Lieutenant Derosier, Colonel Houssong's ADC. Derosier was carrying a small tray of coffee. "Here!" he said, handing me the tray. "Take it to him. Maybe he will listen to you."

"What's wrong with the colonel?"

Derosier shrugged. "Lorilleaux!" he said. "The old man just can't digest the news yet."

I entered the office and closed the door behind me. Stripped to his undershirt, Colonel Houssong was standing at the open window with his forehead resting against the mosquito netting. He was holding an almost empty bottle of Calvados and the room was strewn with papers and broken glass. Slipping the tray onto the desk, I reported. "First Lieutenant Hans Wagemueller, at your request, *mon colonel.*" He turned slowly and came toward me, wiping his face with a towel. Taking another gulp from the bottle, he tossed it into the wastebasket.

"First Lieutenant Hans Wagemueller," he repeated with a hint of mockery in his voice. "Sit down, Wagemueller . . . *Stürmführer* Wagemueller, the Lord High Executioner of the *Waffen* SS . . . or the French Foreign Legion . . . It does not matter which, does it?"

"Would you like some coffee, *mon colonel?*"

"To hell with your coffee," he roared, pushing the tray aside and spilling coffee over his desk. "Leave it!" he stopped me when I jumped to rescue some of his papers. "We have a far greater mess to worry about." He paused for a moment, then dropped behind his desk, turned on the fan and looked at me with his eyes drawn. "Do you know why I called you?"

"*Oui, mon colonel.*"

"You go and put those bloody bastards to rot, Wagemueller," he breathed with hatred in every word. "The whole village . . . they were all feasting over the corpses of Lorilleaux and his men." His fist came down heavily on the table. "Seven hundred and twelve men, Wagemueller. All dead! You go and get those bastards who killed Arnold. . . . Give them a first-class SS treatment. Spare nothing and no one except babes in their cribs. If this is the kind of enemy you were fighting in Russia, then many of your SS buddies were hanged quite innocently. I fought you in the Ardennes, at the Meuse, in North Africa, but now I am beginning to think that I may have fought the wrong enemy all the time."

"*Mon colonel–*"

"Shut up, Wagemueller! Those poor devils must be buried and the murderers put to rot. I know what you wanted to say. I will leave it to you how to go about it. You will manage it somehow. You always do."

"Do you want prisoners, *mon colonel?*"

"To hell with them!"

"*Oui, mon colonel!*"

It was an order I could appreciate: "I will leave it to you how to go about it." In my opinion it was the only sort of order a field commander in Indochina could act upon with responsibility and return with results. After studying the maps and aerial photos it took us less than three hours to prepare "Operation Triangle," one of our most successful raids on a Viet Minh stronghold. Every local landmark on our operational maps was given a German code name. The target village, a heavily fortified terrorist stronghold deep in the mountains (now in Laos), was renamed "Altdorf." Similarly we referred to Hanoi only as "Hansastadt" and to Saigon as "Schwaben." The river which we were to cross, the Nam Ou, we called "Schelde." The expedition was to be an extended one, over two hundred miles, with the last stage of it to be covered on foot.

The enemy was aware of our coming. For three days we had been advancing on the open road, following the tracks of the unfortunate French battalion. Air reconnaissance reported that the plank bridge across the river was still intact, as I suspected it would be. Why should the terrorists demolish a bridge across which Captain Lorilleaux and his seven hundred men had so conveniently marched into oblivion? The Viet Minh invitation had been left open for us too. Intelligence estimated the number of guerrillas in and around the village at more than a thousand men.

Had there not been seven hundred bodies beyond that plank bridge, I could have laughed at the guerrilla's naïveté. The Viet Minh, in fact, always planned with a certain amount of naïveté, seldom conceiving a plan of great complexity. Even today, the Vietcong guerrillas are only repeating the well-worn ruses of the Viet Minh, their forerunners. It was never guerrilla ingenuity but only French ignorance that fostered spectacular terrorist coups. Superior weapons mean little in the jungle and superiority in numbers could also be an unimportant factor. A thousand tough experts may cause more damage to the enemy, spread more terror, destroy more of their ranks than a division of green recruits can. My headhunters had often destroyed Viet Minh detachments three times their number, accomplishing more with their bayonets than other units of the Legion ever accomplished with artillery.

The bridge was intact, open and inviting. The only thing missing was a placard saying "Please cross." On the way toward the river we collected ample evidence of the persistent terrorist surveillance we had been subjected to from sunrise to dusk. As a rule, we trusted no one and considered every native Indochinese a potential enemy, unless half of his or her family had been executed by the Viet Minh. From their ranks we selected our few but trusted guides. They had been truly loyal to us and we respected them highly. We had some routine precautionary measures that we always took, "the rules of survival." If we passed by some rice paddies, for instance, where a few dozen peasants were at work, Eisner would give the word: "*Abwehrmannschaft abtreten!*" and six of our sharpshooters would quietly drop into the roadside underbrush, carrying telescopic rifles with silencers attached – a formidable weapon against guerrillas. The column would march on as though nothing had happened. Sometimes, and as soon as the army was out of sight, some peasants would turn into armed terrorists, taking off after the column head over heels. Our sharpshooters would drop them before they reached the jungle.

It was also one of our tricks to pass a Viet Minh-controlled village without bothering a soul. The column would vanish into the hills, except for the sharpshooters, who would drop back to cover every exit. In ninety percent of all cases, Viet Minh messengers or even groups of guerrillas would emerge from the village and depart in a hurry. The silencer-equipped guns were excellent for dropping them quickly and quietly. Indeed, our marksmen were capable of hitting a dozen terrorists within a few seconds, starting invariably with the last man in a line or group. Erich Schulze had once eliminated five running guerrillas, repeating aloud, "*Mitte-mitte-mitte-mitte-mitte*" – "Center-center . . . ," pulling the trigger at each word which corresponded with one shot per second. We had used the same ruse in occupied Russia and invariably it worked.

Nevertheless we could not have possibly eliminated all the Viet Minh observers. Some vital information, however, we would never let them learn: our exact strength, equipment, and combat order. Where the enemy observed only three hundred men carrying light weapons, in reality there were seven hundred troops equipped with mortars, machine guns, flamethrowers, and two 4 CM rifles.

For three days we had been advancing in a fashion which we called the *Frachtzug* – Goods Train – for it was a slow but very effective process. Group One, code named *ATA*, with myself in command, was the only force the Communists had been allowed to see. We moved openly during the day but never covered more than ten to fifteen miles and always camped down for the night. We set up what was in reality only a decoy camp, for as soon as darkness fell most of our force would quietly evacuate the camp to deploy on the flanks.

Group Two, *ROTKAPCHEN*, and Group Three, *PERSIL*, each consisted of two hundred and fifty men. They were strictly stationary during the hours of daylight and remained camouflaged in the jungle. While *ATA* was advancing, the two other groups rested. *ROTKAPCHEN* and *PERSIL* moved only at night, sometimes toward a predetermined assembly point, sometimes by simply "riding the beam," the radio beeps transmitted regularly by Group One. For a short time we had tried using dogs to guide troops at night but the Viet Minh soon killed them off by leaving poisoned bits of meat along the trails. We never succeeded in training the dogs not to snatch food from the ground.

By dawn, Group Two and Group Three would arrive at the place where Group One had spent the night. Dispersing and taking cover before sunrise, the troops would settle down for another day while *ATA* penetrated deeper and deeper into the hills in plain sight of the enemy. Group One – the decoy.

Helmut Riedl, a one-time Brandenburger, was in charge of *ROTKAPCHEN*. Riedl was a tall blond Prussian, a tough and resourceful fighter who spoke little but did lots of shooting. During the war he had fought in Yugoslavia and in Greece, then spent two more years in Italy. Riedl had lost his wife and children during an air raid on Erfurt in 1943. After his tragic loss he did not care about being killed, which is probably why he had survived without receiving more than a few superficial wounds.

In the spring of 1944, the Americans overran the small Italian village from which Riedl was directing the fire of an artillery battery a few miles away. With Shermans and half-tracks swarming on the main square, Helmut coolly remained and continued to radio trajectories from the tower. When the artillery commander asked him by wireless the target concentration of enemy trucks in the area, Riedl cast a glance at the motorized multitude down below the belfry and replied flatly, "Fire on me." He survived that and received the Iron Cross for it. He wore the medal proudly in Indochina, something most of my men did, wearing their Wehrmacht badges, battle insignias, SS emblems, Marine daggers, belts, and the like. Almost everyone had kept a souvenir from the grand old days of glory. Those old relics seemed to inspire them, or to reinforce their superstitious belief in survival. Before embarking on a particularly perilous mission, they would often say jokingly: "Good luck and fight well. Old Adolf is watching you."

Leading *PERSIL*, Karl Pfirstenhammer was a veteran head-hunter who would take an order and execute it, never looking for an excuse, never lamenting about difficulties. When an especially dangerous mission had to be carried out, Karl would never order any of his men to do the job; instead he would say, "There are some rats in that tunnel. We'll have to smoke them out. Who is coming with me?"

We had our own codes in German, a definite advantage over the Viet Minh. The enemy intelligence had often broken the French Army code (or rather the Chinese or Russian experts had done the job for them). Another important rule we always observed: in order to communicate with a sister unit only two miles away, we never used short-range walkie-talkies but only high-powered transmitters with a range of several hundred miles. In the early fifties the Viet Minh and especially their Chinese patrons possessed some electronic devices, among them the wireless range finder. Tuning in on our short-range sets, the enemy could have deduced that somewhere within a radius of a few miles there was another hostile group to be considered. By using a powerful set to call troops barely three miles away, we could frustrate the enemy experts. And even if the Viet Minh did have the means of breaking a code in German (a very doubtful proposition), what could they have learned from a message which we had for instance transmitted before the big attack in Operation Triangle?

"ATTENTION WAR GAMES: ATA-ROTKAPCHEN-PERSIL. DIRECTION CROCODILE! SAUNA AT SCHELDE FOUR AGAINST ALTDORF TRIANGLE IN EFFECT. BIG

WHEEL! TURNING FIVE TIMES UNDER YELLOW STARS."

In our code "sauna" indicated river crossing. "Crocodile" was the plank bridge. "Big wheel" translated into complete encirclement, "five times" meant five o'clock with the attack to begin upon yellow lights.

We reached the river on schedule, in the early evening hours. We saw nothing of the enemy but that was expected. The Viet Minh wanted to say "good-night" to us on the other side of the bridge and farther inland. The enemy had, of course, observed the arrival of Group One but all details had been obscured by the advancing darkness. Of Groups Two and Three they knew nothing, at least so we hoped. When it was dark enough, I split Group One; Bernard Eisner took charge of two hundred men who were to cross the bridge at dawn and advance "dutifully" into the guerrilla trap, a steep ravine two miles from the river. The "Suicide Commando," as Eisner remarked not entirely without reason. But by dawn, my hundred men and our two other groups would have deployed in the hills around Altdorf behind the enemy. Riedl and Pfirstenhammer were to cross the river five miles upstream from the bridge. My hundred men from *ATA* would ford the river three miles below the bridge and Eisner was to hold the guerrilla's attention on the center group.

The complete encirclement of the enemy before the actual attack commenced had always been our principal tactical aim. The guerrillas dreaded nothing more than having their rear blasted and occupied. They were brave men, capable of standing up to severe punishment, but only as long as they knew that their escape routes were open. The moment their "emergency exits" had been bolted shut, their ranks crumbled into something that resembled a panicky mob, not a fighting force.

Timing was of the utmost importance. We had to reach our positions around the village by dawn. Otherwise, Eisner and his two hundred men would have little chance of surviving a major Viet Minh drive in the valley. The diversion at the village itself should coincide with Eisner's crossing the bridge. "Just keep going in third gear," Bernard said to me before we parted, "or the lightning will sure hit the latrine here!"

Leaving them at the bridge, I led my men downstream to a point where it was shallow enough to ford. We crossed and took to the hills immediately, following a narrow depression that we had discovered on an old, wartime Japanese map. Strangely enough this very important ravine had been missing from every contemporary French map of the area. More than once we discovered the superiority of vintage Japanese Army maps; they were more detailed and more correct. They gave us valuable data on sources of drinking water, possible river crossings, areas frequently foggy, cliffs dominating a particular area, abandoned hamlets, ruins, and so on. Thickly or sparsely foliaged forest had also been carefully marked. Thanks to the meticulously precise Japanese cartographers we covered ten miles in about six hours over a very difficult terrain.

There was good order in Japan – as there used to be in Germany. The French housekeeping was nothing but a giant whorehouse from maps to machine guns. Nothing ever functioned properly. Not even the water closets.

Apart from large rocky sections which delayed us every now and then, we were able to push forward in a relatively straight line and at good speed over the spongy soil, formed by the fallen leaves. The machine guns, rifles, flamethrowers, light mortars, and ammo cases weighed heavily on my men, and to avoid wearing them out, I allowed five-minute rests for every fifteen minutes of climbing.

About an hour after we had crossed the river the moon appeared through the drifting clouds and made our uphill journey much easier. Sometimes we struck open sections where we had to keep to the shadows of the trees, skirting the clearings. No one was permitted to speak except in whispers, but by imitating the clicking sound of the gecko lizards, our advance guard had at times informed us that everything appeared clear. To signal danger, we imitated the call of the jungle owl.

Some three miles from the river the forest ended abruptly and we found ourselves on the edge of an open slope leading up to the crest of Hill 124, our first objective. According to the aerial photos, Hill 124 dominated the valley in which Captain Lorilleaux and his battalion had been slaughtered to the last man. We took possession of the crest and left behind a platoon under the command of Corporal Karl Stolz. We pushed on toward our second and third objectives, Hills 125 and 126. The guns and ammo seemed to have doubled in weight and I felt sorry for Riedl's group, struggling somewhere in the opposite hills. They were transporting the heaviest MGs and the dismantled 4 CM rifles along with the shells.

Another two miles and we arrived at the crest of Hill 125. A few dim lights of the distant village could be seen. The valley, where over a thousand Viet Minh must have been waiting for us to come across the bridge, lay in darkness. The night was warm and we perspired profusely as we labored higher and higher on the slope. We kept carefully on the far side of the crest, so that we could not be spotted as a long line of dark shapes, moving against the background of the moonlit skies. I called a brief halt and scanned the silvery panorama down below through binoculars. I wished that I had a way of knowing how Pfirstenhammer and Riedl were progressing some five miles away on the far side of the valley. And I missed Erich Schulze, who had been wounded slightly in the hip the week before and had been confined to his bed for another week.

Leaving thirty men with MGs and mortars behind, I took my remaining fifty troops to Hill 126, which rose eight hundred feet above the village half a mile away. It was 3 A.M. and there was perceptible lightening of the eastern horizon. The moon hung low above the hills and I could just make out a number of long thatched buildings and huts. Beyond the village lay another chain of undulating hills, densely forested with gentle downward slopes into the valley and the settlement. I could see the dim, whitish ribbon of the narrow road that ran through the village toward Neua in the west.

Having deployed my men on the hill, I sent fifteen men to link up with a similar patrol from Group Two to sever the road to Neua a mile beyond the village. Shortly after four o'clock the patrols established contact. Encirclement was complete. Riedl and Pfirstenhammer were in control of Hills 127 and 128 on the far side of the valley. At 4:25 A.M., Eisner sent a radio message. He was across the bridge and under intense enemy fire.

Then everything began to run with the precision of good clockwork. Our yellow Very lights were instantly answered from every hill, and it began to rain fire and steel. We opened up on the village with everything we had. Where only moments before utter silence prevailed now hundreds of projectiles, mortar shells, and incendiaries were shrieking downward, blasting the road, the huts, the water tanks, turning wood and bamboo into a sea of rising flames. There were about two hundred huts in the village and every one of them seemed to become the focal point of intermittent lines of converging tracers. We could see knots of people as they emerged from the huts, running in every direction in the futile hope of finding a way out of the sudden holocaust. Six minutes later, Eisner called again. The guerrillas were falling back in the valley.

"Now it's beginning to look like the *Blitzkrieg* in Poland," Bernard remarked. "But in the nick of time, Hans!"

I could sense sadness in his voice. "What's wrong?" I asked.

"We lost thirty-two men," he replied quietly.

It was a heavy loss.

Dawn came slowly like the gradual illumination of a stage in the darkness; a repulsive stage with bodies sprawling on the streets, in the doorways, even out in the fields. The survivors ran amuck amidst the bursting shells and flickering tracers, only to be mowed down a few seconds later. From the valley, massive groups of the withdrawing Viet Minh began to emerge. Shooting in every direction, the enemy was moving toward the village. There were over a thousand of them, still armed, still fighting but already doomed. They had no place to withdraw to, and encirclement had always been a German specialty. Under the cover of machine guns and flamethrowers, Pfirstenhammer's platoons were entering the village, burning and blasting everything that still stood. The sun rose higher, sending its first rays into the valley from which came cries of agony and frustration; yells, curses, and explosions echoed back and forth between the cliffs. About two hundred guerrillas had tried to storm Hill 125, which was defended by only twenty troopers. But those twenty had twelve machine guns. Pivoting their guns from left to right, then back again, the platoon took a terrible toll among the exposed enemy.

Once again Eisner called. He had found the badly decomposed and horribly mutilated corpses of at least four hundred French troops strewn all over the valley, hanging disemboweled from the trees, the rocks. Many of the corpses were headless and castrated. The heads had been neatly arranged along the road like a row of macabre milestones. Only they indicated yards, not miles – only yards! This was to be the terrorist reception for us!

The mortars and the two 4 CM rifles were turned on the guerrillas now milling in the narrow depression, seeking a way out of the deadly trap. The acrid fumes of cordite hung heavily over the woods, and as the machine guns chattered I could see a dozen men pitching from the rocks, rolling down the slope, dead or dying. Men with legs or arms shot to shreds or with their clothes on fire were tumbling down on top of those who had fallen before. Under the cover of the MGs and the flamethrowers Pfirstenhammer began to advance. Moving from rock to rock, from crevasse to crevasse, his troopers were burning everything and everyone. Descending slowly on the eastern slope, Riedl's detachment sealed the trap.

Dominating every hill, we proceeded systematically to exterminate the guerrillas. We spared only small children and women. Everybody taller than four feet was gunned down or burned to ashes. Our aim was not to cause casualties but to exterminate; gaining territory was of little importance to us. We could not hold an inch of land for any length of time. The destruction of the enemy manpower was our principal aim. We gunned down every man in sight regardless of whether he carried a weapon or not. They all belonged to the same snake pit. And if they were among the guerrillas we shot down twelve-year-old boys, too. We regarded them as the terrorists of the coming years. The golden reserve of Ho Chi Minh!

The battle lasted for about three hours. The surviving four hundred Viet Minh, most of them wounded, finally surrendered. They should have known better. About a hundred of them, captured by Pfirstenhammer higher up in the hills, were taken to a jutting precipice and cast down one after another. "They aren't worth the bullets," Karl commented.

The captured company commanders, propagandists, commissars, and platoon leaders who were directly responsible for the massacre and mutilation of the French battalion were executed by what Eisner called "shooting to bits." The victim's fingers were shot away one by one. His nose and ears followed; then slugs were fired into their kneecaps and feet. Throughout the process no vital organ was hit and the guerrilla leader was left to die by bleeding.

It was not a senseless act of brutality. It was tit for tat. We wanted to plant such terror in their hearts that they would run, head over heels, when they heard us coming.

Sparing but fifty of the prisoners, we lined them all up against the rocks, facing a dozen MGs. We neither could nor wanted to handle prisoners. We needed the fifty men to gather the corpses of our dead comrades, who were then buried with full military honors. Forty-eight Germans from our own ranks found their final rest in a common grave, over which we blasted thousands of tons of rocks to prevent the enemy from exhuming the bodies.

After the burial we executed the rest of the prisoners except for a single individual. We needed him for sending a message to the Viet Minh High Command. "Go and tell Giap that he had better study the Geneva Convention about the treatment of prisoners," I told the guerrilla. "Unless he behaves in the future he will receive similar treatment in every filthy village he has."

We could find nothing of the corpse of Captain Arnold Lorilleaux.

Walking through the smoking ruins of the Red village, I suddenly remembered Schulze's words to the guerrilla emissary on the road to Yen Bay: "You may run into the jungle when you see us coming, but beware when you see us leaving. You may find no village to return to."

After this incident, the Viet Minh placed a reward of 25,000 piasters for the capture of any German of my group. I enjoyed the honor of being valued at 200,000 piasters, with a distinctive "dead or alive" allowance. Afterward Schulze and Eisner would often remark teasingly, "Hans, before we quit the Legion, your price will surely be above a million. We shall bump you off and sell your guts to Ho Chi Minh. Would you kindly remind us. . . ."

Schulze, Eisner, Pfirstenhammer, and Riedl had to be content with a meager 50,000 piasters per head, "An insulting under-valuation," as Karl put it. "We'll have to work harder to boost the price," he remarked wryly.

6

Humane and Inhumane Interludes

On patrol duty along the Hanoi–Lang Son railway line. Eighty miles there, eighty miles back. Under ordinary circumstances a return trip would not take longer than four hours. We were on the road for the sixth consecutive day, mercifully on the way back and still in one piece. Along the line and at every crossing small bunkers dotted the landscape. Strong platoons patrolled their respective sections. The dominant elevations along the line had been fortified, the forest line cut back to deprive the enemy of cover. At a few particularly vulnerable sections coils of barbed wire stretched for miles. The barren strip of land that bordered the line had been proclaimed off limits to civilians, and unauthorized persons were shot without warning. Large posters in French and in three local tongues warned the population not to trespass in the restricted areas. Legitimate crossings were permitted only at the army checkpoints near a bunker or fortified guardhouse.

The trouble was that a large percentage of the population could not read. Many fatal incidents occurred when old people or children tried to traverse the tracks and were gunned down from a hidden observation post. The guards were jittery. Pulling the trigger was their natural reaction to anything that moved within the restricted area, especially after dusk. All the same, the Viet Minh had managed to blast the line several times and at places miles apart. They had occasionally derailed a train as well.

The road along the tracks was also a principal guerrilla target. Hardly a week went by without a few army vehicles exploding somewhere between Bac Ninh and Lang Son. In order to frustrate the enemy snipers, who preferred to operate at night, our vehicles carried a pair of decoys apart from the standard headlights. The decoys were mounted on thirteen-foot-long steel pipes that we attached to the mudguards as soon as darkness fell. They traveled well ahead of the vehicle, and the first guerrilla salvo would invariably go wild because it was aimed behind the fake headlights where the terrorists thought the engine and the driving compartment should be. The decoys gave us time to switch off all lights and disperse along the road before the snipers could correct their aim.

The vehicles kept thirty yards apart with an old GMC truck leading the way, followed by two jeeps with mounted MGs, a light armored car, and two troop carriers. We fitted the front of the GMC with a pair of heavy steel wheels, in line with the front tires but nine feet ahead. The wheels could be raised or lowered on their hinged mounts by the front pulley. They were ordinary transmission wheels which used to drive the machinery of an old mill; heavy enough to detonate pressure mines yet sufficiently solid not to break easily but rather to lift upward should a charge explode under them. Curved steel plates an inch thick shielded the driving compartment and the tires from fragments. The windshield of the GMC was reinforced with wire mesh and the sides of the truck protected by additional plating. Defense against command-detonated mines was not easy but such mines were also less frequent. We devised a primitive contraption, a sort of narrow-bladed, sturdy hoe which the GMC dragged along the roadside to pick up the wires of such command-detonated mines. A swivel socket with springs prevented the hoe from breaking when it caught a root or a stone.

Naturally we submitted a report on all our workable "inventions," many of them old tricks that worked well in Russia and similarly in Indochina. None of them was ever appreciated, let alone introduced. Our generals were still firmly convinced that the military academy at Saint Cyr had bestowed upon them all the knowledge one should have about warfare and the descendants of Napoleon should not borrow ideas from the ranks, and especially not from the Germans.

Unfortunately, the last two generals known to have taken part in perilous patrol missions in enemy territory were Rommel and Patton – both now dead. The French generals conducted the war the way they would have conducted it in the forests of France or in the Sahara desert. The jungles of Indochina made no impression on them. They were refined, cultured, and dignified men who knew by heart every significant work on warfare except Mao's doctrine of guerrilla wars. No French officer with dignity would even touch Mao. For them the jungle meant only a sort of overgrown Bois de Boulogne, and guerrilla warfare was only guerrilla warfare.

The woman who waved down our jeep was standing on the roadside shading her eyes from the searchlight. She wore a shabby workman's overall fastened with a thin belt around her waist and crude rubber sandals. A small paper bag lay beside her in the grass. When I stopped she walked up to the jeep and wiping the loose hair from her forehead she said hesitantly, "Excuse me, officer, are you going to Hanoi?" She spoke educated French but her voice sounded weary.

"Yes, we are." I nodded, eyeing her with mixed feelings.

"May I come with you? I am very tired."

I looked at Riedl and he said in German, "She isn't Veronica Lake but let her come. I will check her bag."

"Do you carry any weapon?" I asked her, feeling a little awkward the moment I spoke.

"Me?" she exclaimed with wide open eyes. Then she shook her head and replied with a smile, "Oh, no, monsieur. I am not fighting the French Army." Her last words caught my attention for native Indochinese would have said "Legion," not French Army. I helped her aboard.

"Thank you," she said, "may I put my bag in the rear?"

Riedl took her bag and glanced into it. "I hope you don't mind, but we have certain regulations." The girl did not mind.

"Thank you very much," she repeated. I gave the word to move on.

For some time there was silence between us. She was probably a middle-class refugee, I thought, remembering her cultured French. We were accustomed to natives trying to thumb a ride and had our orders not to pick up anyone. There were too many pitfalls; not only the wartime Japanese but the Viet Minh, too, had its *kamikaze* squads. We had just heard of a young terrorist who had been given a ride on an ammo truck – gross negligence on the part of the guard. The passenger had been a quiet little boy who told a sad story about his family having been tortured and executed by the Communists in Cambodia, and about his long way across the jungle. He had said that he wanted to join the army and avenge the death of his family. The troops had been impressed; they had given him food, money, and friendly advice.

When they reached the middle of a vital bridge, the passenger had suddenly pulled a pair of grenades, and, before the terrified troopers could do anything, he had dropped them into a narrow gap between the ammunition crates. Shrieking "Death to the French colonialists," he had dived into the river. An instant later the truck exploded, destroying the bridge and a company of infantry moving alongside on the narrow gangway.

"Have you come far?" I asked the girl finally, to break the silence.

She did not turn but answered tiredly, "Yes, I have come a long way."

No, she was not a country girl, I concluded. She could have been anywhere between twenty-five and thirty, and she was slender, almost fragile, despite the odd-looking overalls she wore. She looked childishly underdeveloped and was not very talkative.

"Where are you going?" Riedl inquired after a while.

"To Hanoi," she replied, "if you will take me that far."

"Have you been in Hanoi before?"

"Once – a long time ago," she said with a persistent melancholy in her voice.

My cigarette was burning away and I reached for the ashtray. "Please don't put it out," she exclaimed, reaching for it.

"I am sorry," I said somewhat puzzled, offering her my

cigarette case and lighter. "I should have asked you if you wanted a cigarette."

She accepted a cigarette. When she lighted it, I caught a glimpse of her hands. They were very small and slender but rough with broken fingernails and some scars of old cuts and bruises. They seemed to be the hands of a manual worker yet she was in no shape to do heavy labor. There was something strange about her. Her cultured way of talking contrasted with her appearance.

She inhaled the smoke deeply, then leaned back, resting her head on the back of the seat. "My name is Hans and my friend is Helmut." I got over the formalities.

"My name is Lin," she said. "You are not Frenchmen, are you?"

"No, Lin – we are Germans," I conceded, surprised.

"I have noticed that from your accent."

"Indeed?"

"Uhm...."

"But you are not a native here either!"

"I am Chinese," she stated.

"Sure, Lin. And if you are Chinese then we are Papuans."

Riedl turned on his flashlight and calmly began to examine the girl's face. Lin certainly possessed some Chinese features, especially her dark almond eyes but her face lacked the strong cheekbones, the roundness so common among Chinese women. Despite the poor light I could see that her face was heart-shaped and her skin almost white.

"My father was British," she admitted finally. "I was born in Hong Kong."

"Hong Kong is not China but England," I remarked. "But still I cannot see how you happen to be on the road between Lang Son and Hanoi."

"Is it so important?" she asked.

"Quite important. For your information, you happened to be walking along a restricted area where the sentries shoot at anything that moves after sundown."

"I must have been lucky," said she.

"Rather!"

She sighed. "My story is a long one."

"We have a long way to go."

She shifted her eyes toward me. "Are you the people the Chinese militia calls 'Yang-Kou-Ce' – the White-Faced Devils?"

"Maybe, Lin." I shrugged. "We are not very popular with the Chinese militia."

"I know that," she stated firmly.

"How do you know that, Lin?"

"I *am* coming from China."

"Without a visa, I presume."

"I've been in a prison camp of the militia." She added tiredly, "For over a year."

"How come?" Riedl cut in.

"They did not ask me whether I wanted to go. I was a prisoner of war, I suppose."

"Did you fight them or something?"

"Me?" She turned sharply. "How old do you think I am?"

I cast a glance at her, pushed the horn twice to signal halt, then pulled up to the roadside and switched on the small map light. Behind us the armored car ground to a halt. Leaning from the turret, Karl yelled, "Anything wrong, Hans?"

"Everything's under control, Karl!" I shouted back. "Just a short break."

"This is a helluva place to have your break," he growled, sweeping an arm about the dark hills which loomed on either side of the road.

"We are overheating," Riedl advised him.

"No wonder with such a cutie riding along," Karl remarked in German. The men in the troop carrier laughed.

I turned the flexible lamp toward the girl. She kept looking at me without a tremor in her eyes. Only her brows arched slightly, as if questioning me on their own. Her lips, slightly apart, revealed small, pearl-like teeth. I surveyed Lin's face almost minutely but found myself as confused as ever regarding her age. I saw wrinkles in the corners of her eyes, which seemed alien there, parasitic. Her face was frail, her eyes dark and bright. The meager rations in the Chinese camp had had their effects. In some ways she appeared only a child, then older again a moment later. Her dark hair hung loosely about her shoulders in waveless strands; she looked uncared-for indeed. Yet I had the feeling that once she must have been very pretty. The bow of her mouth was perfect. She had a prim little mouth, the sort which could relax in a bewitching smile or a kissable quirk. Properly dressed and cared for, she should have been attractive.

My eyes relaxed on her lips and I saw them curving down in a wry smile. Then she sighed and turned away. "I know it is hard to believe but I will be eighteen in September," she announced quietly. My kindest estimate would have been that she was twenty-five.

I switched off the lamp and started the engine. For some time Lin sat staring into the darkness. "You don't believe me, do you?" she spoke finally.

"Why should you lie to me, Lin?"

"I have no reason to lie to anyone!"

She fascinated me. It might have been that quiet, persistent resignation in her voice, her sadness, her way of talking. I sensed some mystery beyond her enigmatic smile and wanted to know more about her.

It was past nine when we arrived at the outskirts of the city. I pulled up and asked Riedl to take over the jeep. "I am taking Lin to eat something," I told him in German. I helped the girl to the pavement. Riedl slipped behind the wheel and handed the girl her bag.

"What's in it, Lin?" I asked, reaching for the bag.

She handed it to me with a smile. "Just a few old clothes. No bombs."

"Nothing valuable?"

"Nothing at all."

I threw the bag into the open field. "Why did you do it?" she asked me. "I might need them."

"Let me take care of what you need, Lin," I said matter-of-factly and turned to Helmut. "I will be back by six."

"Take care, Hans!"

"I will, don't worry."

I took a cab to Ba Dinh square, then we walked until I found the shops I wanted. Half an hour later Lin had a lovely, light-blue "Ao Dai" and a pair of matching shoes.

"Are you satisfied?" I asked and she blushed.

"Satisfied? I don't really know what to say."

"What have you eaten today?"

"Not very much," she admitted reluctantly. "I wouldn't mind a sandwich or something."

I took her to a small restaurant. At the entrance she stopped and asked me with concern, "Won't I embarrass you?"

"Embarrass me? Why?"

"I am . . . not very . . . clean."

"They have a ladies' room and we have time."

Lin took her time but when she returned a good half an hour later, she looked much younger indeed and she was beautiful. "Do I look a bit more acceptable?" she asked turning on her heels childishly.

"Acceptable, Lin? You look smashing!"

"Thank you, Lieutenant," she bowed, casting a deep level look at me. I reached for her hand and she accepted my hand gayly. "Let's go."

The bar was almost deserted. I led Lin to a secluded table in a quiet corner. "Please, Hans," she addressed me by my first name for the first time. "Some sandwiches will be fine – for me, of course."

"You should have a proper meal."

I ordered curried chicken with rice, salad, fruit salad, some wine, and coffee. Lin glanced around with face flushed and eyes gleaming. "It is so heartening to be among people."

The waiter came, placing a bottle of wine on the table. He filled our glasses. Lin unbuttoned the uppermost part of her tunic and showed me a small crucifix on a thin silver necklace, apparently very old. "An old missionary sister gave it to me in the brick works where we used to work," she explained. "She told me that this little cross brought her father back from the Boer War, her husband from Flanders Field, and their son from the Second World War. She gave it to me in the belief that it would show me to freedom."

"And it seems it did. . . . Where have you been in China, Lin?"

"Near Kweiping."

"I am glad you weren't somewhere in the Sinkiang."

She shook her head slowly. "I don't think I would ever have returned from there."

"Was it hard?"

"They were savages!" she burst forth. "You have been a

soldier for many years, Hans, but I don't think that you have seen so many dead people in your life as I have seen in two years. The militia just kept moving from village to village, holding trials, sentencing people to death – sometimes two hundred people in half an hour. . . ."

The waiter returned and I was glad for his timely appearance. I felt that our conversation had begun to slip toward painful remembrances and I did not want to upset the girl. When the waiter finally left, I saw Lin was staring at her plate. "Anything wrong, Lin?" She raised her face. Her eyes were filled and she was trying hard to fight back her tears. I placed my hand gently over hers. "What is the matter?"

"Nothing." She shook her head. "Only . . . you see, I haven't seen a table like this for such a long time and. . . ." Her lips curled down and quivered.

"Then why don't you carry on?" I suggested softly.

Lin ate like one who hasn't really eaten for years. She seemed at a loss and couldn't decide what to take first. She touched everything, mixed up salt and sugar, slipped her fork, and almost upset the wine. Then she glanced up and her cheeks reddened. "I . . . I have forgotten how to eat properly. . . ."

"Take your time, Lin."

A second wave of color flushed her face.

"I am embarrassing you."

"You do nothing of the sort."

When Lin finished her meal with a long, deep sigh of satisfaction there was not much left on the table. "Would you like a drink now?" I asked, reaching for the bottle.

"I might try."

"Cheer up a little, Lin. . . . Things will be better from now on."

As we drank the wine, I looked at her. In the strong light she seemed much younger than before. I knew that she was from a decent family, and I wanted to know more about her past. I had already made up my mind about her immediate future. I would take her to the only possible place I could think of, Colonel Houssong's house. I was certain he wouldn't object. Later on we might contact the British Consul. After all, Lin had been born in Hong Kong and her father was British. She did not tell me where her family was. I suspected that her parents were dead, but her father ought to have relatives somewhere.

I excused myself and went to the phone. Colonel Houssong listened to my story without interruption, then asked me to hold the line. I knew he was consulting with his wife. They had a sixteen-year-old daughter, Yvette, and a fifteen-year-old son, Jacques. Madame Houssong, I knew, was generous to charities, and she was spending much of her spare time and household savings on refugees.

The phone clicked, and I again heard the colonel's well-known, throaty voice. "Well, bring her over, Wagemueller," he said. He could not refrain from adding teasingly: "Your humanitarian aspirations are truly overwhelming. You should have joined the Salvation Army instead of the *Waffen SS*."

"*Oui, mon colonel.* . . . It might have been a better idea."

I returned to the table and sat down. "Lin, you are coming with me."

"With you?" she exclaimed. "Where to?"

"To some place where you can sleep."

She blushed. I gave her a mysterious look and her eyes widened.

"I . . . I cannot do that," she muttered, barely audible. "I . . . please. . . ."

"I hope you are not afraid of me, Lin?"

"Still. . . ." She lighted a cigarette nervously, then averting her eyes she asked, "Are you . . . living alone?"

I laughed. "I am not taking you to my place or to a cheap hotel, if that's what you are thinking, Lin." Instantly she seemed relieved. "I am taking you to a very nice family where you will find a girl of your age and a temporary home. Then we shall see what we can do about your getting a British passport."

"I am so sorry. . . ."

"I understand you, Lin. Don't worry."

The colonel's family was waiting for us. They all eyed Lin with sympathy as she sat on the edge of a chair twisting her hands. She looked like a frightened little bird. "Please, excuse me." She was finding it hard to form her words. "I really . . . I did not want to disturb you. . . . If only I could stay for the rest of the night. . . ."

"Of course you will stay!" Madame Houssong reassured her cheerfully. "We have enough rooms."

Yvette stepped forward. "I am Yvette," she said reaching for Lin's hand. "Do you really come from China?"

"Yes, Yvette."

"It must have been awful. . . ."

"It was hell!" Lin exclaimed. The surprise in Yvette's face dissolved in a warm smile. She embraced Lin lightly and I saw her parents exchanging glances. "Now you will be all right, *chérie*," she said softly. "You will stay with us."

Lin made a swift half-turn, raising her hand to her eyes. Her shoulders quivered under the sudden strain of emotions which she tried to control.

"Let her relax!" Madame Houssong ushered Yvette aside.

The colonel interposed. "Why don't we go into the salon?"

Lin turned. "Please, I feel . . . so filthy. . . ." she muttered. Her voice trailed off and her cheeks flushed.

"Do you want a bath?" Yvette asked.

"I would like it very much," Lin replied, her face now ablaze. She felt embarrassed, but Madame Houssong came to her rescue. She called the maid and ordered her to prepare a bath for Lin. The maid took the girl to the bathroom and we sat down. The colonel prepared drinks and questioned me briefly about our trip. Then Yvette turned to me.

"How old is Lin?"

"She will be eighteen in September."

Yvette turned on her heels and disappeared into the other room. When she returned her face was flushed with excitement and she was carrying a pile of clothes which she cheerfully dumped onto the couch. "I think we can give these to Lin," she explained. "I really don't need them and we are about the same size." Her generous offer warmed my heart and I noticed a smile of approval on her mother's face. "Tomorrow I will buy her a pair of nice shoes."

"Have you any money?" the colonel asked nonchalantly.

"I have my savings."

"I thought you wanted to buy a stereo set."

"Well," Yvette sighed, lifting and dropping her shoulders, "poor Lin needs more important things now."

When Lin reappeared, we all looked at her astonished. Her cheeks were pink, the weariness in her eyes was gone, and with her hair washed, dried, and tightened with a blue ribbon, her face was transformed. All the hardness had vanished from her features and she looked younger than Yvette. Her legs were beautifully shaped and the light summer dress that Yvette had given her made her look even more slender. I could have encircled her waist between my hands.

After coffee, Lin began talking about her life – and soon our cheerfulness was gone. The air in the room seemed to grow heavier and heavier.

"We used to live near Hankow beside a wonderful lake," Lin began. "My father built a cottage there. He was an architect. They were building a hospital at Hankow. My father's name was Carver, John Carver. My mother was from China. She was the best mother, good and beautiful like an angel. I was their only child and they loved me more than anything on earth. My mother used to call me 'my little blue sky.' They bought me the best of everything and every summer we went to the sea near Shanghai. When the Communists approached Hankow my father refused to evacuate. He did not want to give up everything he had been working for. He wanted to finish the hospital and said that not even the Communists would prevent him from building a hospital for their own people.

"When the siege came he took me to a friend of his, a missionary doctor who lived in a small Christian colony with his wife, also a doctor. My parents thought I'd be safer at the missionary station. There were only teachers, priests, nurses, and doctors caring for old people and children. They did not think of themselves, only of me. My father decided to stay in the partly finished hospital. There were already hundreds of crates of expensive surgical equipment stored in the cellars, gifts from the American and British people. He was afraid that the ignorant soldiers might loot the containers or destroy the machines. My father was sure that once he spoke to the Communist commander, he would be permitted to continue with his work. How wrong my poor father was. . . ."

She sighed deeply and her eyes clouded. "The fathers and sisters at the missionary station worked night and day. More and more people were brought in, most of them wounded. Many of them had to sleep in the open and the doctors operated on a table in the yard. I have seen so much suffering – and as the front came nearer and nearer. . . ." She broke off again, lifting her hand to her eyes nervously. Madame Houssong urged her not to continue if she felt tired. But Lin only shook her head. "Oh, no, if I won't make *you* tired. . . ."

Colonel Houssong then shook his head.

"One morning a couple of wounded soldiers came and told us that the Communist army had already occupied the hospital compound for three hours but had been driven out again. Of my parents they knew nothing. When they told me that, I just picked up my little doll and ran out of the station. I ran like a maniac all the way. I did not hear the explosions or the bullets, I did not see the burning houses. I just ran, jumping over debris, broken furniture, and deep craters – many of them full with corpses."

Lin flushed and her breasts heaved; her breath came in little gasps but she went on bravely. "I found our housekeeper standing at the gate of the hospital. I noticed immediately that he was wearing my father's leather jacket, but I did not pay much attention to it. I was glad to see him alive and grasped his hand. 'Huang, I am so glad to see you. Where are my parents? How are they? Please. . . .' He pulled away from me and acted so strangely cool, so hostile. But my thoughts were with my parents. 'Please,' I cried, 'where are they?' He pointed toward the main building. 'You will find them in there,' he said and smiled. But his smile frightened me. I could not imagine what was wrong with him. I rushed toward the main building and as I entered I saw . . . I saw my father . . . in a pool of blood. . . . When I fell on him, he was icy cold . . . then my mother . . . she lay in a nearby room with bullet holes in her breasts . . . and, and. . . ."

She could not continue. Her words faded into a stream of tears. Her frail body shook as she buried her face in her hands. Madame Houssong rushed to her and caught her in her arms, herself crying. Yvette was weeping too and the colonel covered his face, shaking his head slowly. "Don't talk, *chérie*," I heard Madame Houssong speak to Lin gently. "We have heard enough for tonight."

Lin, with her eyes closed, her tears rolling freely, grabbed Madame Houssong's hand and pressed her face against it. "I must . . . I must tell. You are so good to me . . . I could never tell anyone how much I was hurt."

Lin had to tell us the rest of her story. We could not stop her. She talked as if she wanted to cast away those tragic memories forever. "When I left the hospital, I saw Huang talking to some strange soldiers. They were the Communists. I still cannot imagine why he had turned so hostile. We were always good to him. When his son was ill, my father drove them all the way to Shanghai, to the hospital. We gave them food, clothes, toys for his children. But then I saw he was wearing a big Red star – like the ones the Communists wore. I tried to run away but the soldiers caught me and . . . dragged me . . . into . . ." She began to weep again. "I . . . I cannot tell you what they did to me . . . until I was pushed into a wagon with many other people. . . . They took us to a camp, and we had to work in a brick factory three miles away. We walked there and back, every day. By the end of the year over a hundred of us had died. Our huts were cold and wet and the food was something we could chew and swallow but it was not food. They always told us that if we worked well we would be taken into better barracks in another camp with good food. We worked like animals to gain admittance to that other camp but they never moved us. We were taken out to bury people whom they had shot. There were thousands of people executed every week. . . . Then one night a big storm came and the wind wrecked the watch towers and a part of the fence. I fled." She glanced at me. "I walked for two weeks eating only what I could find, then I crossed the border and walked . . . until the cars came."

Daybreak was showing through the slightly opened shutters when at last Lin fell silent.

"You had better get some sleep now," Madame Houssong said. "Come, *chérie* – and try to put those things forever out of your mind."

Lin rose and looked at me deeply. "Thank you," she said. "Thank you. . . ."

Lin's story had a truly happy ending. Colonel Houssong wrote a long report on her to the British Consul, who in turn forwarded the data to a competent authority in Hong Kong. Three weeks later Lin received her British passport and a letter stating that a search to find her father's relatives in England was under way.

During the next two months we saw each other often; I took her out to a dinner or to dance and became rather attached to her. I think she too felt the same way. "What's bothering you, Hans?" she asked one evening after a long and passionate kiss. "Something's wrong?"

I only embraced her again and held her close. There was plenty wrong, I thought. She was only eighteen. I was thirty-six and still a "death candidate." When Lin was born, I was already entering the army. We were far apart both in time and in space. It was painful but also a relief when her uncle came flying down a week before her birthday. He was a jovial, middle-aged English businessman who was completely overjoyed at having found his niece after three years of gloom. He had been informed of John Carver's death in Communist China and Lin was listed as "missing," probably dead too.

"If you ever need anything, or if you ever come to England please do not fail to call me," he said before their plane departed for Singapore and from there to London. He handed me a small envelope and we shook hands. I embraced Lin and she kissed me openly. Her eyes were filled as she whispered, "Please write me soon. . . . Write always."

"*C'est la vie*," Colonel Houssong said quietly as the plane started to take off. "Had it not turned out so well, we would have adopted Lin . . . but it is better this way."

In the envelope I found a very nice letter of appreciation and a check for five hundred pounds. A small card with Lin's letter read: "I love you . . . I love you . . . I love you."

The cruel war went on.

Near Hoa Binh we discovered the mutilated corpses of two German legionnaires. Both men had been disemboweled and castrated, with their private parts cut away and placed in their hands. A macabre Viet Minh joke.

Two days later we captured the four terrorists responsible for the murder and mutilation. They were stripped, and a thin cord was fastened around their private parts with the other end tied to the jeep. The vehicle was driven at a speed that the prisoners could pace by easy running and so avoid having their testicles torn from their bodies. In such fashion we brought them to the dead legionnaires, about two miles down the road. Then the driver shifted gears and accelerated. The jeep sprang forward and the prisoners tumbled. Screaming in agony they rolled in the dust. We bayoneted them as they lay bleeding. The score was settled.

Bomb for bomb! Bullet for bullet! Murder for murder!

We were never particularly soft toward captured terrorists but for murder and mutilation we retaliated with the most brutal third degree that man or devil could conceive. Among them were methods learned from Karl Stahnke. The one-time Gestapo agent and our former companion had entertained us with stories of their use during our long sea voyage from Oran to Indochina. Stahnke used to call his methods "educational exercises." All of them sounded incredibly uncivilized and inhumane but every one of them worked. After what Stahnke had told us, we understood why our former State Secret Police could invariably obtain all the information it wanted to gather. But has there ever been an unsuccessful secret police in history? No one had ever refused to sign the "statement" for the French *Deuxième Bureau*. In the dictionary of the secret police such words as "failure," "blunder," or "innocent" are seldom present. All secret police prefer results and they do not willingly admit failures. How the Soviet GPU or NKVD handle their prisoners is well known. The brutality of the Gestapo had been featured in countless publications. But I have also spoken to a former German POW who had to submit to the entire range of CIC third degree, and the Americans proved themselves not much gentler than their so much publicized Nazi or Red counterparts had been.

The POW was not beaten and he was burned only occasionally with cigarette butts. But he was kept chained to a hot radiator, naked of course, for ninety-six hours in such manner that he could neither sit nor bend. On the second day his ankles began to swell. At the end of the ordeal they were swollen to the size of grapefruits and he could not flex a muscle. During that ninety-six hours, he was given very spicy food and only one small cup of water per day. Installed twenty inches from his ears a pair of loudspeakers kept blaring distorted music without a break. Occasionally the music stopped and he could hear the desperate screams and pleas of a German woman, coming from a nearby cell; she was obviously being tortured and abused in the most brutal fashion. Every now and then a CIC agent would enter the POW's cell to inform him about the mental or physical state of his wife confined next door. The agent also made a few acid remarks related to the woman's private parts or sexual behavior. The prisoner could often overhear the tormentors calling the woman "Sigrid," which was indeed the name of his wife. Only months later did he learn that his wife had been at home all the time and no one had ever questioned her about anything. There had been no woman at all in the next cell and the brutal torture scenes had been only cleverly recorded sequences. The cruel ruse had caused the prisoner weeks of mental anguish and in order to save his wife from further "torments," he confessed to everything the American Counter-Intelligence wanted him to confess to.

Who knows how many "war criminals" went to the gallows because their "confessions" had been obtained in a similar fashion. Sometimes a man is ready to die if his death will save the lives of his loved ones.

The Americans proved that results can be obtained *without* beating a prisoner into an insensible pulp of swollen flesh. Instead of squeezing a prisoner's balls, they would squeeze his soul. Some American parents should see what their clean-cut sons are doing in some CIC interrogation chambers. But whatever they do, it is done behind yard-thick concrete walls and steel doors. No books were ever printed about the American Counter-Intelligence except maybe a few glamorous adventure stories in the tradition of James Bond.

To dictate his statement, the naked POW was taken upstairs and made to stand at the wall while the two CIC investigators and an extremely pretty American secretary took down his confession, smoked cigarettes, and drank coffee. A few months later the man managed to escape and beat his pursuers to the Foreign Legion. He was serving in my battalion.

The only people I cannot picture committing similar brutalities were the British. But the MI-2 or the MI-5 had all the time on earth to investigate and conclude an affair. (Besides, their clients could always count on at least half an hour of relaxation daily, during the fifteen-minute tea breaks, which no Britisher would ever forego unless the room were on fire.) There were scores of Germans among us who had been imprisoned by the British military in Germany. A few of them did receive a couple of kicks in the ass just to remind them that they were "bloody-goddamn Nazi bastards" but no one had been mistreated. Brutality and British temperament just do not seem to go together.

In a captured Viet Minh village we unmasked a long-sought terrorist, "Hai Si," a corporal. His name was Trang Ghi Muong and he was responsible for the massacre of eight French prisoners and a German comrade. We were always mad enough when we came across the bodies of French comrades, but the discovery of a German corpse, minus nose, ears, tongue, and testicles always sent us "off our rockers." The moment Muong was identified I knew that there were more terrorists whom we did not personally know, but who were, nevertheless, responsible for similar atrocities by the Viet Minh in the area.

The presence of a guerrilla battalion less than ten miles from the village prevented us from embarking on a complicated investigation, so we had to resort to some of Karl Stahnke's methods. We wanted to wipe out as many terrorists as possible before leaving the locality. Certain that the captive terrorists could tell us all the names we wanted, I decided to give Muong the well-deserved Third Degree.

He was stripped. A naked man always feels inferior and more defenseless in the presence of persons fully clothed. Especially Orientals, who are, by nature, shy about exposure. Whenever someone had to be "worked over," he was first stripped.

"Well, Muong, this is the end of the road for you," Sergeant Schenk remarked, pushing the prisoner through the cloth-covered entrance of a vacant hut. "In you go . . . and whether you will come out again depends on you." The prisoner staggered inside and stood blinking in the semidarkness, his hands covering his loins protectively and his eyes flitting back and forth among Karl, Eisner, and Krebitz.

"Can't you at least say '*chieu hoi*' when you come visiting?" Sergeant Krebitz bellowed, greeting the terrorist with a stinging, openhanded blow which sent the man reeling against Pfirstenhammer who was still busy rolling up his shirt-sleeves. The two crashed into the mud wall, with the naked Viet Minh embracing Karl.

"Watch out, Karl! He is about to rape you," Eisner chuckled.

Pushing the prisoner away, Karl drew his right knee up, feinting a kick. As the man doubled up instinctively, Karl's fist lashed out. With a cry of anguish, Muong went flying back toward Krebitz, who in turn dispatched him to Eisner. Bracing his back against the wall, Eisner received the prisoner with his boot lifted high. A powerful kick returned the terrorist to Karl's feet. For some time the ball game continued without causing the delinquent any serious injury; only the corner of his mouth split and his nose began to bleed profusely. Sergeant Schenk, too, had joined the game and though the terrorist did not understand a word of what was being yelled at him in German, the men entertained themselves with filthy oaths and wisecracks just to keep up spirit. Finally the prisoner tumbled and fell on the hard ground and remained folded up with his hands protecting his loins and his head between his knees. Schenk grabbed Muong by the hair and pulled him to his feet.

Whack!

Crashing into the straw-and-mud wall with an impact that almost brought the roof down, Muong dropped again and sat moaning. Krebitz kicked a low stool to the center of the room. "Stand up!" he commanded, pushing the sobbing wretch toward the stool. "You may be sitting a lot after we break your legs. . . . On the stool!"

Trembling and already half paralyzed with fear, the man climbed onto the stool. "Which one of you is a Dang Vien?" Eisner shouted. "Who is the Agitprop secretary?" Karl cut in, stepping closer and swinging his belt. "Who is your commissar Muong? . . . Who is the resident cadre of the Lao Dong?"

Wielding four-foot-long bamboo clubs Krebitz and Schenk began to hammer away at the terrorist. Eisner drew his bayonet and held its point gently against Muong's belly. "Steady, steady. . . . Watch out which way you jump."

"Mercy . . . mercy. . . ."

"Sure, Muong . . . You've given plenty of mercy to the legionnaires, haven't you?"

More beating followed, then more questions.

"Who is your commissar?"

"Who are the Dang Vien?"

"Who participated in the July massacre at Bo Hac?"

"Where is the Lao Dong agitator? . . . Who is the resident cadre?"

Eisner grabbed him by his hair. "Are you going to sing, or do you prefer some more beating?"

"Sing!" Sergeant Schenk yelled. "Sing 'Father Ho is a filthy swine.' "

His cane came crashing down on Muong's buttock, leaving an inch-wide red strip of burning flesh. "Sing!"

Sergeant Krebitz jerked the terrorist around. "You had better start talking, my friend, or your ass will soon look as red as a First of May parade in Moscow."

"Father Ho is a filthy swine," Schenk repeated.

"Pull his beard and he will whine." Pfirstenhammer improvised a rhyme. The quartet broke into laughter. Muong tumbled from the stool but was dragged back onto it instantly.

"Steady!" Eisner pushed his bayonet between Muong's thighs. "If you keep jumping, you will lose your balls, *Liebchen*."

The guerrilla cried out in pain. "Don't howl, only sing," Karl urged him. "Sing!" He smashed the guerrilla in the nose. Muong fell from the stool with blood splattered all over his face and chest. He screamed. As he slipped from the stool the bayonet slashed him between the thighs.

"I told you to keep steady," Eisner snapped. "What will you do if you lose your pecker?"

"Yes . . . Father Ho is going to be mad at you, Muong." Schenk chuckled. "He needs lots of little Viet Minh. In the future, that is if you have a future, Muong, no girl will look at you. So you had better wise up."

"I have nothing to tell you," the guerrilla sobbed. "Nothing."

The joking stopped and the real work began. Calling in a couple of troopers, the terrorist was bound and beaten again while questions were shouted from every direction. "Where are your weapons? . . . Where is the rice for the section? . . . Where are the tunnels?"

"Aren't you going to talk?"

"Haven't you had enough?"

After fifteen minutes of intensive beating the man fainted. A bucket of water was thrown over him; the quartet waited a while then resumed the treatment. The resistance of the terrorist was truly astonishing. Ever since the "going over" started, except for screams and moans, he had uttered not a syllable.

"*Merde!*" Pfirstenhammer swore. "Does he feel no pain?"

"Maybe he is a fakir," Krebitz suggested.

The beating continued. Suddenly Muong emptied his bowels and began to urinate. Schenk drew aside swearing. The guerrilla's face was a swollen, contorted mass of battered flesh. Eisner brought in a pair of pliers and shoved it into Muong's face.

"Look here, you canaille, either you talk now or I am going to yank your teeth out one by one, squash your balls, then break every bone in your fingers. You can still recover from what you have had up till now, but by the time we are through with you, you will be crippled for life."

"If you talk, I will set you free," I interposed, allowing the prisoner a ray of hope to survive, an important tactical move. By then, Muong was all set to die and thought we were going to kill him whether he talked or not.

"You . . . will . . . let me . . . go?" he muttered.

"I will let you go," I repeated firmly.

He was ready to talk. In short, high-pitched, hysterical gasps his words came. Eisner rose and put away the pliers. "Give him something to drink," he told Schenk, and taking a bar of soap from his kit, he began to wash his hands. The smell of blood, urine, and excreta in the hut became overwhelming. The rag cover of the door was flung back and Riedl appeared.

"Phoooi," he exclaimed twisting his nose. "It stinks in here. How can you stand it?" Turning to Eisner he asked, "How's the dirty work coming along?"

"Shut up and get out of here!" Bernard snapped. "Someone has to do this. Be glad it's not you."

Riedl grinned. "I *am* glad. I never saw so many shitty bastards in my life." Holding his nose mockingly, he turned and left for the open.

"Get some more water and call in a few villagers to wash up the wretch." I gestured toward the guerrilla.

"What for?" Schenk queried. "We can shoot him shit and all."

"We are *not* going to shoot him," I said quietly.

"My good God, Hans, you are getting soft."

"We made a bargain with him which I intend to keep. . . . Besides, he is a brave man, Victor. How long do you think you would have stood up to what he was getting?"

"Me? I would have pissed you between the eyes in the first five minutes," he replied. "I am a small, weak creature . . . very delicate and – "

Karl gave Schenk a friendly kick in the bottom. "*You* would have given *us* away all right."

"Given you away?" Schenk cried. "I not only would have told them everything but would have helped them to put the rope around your neck, Karl."

"Set him free!" I ordered the troopers as we left the hut. "After what he told us he won't be playing the liberating hero much longer. The Viet Minh will kill him."

We rounded up the party members and the Viet Minh activists whom Muong had named, some twenty men altogether. We bayoneted them in a small ravine behind the village.

The cruel war continued.

7

The Man-Hao Incident

THE village elder had refused to accommodate the Communist agitators; now he lay in his own doorway with a shattered skull. A frail little woman had tried to prevent the terrorists from recruiting her son. She too was dead among the smoldering ruins of what had been her house. The son, his hand still clutching the ax with which he had tried to rescue his mother, lay in a ditch filled with filth. In a small bamboo hut we discovered seven bodies; father, mother, grandfather, and four children – everybody stabbed, cut open, beaten to death, including the smallest of the victims, a baby in her crib. A girl, slim and pretty, lay across a low fence over which she was trying to flee when the bullet struck her. Her hand still clutched a broken doll and her lips were blue with death. Nearby a scraggy mongrel whined at the corpse of a man.

Along a low palisade we found the naked corpses of eleven legionnaires. Their flesh was beaten into a swollen bluish pulp devoid of all human semblance and mutilated beyond description. They were all Germans, our veteran comrades for many years. Receiving the village elder's urgent request for evacuation, I had sent them forward to reassure the terrified people. Having refused to cooperate with the Viet Minh, the inhabitants had expelled the guerrilla agitators and had beaten one of them up in the heat of an argument. They had not done it because they were pro-French or hated Communists but for the simple reason that the war had so far avoided their hamlet and they had desired to preserve peace in their dwellings.

The Viet Minh revenge had been swift and ferocious. The Communists, who can exist only where terror prevails, decided to give a lasting example of what happens to the enemies of Father Ho's "soldiers," the guerrillas. The small platoon could not stem the human tide that descended on the community. It had been crushed by the sheer weight of enemy flesh.

We recovered ample evidence of their desperate last stand. The piles of spent shells around the palisade told us the whole sad story. There were no enemy corpses in evidence. When not pursued immediately, the terrorists would always carry away their dead to bury them secretly near their homes or in the hills. From the blood-soiled ground where they had fallen we computed the possible number of enemy casualties: one hundred and six altogether.

Walther Grobauer from Munich, Adolf Greilinger from Kiel, Kurt Heinzl, a veteran of the battle for Leningrad, Hans Aigner, Erich Stumme, Erich Windischmann from Berlin, Rupert Winkler, Max Hartmann, Hans Weber, the one-time *Panzer* driver of the *Afrika Korps*, Friedrich Zimmermann and Alois Krupka, the two veterans of the last great battle on the Vistula. They had fought Communism for over a decade and had come a long way to fight it again and die. They will be forgotten heroes.

The survivors of the community, about sixty families, were leaving the village that could no longer offer them either food or shelter, let alone security – weeping, sagging people who had lost everything and everyone in a brief fury of hatred that had obliterated their past, present, and future. We stood in silent sympathy as our three tanks took positions at the foot of the hills. Our convoy of thirty American trucks looked strangely new and powerful as they loomed over the collapsed, blackened huts – a bit of the present dominating the ancient, the Stone Age. Yet all that those people had ever wanted was to be left alone to live their Stone-Age lives and never encounter anything "civilized." To them civilization meant tanks, machine guns, warplanes, death! But the entire world of "civilized" nations with all their humanitarian institutions and their United Nations could not fulfill the modest desire of these simple people: to be left alone, not to be bothered, not to be given anything except peace.

The civilized world is very generous. It provides even for those who neither sought nor wanted to receive its gifts.

Wherever we turned, corpses sprawled on the ground for acres around; here one, there in groups of five or more. Those who had escaped the massacre were trying to gather what was left of their possessions, pushing and pulling at the burned debris, still in a state of semistupor. Men, women, and children wailed over their dead or just stood petrified, gazing at the corpses in silent perplexity.

In and around a small Buddhist temple the survivors gathered. Erich and Helmut were busy opening tin cans to distribute corned beef, condensed milk, rice, and drinking water. The wells of the village could not be used. The terrorists had dumped corpses into them. Behind the temple, Eisner set up a first-aid station to care for the wounded. Some of the people had been hurt badly and for them Sergeant Zeisl, our chief medic, could do little beyond easing their pain with morphine. Others, only slightly injured, sat sullenly on the ground, holding a hand or a dirty rag over their wounds, waiting their turn.

Around eleven o'clock the sun was blazing furiously. Perspiration could not evaporate in the ninety percent humidity. We were all soaking wet and a great stink enveloped the crowd around the ambulance. The air was pregnant with the scent of sweat, blood, and human filth. From the ruins little groups of people dragged forward. Fathers pushed carts, the women hauled them with ropes. The children and old people rode in the carts, some wailing, others just staring with vacant eyes.

I was thinking of the villages which we had had to destroy in the past. It was always the civilians who suffered, whichever side they adhered to. Even if they wanted to take no sides and remain out of trouble, the war struck them down. If they refused to accommodate the Viet Minh, the terrorists liquidated them without mercy. If they went "Red," the Foreign Legion exterminated them directly or indirectly. The people were trapped between the cogwheels of a murder mechanism which turned inexorably, churning up and crushing everyone it caught. It was easy to say, "*C'est la guerre.*" We were not any better than the Viet Minh and we knew it. But we did want to fight a clean war and we were not the ones who started the atrocities.

We only retaliated in kind. We could do nothing else. The French tried to remain humane and their troops were dying like flies. We had no desire to die in Indochina. We knew that if anything could ever induce the Communists to recognize military conventions or even the fundamental principles of human law, it would be only their own terror. That might convince them that they had better fight a man's war instead of a war of the wolves. The Viet Minh had to suffer immensely before they would do as much as recognize a Red Cross emblem. The Communists understand no language other than the cries of agony, to which they are accustomed. Kindness and sympathy or a humane approach will only make them suspicious. They know the world hates them, and that they can exist only by the force of arms, blackmail, fire, rebellion, destruction, death! We were resolved to make their lives a long cry of agony.

Still there was a slight difference between our opposing groups. We did feel remorse whereas they felt none. We could shed tears over a single fallen comrade. The Viet Minh were throwing away men the way we discarded cigarette butts. For us, spreading terror was the sole means of survival. The Viet Minh killed and mutilated for the sheer pleasure of seeing suffering and shedding blood.

I watched Schulze and Riedl as they distributed food, smiled and joked to cheer up the apathetic children. I recalled some past events when those very hands, my hands included, had gunned down similar children at another place without batting an eye. It was all so senseless, like a schizophrenic vision that would haunt us forever.

It was difficult to stay within reason when one beheld the abused corpse of a comrade for whom, the enemy thought, death alone had not been enough punishment. Nothing except our own survival could justify what we did and no sublime Communist slogans about "liberation" and "independence" could ever justify the ruthless genocide committed by the patriots of Ho Chi Minh. But in the end they will get the worst of the deal. Because one day we will depart. The assassins of the Viet Minh will have to stay to face their victims again and again, bracing against those who seek revenge. And there will be tens of thousands of people who *will* one day, seek revenge; fathers, sons, or even mothers whose loved ones had been murdered by the "liberators." People can always be subdued by terror but nothing can make people forget. Neither the bayonets nor the secret police.

Corporal Altreiter and a platoon gathered the sad remains of our comrades. We buried them in a common grave over which Schulze planted a crude wooden cross which bore no names, only the short notice:

"Eleven comrades. Deutschland–Russland–Nord Afrika–Indochina" and the date. We will always remember their names. Others won't care who they were anyway.

The killers had to be punished but there was no need for us to hurry. The village lay only eight miles from the Chinese border and the assassins were low on ammunition; they wouldn't stay in the vicinity. Most of the victims had been stabbed or clubbed to death. The terrorist unit was on its way home to a base near Man-hao, China. They must have already crossed the border. The survivors insisted that there were many Chinese "officers" with the Viet Minh. The village had been attacked by at least three hundred guerrillas.

"I think this is Ming Chen-po's handiwork," Eisner remarked and I agreed. The people spoke of a "one-armed Chinese" who seemed to be in command of the terrorist group. Ming was known to have lost an arm to the Japanese artillery in 1939, and I had seen some of the hamlets overrun by the troops of this one-time bandit and now People's Commissar

It was a known fact that Chinese "experts" and even militiamen were actively engaged in terrorist ventures within French Indochina. I had sent several reports to Hanoi drawing attention to their activities in the border provinces but the High Command could do little to retaliate. "Kill as many of them as possible," said Colonel Houssong, "but take no Chinese prisoners. Mao couldn't care less about losing a million volunteers in Indochina but if we displayed a single Chinese prisoner, he would be pushed into saying something to the world. And Mao would never admit that he was guilty of armed intrusion into French territory. He would demand the release of a Chinese officer whom the French had kidnapped from Chinese territory (where he was probably engaged in the peaceful activity of planting potatoes in the garden behind the guardhouse)." The Communists are superb liars. They are quite capable of delivering a fat lie so convincingly, or at least vehemently, that even their victim will later apologize for having erred.

Ming had a base across the frontier and was wary enough never to venture too deep into Indochina. We suspected that the terrorists had established a base, a sort of advance command post, somewhere within a fifty-mile radius of Man-hao. The Chinese advisers remained there, while the native Viet Minh embarked on more distant missions. Whenever the Legion pursued them, they quickly retreated into their sanctuary where no French troops could follow them. Ming was an old quarry of ours. Twice in seven months we had been compelled to abandon pursuit because of the border.

Now I felt it was time to get even with the terrorists of Ming, wherever they might be. I decided to demolish their home base some twenty-odd miles inside China. Should we succeed we could keep our mouths shut and enjoy being rid of Ming. Should we lose, none of us would give a damn what Hanoi or Peking might say or do. With a bullet in the head one has no worries. Both Hanoi and Peking were far away. Our enemy was temptingly close.

I turned the thought over and over in my mind, checked our stores, the maps, and found the idea feasible. The battalion had refrained from crossing the frontier before. The enemy would not suspect us now. I summoned my companions and motioned them to sit down around a table in the ambulance tent.

"What's up, Hans?" Schulze queried. "Anything's wrong?"

"Nothing's wrong," Eisner spoke before I could answer. "I think we are going to leave here soon." He jerked a thumb toward the Chinese frontier. "That way!"

I nodded and announced without preliminaries. "We are going to blast the camp of Ming Chen-po!"

Pfirstenhammer gaped. "At Man-hao?"

"That's right."

Riedl whistled and Karl pursed his lips in a grin. Schulze began to rub his scalp. "Well?" I asked them. "What do you think of it?"

Riedl shrugged. "I always wanted to see China."

"You won't be seeing much of it," Schulze chuckled, "but if we want to say good-night to Ming this is the time to say it. We don't have to walk far."

"That's right," Karl agreed as Eisner remarked, "Headquarters will be mad as hell."

"Who cares?" Schulze hitched his chair closer. "Let's have a look at the maps." He glanced at me. "I presume this is going to be a strictly private enterprise, Hans?"

"Naturally. We cannot request a permit to enter China and we can never admit having done so."

"How about Colonel Houssong?" Karl inquired. "I am sure he would love it. Provided, of course, that we return without leaving corpses behind . . . our own corpses."

Eisner thought the raid was within our "means," and Riedl said that for him it was *alles Wurst*. He suggested that with the Man-hao business done we might as well take the train to Peking and free the Republic. "After all, Mao has only about seven thousand divisions and of these only seven carry guns, the rest clubs," he said.

We quickly decided to leave our uniforms behind, along with identity tags and personal papers. Pfirstenhammer swore because we selected him to remain with the convoy and take care of the villagers. "We need a competent man to maintain the perimeter. I cannot leave the convoy to a corporal," I stated flatly. "Some of us will have to stay, Karl."

"How about Riedl?" Pfirstenhammer exclaimed indignantly. "He is just as competent as I am." He turned toward Riedl. "Aren't you, Helmut?"

"Why pick on me? I haven't got a sore leg. Besides I can shoot a lot better than you ever will."

"Let's bet on it," Karl exploded.

"Keep your shirts on, men!" I snapped. "This is not going to be a pleasure trip into the bordellos of Man-hao and I am still the one who decides who is to stay."

"Why not Eisner?" Karl argued. "He is old anyway."

"Who, me?" Bernard turned sharply and began to rise. "Would you care to prove it, Karl? How about stepping behind those trucks for a moment?"

"Sit down!" I pushed him back. "And now shut up, all of you. Karl, you still have a sore leg and we cannot expect you to walk the sixty miles there and back."

"I like your good heart, Hans," Pfirstenhammer growled but he sat down.

I estimated the expedition would last for about four days and that we could never enter China without a proper guide. We needed a map or diagram of the area so that we could make a rough plan. Fortunately smuggling was a common and respectable profession in the border villages because French wares fetched good prices in China. Eisner thought that it should not be difficult to find people who were familiar with the other side of the frontier. Calling for our interpreter, he left for the temple to talk to the survivors.

After a while Eisner returned with two men and a girl about twenty years of age. Although her high-necked smock was burned and soiled, I noticed immediately that she belonged to the "upper class" of the community.

"You may trust *them*," Eisner advised me in German. "Phu has just lost his wife and child, Cao's father and mother were gunned down, and the girl, her name is Suoi, lost her entire family of six. She is all alone now. She has been in Man-hao."

"And the men?"

"They know some trails across the frontier."

Before the war Suoi had attended a French missionary school at Lao Kay, and she spoke good French. She was a very pretty girl with long black hair which she wore in braids. Small but beautifully proportioned, she had almond eyes and a slightly upturned nose. Now her eyes were swollen but dry, for she could no longer cry. Looking at her as she sat staring at the table, still in a semi-stupor, she reminded me of Lin. How identical were their stories. Separated from one another only in time and space, they were victims of a common enemy. It pained me that we had to torment her with questions.

Her male companions were deeply shaken but in their eyes I could see nothing but murder. It has often astonished me how much suffering the Orientals can bear without breaking down. Pain which would have sent a white man raving mad they often withstood without a moan. It might have been their heritage of countless centuries. Death came often and unexpectedly into Oriental homes, even in times of peace.

"We shall go with you," Phu stated resolutely. "Will you give us weapons, so that we may kill?"

"We want to do nothing but kill . . . kill . . . kill every Viet Minh and every Chinaman," Cao added vehemently. "When a thousand enemy die, we will rest . . . but not before."

"You might kill, too," Schulze nodded. From his map case he took a sheet of paper and laid it on the table. "We are going to punish the terrorists who killed your people. They have a camp in China where they feel safe. You can help us to wipe them out, but first of all you must tell us everything you know about the land between the border and Man-hao."

Erich drew a line across the paper which followed roughly the contours of the border. "This is Lao Kay and here we have Ch'i-ma-pa." He put a few minute rings on the paper. "Here we have Muong . . . and the line here is the Song river . . . they call it Kiang in China." Working briskly he added more and more details, carefully adopting the approximate positions from the map. "This is Man-hao with the railway line to the north connecting Lao Kay and Meng-tzu." He glanced at the two men.

Phu nodded. "You draw well," he remarked with appreciation which Schulze acknowledged with a quick smile.

"Now tell me about every hill, road, path, creek, stream, ravine, settlement, or lonely hut that you know of between this village and Man-hao. Try to recall the distances between them."

With the interpreter translating, Schulze began to question the men expertly, mapping details however small or insignificant. He interrupted the men every now and then to double-check miles, yards, or even paces between the various topographical objects, which he then marked on the map. Phu and Cao knew the frontier area well but they had never ventured as far as Man-hao. "There are Chinese militia posts here," Cao announced suddenly. He pointed at a spot on Erich's diagram.

"How many posts are there?"

"Two posts. One right along the road, the second farther up on a small hill." Schulze drew a wavy circle marking the hill. "What is the distance between the posts, Cao?"

"About five hundred yards."

"Is it on the left or on the right side of the road?"

"On the right side," Cao said without hesitation.

"I see," Erich nodded. "How high is the hill?"

"Not very high. Maybe four hundred feet."

"Is it forested?"

"No trees. The militia cut the trees. Otherwise they could not see the road and the railway line."

"There are trees," Phu interposed, "but only halfway up the hill."

Schulze shaded the hill accordingly. "Are there trees all around?"

"Yes," said Cao. "And there are two paths up to the guard-house, one facing the road, the other one leading into the hills." He leaned closer to the diagram and drew a line with his finger. "This way the path runs."

"On the northern side?"

"Yes."

Schulze was very talented in drawing accurate maps of uncharted lands. Questioning the villagers on details, he proceeded from sector to sector. More than an hour went by before he finally announced, "I think it will do, Hans."

We had a diagram of the Chinese side of the border; every creek, path, ravine that the men could recall had been marked with numbers indicating the approximate distances, grade of elevation, and similar data. Eisner sent a trooper for tea and sandwiches.

"Eat something, Suoi. You must be very hungry," he said to the girl. She shook her head at the food but accepted the tea, then burst into tears once again. "We know it is difficult for you to talk now," Erich said softly, "but you must help us. You are the only one who knows Man-hao, where the guerrillas are hiding, Suoi. If we don't smite them now, they will return to murder more people."

Burying her face in her hands, she sobbed.

"Let her be!" Riedl exclaimed indignantly. "She is only a young girl trying to bear a terrible grief."

swore between his teeth. "They didn't spare a soul in her family. She is alive only because she was visiting another family when the raiders came, and escaped into the jungle."

Schulze prepared another sheet of paper and waited patiently for Suoi to gather herself. Phu spoke to the girl quietly in her native tongue, and after a while she dried her eyes and announced that she was ready to help us. Erich drew her closer and ran a line across the center of the paper, explaining softly, "This is the river right across Man-hao. Can you recall how many bridges are there, Suoi?"

"*Oui, monsieur.* There are two bridges," she replied.

"In the center of the town or outside it?"

"One of them is in the center, at the marketplace. Near a small temple."

"So we have a square with a temple," Erich noted down, sketching rapidly. I was thinking of the excellent maps of the Chinese cities gathering dust in the reference section of our *Troisième Bureau.*

"How large is the square, Suoi?" I heard Erich asking.

"It is not a very large square. Maybe a hundred paces across."

Schulze's pencil worked but he kept talking to hold the girl's attention. "And the bridge . . . is it opposite the temple?"

Suoi shook her head. "No, *monsieur.* It is on the right side."

"A stone bridge?"

"*Oui,*" she nodded. "The other bridge is near the end of the road to Meng-tzu," she added, placing her finger on the drawing. "Here, along the river is a market with many shops."

"Very good, Suoi." Erich paused for a short while, then glanced up. "Do you remember how many streets enter that square?"

Suoi was thinking. "I think five. Three streets run opposite the river, two others parallel with it, on both sides of the square. The right side road goes uphill to where the militia barracks are."

Schulze looked up sharply. We were on the right track. I nodded. "Go on, Erich. You seem to be doing fine."

"Now this is very important, Suoi," Erich went on. "Is it the only road to the barracks, or have you seen other roads too?"

"The other road goes to Meng-tzu," she said.

"I see. Now about those militia barracks. Have you ever been close to them?" Suoi shook her head. "No, *monsieur*. No one is allowed up there. The soldiers have barriers on the road."

"How far from the barracks?"

"At the bottom of the hill," she said. "With guardhouses."

"Is there a wall around the camp?" Eisner cut in. Suoi turned slightly and shook her head. "Only a wire fence."

"No trees?"

"No," she replied, "the hill is bare."

"We will take heavy MGs," Eisner remarked rather to himself.

Erich lifted his legs and swung around on his chair. Surveying the neighborhood briefly, he pointed at a nearby hill. "Is the barrack hill as high as this one, Suoi?"

The girl turned, observed the elevation briefly, then replied, "Not as high – and not as steep."

"More like the one over there?"

"Like that one!" Suoi exclaimed pointing toward a hill. "It is very similar to that one."

Erich questioned her about the hills near Man-hao and gradually his design began to fill with details. Adjoining the militia barracks, we thought, should be the Viet Minh compound. Unfortunately Suoi could not tell how many barracks were there or how large, information which would have enabled us to compute the number of troops the buildings could accommodate. She thought the barracks were of wood but she could not say for sure.

"We will have to send in a reconnaissance party before the attack," I said, satisfied with what we got on Erich's diagrams. "Their going will be a great deal easier now."

I had confidence in our chances. With the advantage of surprise on our side, we should be able to destroy some of the installations and deliver a crippling blow to the enemy manpower – if only for a few weeks. We were almost seven hundred strong, but I decided to take along only two hundred men. With the aid of Schulze's diagrams we prepared a rough plan, subject to adjustment later on, according to the reconnaissance findings: a two-pronged attack with Eisner and myself moving in from the east, while Schulze and Riedl would advance from the north. The raid would be timed for 11 P.M., late enough for the troops to be in bed yet still early enough for some important buildings to remain illuminated.

Since we were to cross the railway line, Riedl suggested that we might as well blow a couple of holes in the tracks. But as far as I knew, there was no railway traffic between Meng-tzu and Lao Kay. Therefore I opposed the idea of wasting time on a line that was not in use. If we wanted to damage the Chinese communications the right place to do it was farther up between Man-hao and Meng-tzu, a fifteen-mile diversion which I dared not risk. The Chinese had considerable forces at Meng-tzu, barely fifty miles away from our intended place of attack. They could rush reinforcements to Man-hao within an hour – if not to the town itself, then to block our way of retreat farther north.

I decided to depart the same evening on a rarely used smuggler's trail which Phu and Cao had known since childhood. The trail was far removed from the regular patrol routes of the militia. Schulze and Eisner left to select weapons for the coming action: twenty machine guns, thirty light mortars with ten rounds each, twelve bazookas, and a dozen flamethrowers, which latter I consider the most effective weapon against guerrillas. We also packed grenades and demolition charges. For ammo, Eisner selected tracers, which were psychologically more effective than ordinary bullets. The glowing ribbons of tracers always panic the enemy. The more fireworks we displayed the greater their confusion.

Ordinary bullets deliver a sudden and invisible death; an instant before the fatal hit the enemy gunner still fires his weapon, and may cause casualties. With tracers it is different. "Death" can actually be seen as it creeps closer and closer and when the glowing ribbons of destruction begin to flicker overhead the enemy gunner will stop firing and will, instinctively, seek shelter. By cutting down the enemy's "time of activity," if only for seconds one may save the lives of a few comrades. A small tactical point which, naturally, was never incorporated in the Legion's *Les Principes de la Guerre*.

The actual raid, I thought, should not last longer than fifteen minutes. "Do not get wounded," Eisner warned the troops. "Stay under cover and take no chances. You know the rules."

They knew them. We could not leave corpses behind to provide the Chinese with evidence. Casualties were to be destroyed with grenades and flamethrowers. A macabre arrangement but we had no choice.

The most important part of our venture was to find a safe place which was secluded enough to conceal two hundred men for a whole day. It was impossible to reach our destination in a single night and the enemy should not detect our presence prematurely. On the return leg of the trip we planned to march through, covering the entire distance in about fifteen hours. Phu recalled a cave on the Chinese side which, he insisted, was large enough to hold us during the hours of daylight. It was also close enough to Man-hao. By questioning Phu again, Schulze was able to pinpoint the approximate location of the cave and mark it on his diagram.

When dusk fell we changed into native pajamas. Eisner had some difficulty finding a pair of boots small enough to fit Suoi's little feet, but Erich solved the problem with additional padding. The trip was to be a tiresome one and her sandals would not have lasted long. She, too, had changed into man's clothes. I advised her to stay close to me all the time.

"I don't care if they kill me," she replied and her remark drew a sharp reproach from Schulze.

"You should not say such a thing, Suoi. We also have lost many people whom we loved. There is not a man among us who has not mourned someone."

"You have each other," she said quietly. "I am alone in the world with no place to go."

"You are not alone, Suoi," Erich answered. "You do have a family, a very large one. A whole battalion." He reached under her chin and tilted up her face gently. "Will you accept us to be your family?"

She smiled through tears. "If you don't expect me to cook for you...."

Looking at Schulze and Riedl as they flanked the girl, I saw Eisner was suppressing a grin and instantly I realized that my battalion had indeed "adopted" Suoi. If not the battalion, then at least Erich Schulze.

"What will you do with her, back in Hanoi?" I asked nonchalantly.

Erich shrugged. "Oh, hell, we will put her up somewhere. If every one of us gives her a hundred piasters every month, she can live like a princess."

"When we move out again, she can join us," Riedl added enthusiastically.

"Like hell she can! We have enough trouble without girls in the show."

"She is a clever girl, Hans. She speaks good French. We can always use a good interpreter," Erich argued.

"Do you want to see her killed?"

"We have been in business for a long time and we are still around. Not every bullet stings."

"No . . . only the one you bump into. How about that bullet they dug out of your ass?"

Eisner cut in. "I like the way you are discussing the girl's future. Shouldn't you ask *her?*"

Schulze waved him down. "Later I will ask her."

We moved out at 9:30 P.M. with our footwear wrapped in cloth to deaden sound. Phu and Cao received their machine pistols and were leading the way with steady strides. We crossed the rugged frontier without difficulty. The men kept at arm's length. Our guides must have known the path indeed, for they marched without hesitation in what seemed to me utter darkness, giving an occasional warning on obstacles or steep descents. Gradually the clouds dispersed, allowing the half moon to shine dimly. Around two o'clock we were already three miles inside China and the going was still good. I held four brief pauses mainly for Suoi's benefit. The little native girl was following me bravely and without complaining. She accepted my hand whenever we hit an obstacle or held onto my belt when we had to climb.

"Say, Hans," Schulze turned to me during one of our short halts, "you aren't booking the girl for yourself, are you? I am kind of interested in her."

"I've noticed that already, Erich, but for the time being I prefer your concentrating on our expedition."

The sun was rising when we arrived at the cave. It was a quarter of the way up a precipitous cluster of rocks that towered a hundred feet over a gorge. A narrow path led to the opening. Only one man at a time could climb up. The place was entirely surrounded with densely forested hills. Phu reassured me that there were no people for miles around. The cave was large, at least three hundred feet deep and thirty feet high. Examining our hideout, Schulze expressed his surprise at the Viet Minh's failure to utilize that natural strong-point so well suited for storing weapons. Cao, however, explained that when it rained, and especially during the monsoon, the cave filled with water and became useless.

"And apart from that," Eisner added, "you forget that we are in China proper where the Viet Minh have depots right along the road."

Farther inside, where the bottom appeared sloping inward, I saw a large pool of clear water. It solved our cooking problems. Everyone selected a relatively dry spot to stretch out and settle for a nap. The place was rather warm but a slight, persistent draft felt refreshing. With the cotton paddings from some ammo boxes Schulze improvised a comfortable cot for Suoi. She lay down and quickly fell asleep. I ordered Corporal Altreiter to post guards at the cave's entrance, then I, too, stretched out with a rucksack under my head. Sleep, however, evaded me for a long time and thoughts flooded my mind to keep me awake. I was thinking of the ruined village, the Viet Minh, the Foreign Legion with its vanishing *gloire*, the rising Chinese monolith in the north that should never have been permitted to be born, let alone to live and grow – the whole insane situation, with us killing hundreds of little yellow men here, trying to rescue other hundreds of the same stock somewhere else. . . .

Thinking of America and England now fighting their own little war in Korea, I could have laughed, had not the fate of the entire civilized world been hitched inexorably to their shaky wagon. The two great pillars of democracy and freedom had been chivalrously allied to Stalin, whom they could have sent reeling back to Russia's prewar frontiers in 1945, when only the United States had the nuclear bomb and Russia was at the end of her endurance. A simple ultimatum would have sufficed to preserve Europe and maybe the world from Communism. There would be no People's Democracies now, no Red China, no Korean war, and no Viet Minh.

I could not regard the Viet Minh as other than subhumans, whom one should squash without the slightest remorse. To me they were nothing but one of the loathsome heads of a many-headed dragon who might belch fire at any part of the world if not stopped. To be sure, there were the rare occasions when mutual sanity prevailed in Indochina. Fighting near Muong Sai, two French officers and thirty men were captured by the guerrillas under the command of a young Communist troublemaker Bao Ky. Bao retained a certain degree of common sense. Having disarmed the prisoners he stripped them to their underwear and sent them away saying that he had neither place nor food for prisoners.

When five months later we had the pleasure of capturing Bao with twelve guerrillas, we likewise only stripped them (bare, of course, for they wore no underpants), decorated their bottoms with a painted Red star and sent them away unharmed. It was against our standing orders to set prisoners, especially guerrilla leaders, free, but to be frank we never cared much for certain orders coming from above and did as we considered right in a given circumstance. By releasing Bao and his men, I hoped to spread a bit of goodwill in the jungle. And when, capturing a Viet Minh camp, we discovered two wounded legionnaires in a hut, bandaged and properly fed, I ordered food and medical treatment for the captive guerrillas, who were then transported to a prison camp instead of being lined up and bayoneted, our customary treatment for captive terrorists. Unfortunately such events were as rare as a white raven.

There were four classes of guerrilla leaders in Indochina. Those who had received indoctrination and training in China were the worst ones, and for whom no brutality seemed cruel enough. The bloodiest atrocities, murder, and mutilation were not only tolerated but encouraged by them. They believed that military or ideological discipline should be maintained on pain of severe punishment: beating, mutilation, or death. Their method was as brutal as it was naïve. The Chinese-educated commissar invariably tried to further the cause of Communism by denying the people the barest necessities of life, or by simply beating a "candidate" into submission. (I believed that our long-sought foe, Ming Chen-po, was a sadist; a mentally ill person who tortured in the most cruel fashion for the sheer pleasure of seeing blood and corpses. Ming was about fifty years old, a born marauder and a common bandit before he joined Mao's rugged army on the Long March north. He had fought the Japanese, then Chiang Kai-shek and afterwards the "class enemy" within China. To save ammunition and time, he is said to have executed two thousand Nationalist prisoners by dumping them bound and gagged onto the Yunnan railway line and running a locomotive over the lot. He called his "system" the cheapest and fastest way of decapitation.)

Guerrilla leaders coming from the Soviet school showed more common sense and were more sophisticated in their manners and methods. Few of them would resort to senseless terror to win popular support. While the Chinese type of revolutionary would move into a village and allow fifteen minutes for the population to choose between joining the party or receiving a bullet through the head, the Russian-educated commissar would talk to the people about their problems, give them brief lectures about the aims of the liberators, or even help the peasants with their work. They took great pains to depart, at least for the time being, as friends who would one day return. And even if the people did not become convinced followers of Lenin outright, they would not betray the guerrillas either.

Members of the third group had been educated either in French schools or in France proper. They seldom committed excesses and usually kept to a sort of military code of honor. But such leaders lived in a kind of Red limbo, for the hard-core Communists never trusted them enough to give them any significant role in the game. The French-educated rebel leaders seemed more interested in establishing a truly independent Indochina than a Communist slave state.

The fourth category consisted of leaders who rose from the local masses. They may have commanded a large band of terrorists but they never ventured far from their own villages. And there was also a fifth group of "freedom fighters" which consisted entirely of common marauders without any political aim. They fought only for spoils and were treated by the Legion accordingly.

After four hours of rest Altreiter, three men, and Phu departed on a reconnaissance mission to Man-hao, which I estimated lay about twelve miles towards the southwest. We spent the morning cleaning weapons, playing cards, or holding language courses. Riedl gave Suoi a small automatic pistol and taught her how to handle it. "Just in case," he remarked – although I had no intention of taking the girl into any skirmish with the enemy. Both Riedl and Schulze were obviously very fond of Suoi and were trying their best to comfort her.

Suoi told us the whole tragic story of the previous day's attack. Her father had been wealthy until the terrorists struck. He had owned five hundred acres of rice paddies, a giant estate by local standards and the reason why her family had become a primary target of the Red exterminators. They had wiped out all the other families of means. "They came to the village before but never killed people, only took a toll in grains and livestock which we gladly parted with for peace in return," Suoi explained. "Whenever they visited us my father gave them money to ransom our safety. My father would never consider leaving. 'Communism, like a bad disease, will pass,' he used to say. He believed that his money was buying medicine for that disease. But in the past there were no Chinese among the guerrillas."

"How many Chinese were with them yesterday?" I asked.

"There must have been over twenty militiamen among the Viet Minh."

"Do your parents have relatives, Suoi?"

"My father's brothers are dead. My mother's brother lives in France. We received some letters from him but those were in the house. I don't even know his address."

"Don't worry, Suoi," Riedl said. "We will find him somehow."

Schulze nodded. "We sure as hell will."

"I have nothing left on earth, not even money to buy food or clothes," the girl whispered as her eyes filled. "What money my father kept at home the Chinese took away. He has much money in a Hanoi bank but I don't know which one or how to get it."

"Of course she has money!" Erich exclaimed in German. "Her father must have kept funds in reserve. He was a wealthy man."

Suoi could not tell us anything else. Whatever papers her father may have had relating to his finances and the family holdings must have been destroyed in the fire.

"A twisted, burned copper chest was all we found in the ruins," Eisner explained. "Even the corpses were burnt beyond recognition. Nothing as inflammable as paper could have escaped the holocaust."

"When we get back to Hanoi we will go from bank to bank until we find the right one," Schulze stated determinedly.

"I doubt if the bank will give her any money before a legal process establishes her as the rightful heir," Eisner commented. "Why, she cannot even prove who she is."

"Like hell she can't," Riedl exclaimed. "We can testify!"

"That might not be enough, Helmut."

"You leave the legalities to me," Schulze said firmly. "Once I get to the right counter she will receive what belongs to her if I have to blast the manager for it."

Knowing him, I had no doubt that Erich meant what he said. But blasting Viet Minh terrorists and blasting Hanoi bank managers were two different things.

"We will talk to the colonel about Suoi's inheritance," I suggested. "You remember Lin? Houssong won't refuse to help Suoi either. He might vouch for her or get the high brass to interpose."

"You take care of the colonel; I will take care of the bank," said Erich. "No red tape is going to deprive the girl of what is still hers."

"I will handle both the colonel and the bank manager, Erich," I said somewhat sharply.

"As you wish, Hans."

The reconnaissance party returned about four o'clock in the afternoon, soaking wet and muddy but bringing good intelligence. Corporal Altreiter had observed the military encampment for over two hours and had drawn a diagram of the area. There were twelve wooden barracks in the compound. Adjoining it, the Viet Minh camp had only tents. The barracks were each about sixty feet long, with eight windows on either side and exits at both ends. One of the buildings, probably the command post, had wireless aerials. Another barrack with more chimneys was obviously the kitchen and mess hall.

That left us with ten living quarters. Since the eight windows were most likely at the intervals between the bunk beds, a quick estimate established the number of bunks at either 30/32 single, or 60/64 double, giving a total number of troops as either 320 or 640. The tents could accommodate about 200 guerrillas.

The possible number of enemy troops in the camp ruled out a direct assault on the enclosure. Hand-to-hand combat was likely to develop and I dared not risk heavy casualties. The presence of fourteen heavy trucks in the compound was welcome news. According to Altreiter the vehicles had just arrived with supplies, most of them ammunition. He saw militiamen and guerrillas unloading the crates and piling them up alongside the barracks. The crates were covered only with tarpaulin sheets. This casual arrangement of storing explosives suggested one of two alternatives, either that the underground ammo depots were loaded to capacity or that the new supplies were to be moved again shortly, for all we knew maybe into Indochina. Either way it was a most fortunate coincidence. A few direct hits on the crates could dispatch the entire camp into the Great Beyond. On his sketch Corporal Altreiter had also marked a row of large drums which he believed contained diesel oil or gasoline. The drums were fairly close to the underground ammunition dumps that the reconnaissance party had detected as a number of earth mounds with ventilation chimneys.

The railway line which we were to cross and recross ran only three miles from the cave. Contrary to my belief, the line was still in use, Altreiter reported. The Chinese used it to ferry supplies to the various border posts facing Lao Kay. "There is a small steel bridge not very far off," he said. "Sentries are posted on the bridge itself."

I decided to demolish the bridge and its guardhouse on the way back. Phu said that the adjoining hills were densely forested and offered ample cover. Except for Phu, whom we were resolved to carry if necessary, I wanted the reconnaissance party to remain in the cave. Weary as they were, the men insisted on making the trip for a second time. "We have earned our right to be present at the party, Commander," the troopers insisted. I consented. And since I no longer intended to storm the Chinese compound I decided to leave Suoi and half of the troops behind. Due to the successful reconnaissance it was unnecessary to take the girl along on the perilous journey.

We departed at dusk, a hundred men altogether, moving at

good speed through the hills. Unencumbered by our close-combat weapons which we had left behind, we could move faster. Phu reassured me that except for the guardhouse near the bridge – which we were to bypass by two miles – there was not a soul around. But on arriving at the railway line we almost ran into four militiamen patrolling the tracks. Fortunately Phu spotted them in time and we were able to retreat a few hundred yards and then to proceed half a mile farther west. Apart from this interlude our trip was without excitement.

By eleven o'clock we were deploying on the two hills that overlooked the militia barracks some five hundred yards to the south. No raiders could have hoped for an easier target. The windows of the command post were ablaze with lights and we could hear faintly the steady drone of an electric generator. The barracks and the tents were dark but a multitude of external lamps illuminated the entire camp. Beyond the hill the town of Man-hao was blanketed in darkness. Only the militia had the privilege of electricity. The population had to make do with their oil lamps.

Faithfully following the teachings of their great Mao, the Chinese kept a vigorous daily schedule in their army camps. At 10 P.M. sharp, the troops had to be in their bunks: "Men who sleep well at night shall march better the next day," Mao said. For once, Mao was wrong. At least at Man-hao, where his militia would march nowhere the next day, except into oblivion.

At precisely 11:10 P.M. we opened fire on the camp with twenty fifty-caliber machine guns and thirty mortars. The rest of my men fired at individual targets with their rifles. The effect of our unexpected attack was instantaneous. Screaming lines of tracers tore across the valley, peppering the barracks, ripping the tents, blasting the parked trucks, mowing down men. Some shells of the first mortar salvo landed short but thereafter every projectile was on target. Instead of turning out the lights the bewildered militiamen turned on even those that had been out. Our riflemen shot through the lighted windows. Groups of yelling, screaming men ran up and down in the compound and fell under a hail of steel.

Two minutes after our first volley half a dozen mortar shells hit a pile of ammunition crates which exploded instantly with a blinding flash of fire. The blast demolished both the command post and the mess hall, along with the barracks immediately behind them.

Seconds later the dumps began to blow up one after another, sending crazily zigzagging fireworks about the hill. The lights went out, but by then the hilltop shone like the rim of a volcano. I doubted if a single soul escaped the ensuing fire and multiple explosions.

The camp had turned into a sea of flames. The drums, containing diesel oil and gasoline, began to burn and burst. The oil leaked into the underground depots like lava. The depots, too, began to explode, ripping hundred-foot-wide gaps into the hillside.

I ordered cease-fire. The troops assembled and we marched away. The job was done. The time was 11:23 P.M.

Reaching the railway line, Riedl went ahead with a small party. He found the eight guardsmen crowding atop the guardhouse. They were watching the firelit skies, chattering excitedly. Helmut mowed them down with a single burst of his submachine gun, then tossed a couple of grenades into the writhing mob for good measure. The guardhouse and the bridge were demolished. Schulze proceeded to plant our remaining mines along the line and the adjoining footpath "to get a few of the bastards later on," as he put it. Our two Indochinese friends asked my permission to collect the weapons of the dead Chinese, saying that they could use the rifles later on, at home.

It was becoming light when we arrived at the cave where our comrades had been waiting tensely. "You have not missed a thing," Schulze consoled them. "A bunch of boy scouts could have blasted the camp with all the ammo crates scattered around. You just spared yourselves a long walk."

The company arrived at Suoi's village at dusk – dead tired but in very cheerful spirits. We had no way of knowing whether Ming had been among the Man-hao casualties but he was never again spotted in Indochina.

"There was a mighty blast in Man-hao," Colonel Houssong remarked two weeks later when I submitted to him my report on our recent activities. "The whole militia went up in smoke and the Chinese suffered nearly a thousand casualties, among them a corps commander from Yunnan."

"Well, isn't that something, *mon colonel?*" Schulze exclaimed with enthusiasm. "It's the first good news for months!" He turned toward me with pretended innocence. "Imagine, Hans . . . we were only about thirty miles from the place."

"That's exactly what I was thinking," Colonel Houssong cut in, stressing his words.

"We didn't notice a thing, *mon colonel*," I said.

"I wonder."

"*Mon colonel*, everyone knows how careless the Chinese are. They probably stored ammunition crates in the open and lightning struck the dump. It has happened before."

"Lightning my foot!" he cut me short. "There has been no storm around there for weeks. A couple of eighty-caliber lightnings with fins maybe. I wonder if I should check your inventories on the ammo you received and what you brought back. Come on. Wagemueller, how did you pull it?"

I told him the whole story and he sent a report saying:

"Terrorist group of about two hundred men and a large quantity of ammunition destroyed 35 miles northwest of Lao Kay."

Needless to say, the General Staff would never bother to check that anyplace thirty-five miles northwest of Lao Kay was well within Red China!

8

Raid Into China

THREE weeks passed before the full impact of our Man-hao raid finally reached Hanoi. We had reason to believe that certain general officers in the High Command suspected the truth but none of them seemed interested in pressing for details. Too much information inevitably leads to too many written reports and those in turn demand the attention of too many people, including civilians, whom the generals scorned and despised, whether members of the press, politicians, clerks in the ministry, or the prime minister himself.

Fortunately for us the raid had been successful. We left no evidence on the scene, neither French Army equipment nor corpses. The Chinese could only sulk over their losses but they were unable to prove anything. Moreover, some diehard Nationalist battalions were still active in the remote southern provinces of China and it would have been easy for the French to credit the Man-hao debacle to Chiang Kai-shek. This token Nationalist presence in what was now Mao's empire and the total success of our totally illegal expedition seemed to inspire our commander to venture a similar foray but on a much larger scale.

The indirect effects of our raid were soon felt in western Indochina. There was a sharp decrease in terrorist activity in the province, even in the exposed frontier areas of Lao Kay. For the first time in many months the local peasants could harvest their crops and cart their surplus to Lao Kay without being robbed on the road by terrorists requisitioning food and money. Since our raid no French troops had been ambushed and no roads had been mined. Somewhat over-optimistic, Schulze insisted that a few similar "house-cleanings" across the border could throw Giap's marauders back into the "good old days" of the bow and the spear.

After the Man-hao coup, our relations with Colonel Houssong became even more intimate. He began to regard us more as "fellow conspirators" than mere subordinates, and he bestowed on us certain privileges which were denied to other units of the Foreign Legion. The permanent gate pass was the one we appreciated the most. Whenever we returned from a mission my men were free to leave the Army compound from five P.M. till eight A.M. every day. I had free access to the supply dumps and could requisition any amount of food, weapons, and ammunition by simply signing for them. I was given unrestricted access to the top secret intelligence files which dealt with guerrilla activity in certain districts.

Colonel Houssong was proud of us, and I may add without bragging, rightly so. Apart from the famous Paras, my unit was the only force that went into action and returned with results; and more often than not, without a single loss of life. In Indochina it was called a "good result" when troops on a distant mission returned without having accomplished anything, only returned with minimum losses. Many troops of the Legion have entered the jungle never to be heard of again.

Ten days after our return, Colonel Houssong summed us to his office. We shook hands and he said without preliminaries, "Sit down, *messieurs*, for what I am going to tell you now will make you sit down anyway." He placed a fresh bottle of Calvados on the table and suggested with a mysterious smile, "Have a drink, you will need it." Evidently the colonel was in a good mood. His eyes danced with amusement.

"Is it going to be as bad as that?" I asked him, taking my seat opposite him. Eisner and Schulze sat down and placed their map cases on the table. Pfirstenhammer opened his notebook, Riedl took pencil and paper. We were ready for the briefing.

"It depends on the way you look at it," the colonel answered my question. Reaching for the bottle he poured drinks for us, filled his own cup, and lifted it slightly, "To your success with the Tien-pao raid."

"You mean the Man-hao raid, *mon colonel*," Eisner corrected what he thought was a reference to our excursion into China.

"I said *Tien-pao*," Houssong repeated, stressing the last word. "That is the place you will be going shortly."

There was a curious silence while we digested the implications of that short sentence. "To Tien-pao?" I repeated cautiously.

"To Tien-pao," said the colonel. His eyes kindled. "You have convinced certain gentlemen in the upper regions that such raids are feasible and can be executed without complications. So, off you go. But this time it isn't going to be a pushover, *messieurs*. You will have to work hard to earn a victory."

"To earn a victory?" Schulze commented with a chuckle. "I will be happy if we can earn a simple return ticket, *mon colonel*."

"And rightly so," Eisner added with emphasis. "There are some thirty thousand Chinese troops at Tien-pao."

"Eighty to one against," Riedl said.

"Sometimes it was worse in Russia," Karl added and lit his pipe.

"I am glad to note your good spirit; a spirited action is already half a success," the colonel remarked. He unfolded a large map of northern Indochina and spread it on the long table. The map covered the district north of Cao Bang, including Chinese areas as far as the Siang river, thirty kilometers north of Tien-pao. Tien-pao was the town where we believed that Ho Chi Minh's "government" had been hiding out for the past two years, although Ho himself was thought to be residing in Nanning, farther to the east.

Holding his pen lightly over the map, Colonel Houssong swept the upper regions of the map, then circled a smaller area and looked up. "Do you think you can make it here, Wagemueller?"

"We can always make it there, *mon colonel*. The question is whether we can also make it back?"

"You had better make it back – and without leaving corpses behind. It must be a clean job like the one in Man-hao."

I rose slightly and bent over the map. It was not just a map but an operational plan with the essential details already incorporated: the routes were marked out, time elements considered and noted down in brackets: the area between the border and Tien-pao, and eastward to the Sengen highway, featured a number of small red stars, some of them placed within rectangles, others in circles.

"As you can see, I spent some time arranging your action in effective patterns," the colonel said good-humoredly. "The stars are known Viet Minh bases and Chinese garrisons."

"The size of which, *mon colonel?*"

"The size of which we can only guess. But it does not really matter for you are to avoid them anyway."

"But do they know that, *mon colonel?*" Eisner cut in and everyone began to laugh.

Colonel Houssong paused for a moment, then joined us over the map. "Your principal target will be the establishment marked 'A', which must be destroyed before anything else. It lies thirty kilometers north of the frontier."

"As the crow flies. Overland it will be fifty," I remarked.

"*Sans doute*. Nevertheless you will have to get there. The second objective, 'C', is located only half as far inland but more to the east. As you can see, objective 'B' is unfortunately off limits. It is much too close to Tien-pao and the main garrisons. Two objectives should suffice for the time being. They are large enemy bases and training camps."

"What are the X-es, *mon colonel?*"

"Small Chinese guardhouses along road bridges with three to five men in them."

"What about them?"

"Don't ask me, Wagemueller, suit yourself. If you find time to demolish also a few bridges it will be an asset."

The conference lasted for two hours. With all the important problems discussed, the colonel announced, "Needless to say this whole business is strictly between us, *messieurs*."

"Of course, *mon colonel.*"

"Your Man-hao raid was a big shock to the Viet Minh and especially to the Chinese. They have many bases along the border and General —— thinks we should hit them at least once more before Peking decides to decentralize." He added with a smile, "*Il faut piquer dedans* – we should hit them where it hurts." His eyes focused on the map. "Alas, most of the Viet Minh training bases and supply dumps are still just across the frontier, but soon Giap will move his establishment farther north, to safer locations." He lifted his eyes to me. "What do you think of it?"

"It seems to me either glory or court-martial, *mon colonel.*" I said jokingly.

"You had better forget about the second alternative," said he. "Since your Man-hao business I am, er, your accomplice in crime."

"In crime, *mon colonel?*"

"What else can you call it? We are not at war with China."

"Peking doesn't seem to know it," Eisner remarked. "We should call such actions only an exchange of mutual courtesies, *mon colonel.*"

"How about those garrisons at Tien-pao, *mon colonel?*" I asked, thinking of the thirty thousand Chinese troops.

"They have no transports," the colonel explained. "Fifteen trucks and some derelict jeeps are all they have. The troops are armed mostly with vintage Russian rifles and for the present their ammo is restricted to about five cartridges per weapon."

"That's comforting," said Karl.

"So keep quiet until you arrive at objective 'A' and the garrisons won't be able to interfere with you in force."

He folded the map and handed it to me. "This is the only map covering the operation," he advised me. "Prepare two copies for yourself, then bring it back. Don't bungle this job, for if you do, you might as well remain in China and go down fighting."

"I understand that, *mon colonel.*"

"You will be wearing civilian clothes, of course –"

"Of course."

Of course, I thought. No papers, no identity tags, no army rations, only native pajamas and foodstuffs.

"What will you do about possible casualties, Wagemueller?" he asked cagily.

"The Chinese will find neither corpses nor graves, *mon colonel.*"

"So be it."

He extended his hand. We avoided discussing the gory details Corpses were to be destroyed either by grenades or by flame-throwers: blasted to bits, burned beyond recognition, and should there be gravely wounded comrades who could not march while the enemy was pressing us, it was also our duty to turn them into corpses, so that they wouldn't turn into evidence in Chinese hands.

"You will have a good chance to succeed," the colonel said before dismissing us. "I have selected your guides personally. They know the area well and they are also professionals."

We code-named the operation "Longhand" because of its far-reaching implications.

"Here we go, one hundred against half a billion," Schulze remarked, gazing back toward the moonlit ridges of Bao Lac. Ahead of us loomed the sinister hills of China. We crossed the frontier following the remote trail which native warriors must have cut across the virgin woods decades before. It must have been maintained by smugglers then cleared again, probably by Nationalist warring parties. After a few miles on the trail I knew that Colonel Houssong's "blueprint for aggression" had been based on precise data, the result of exhaustive intelligence and even aerial reconnaissance. The colonel did not believe in venturing an important job on the spin of a coin. And since our lives depended on his meticulous exactitude, we indeed appreciated it.

The company advanced in a long line, the men keeping about ten paces apart: pajama clad dark shapes, wearing coolie hats and crude rubber sandals fashioned from old automobile tires. Everything had been blacked with soot, our faces, our hands, the weapons; nothing glinted in the bright moonlight.

Although we carried only the absolute minimum, the load on each man weighed about fifteen kilos. That included a submachine gun with ten spare mags, food, burlap, a small medical kit, magnetic compass, flashlight, bush knife, mosquito net, and hand grenades. The field gear of *Gruppe Drei* was divided among the troops.

Gruppe Drei was our advance guard, the "Trailblazers," the unit on which our existance depended. It consisted of only thirty men but they were specially trained. Every member of the group had completed a rigorous six-month training schedule that included bomb detection and demolition, trap detection, tracking, and general woodsmanship. Their tutors were some of the foremost experts of antiguerrilla warfare, both French and foreign: an ex-captain in the British Army who had fought the Communist insurgents for three years in Malaya and a former Japanese colonel, the one-time commander of a counter-intelligence unit of the *Kempe Tai* (former Japanese Secret Police) during the war. Both men wore the uniform of a colonel of the Colonial army but they did not formally belong to the armed forces and received civilian wages, as per contract.

A hundred meters ahead of us marched the advance guard led by Krebitz. Still ahead of them marched four Nationalist Chinese officers, one of them a former guide to the forces of Chiang Kai-shek. They knew the area well. Some of the last Nationalist battles had been fought in the province before the vanquished party was compelled to withdraw into the jungles of northern Burma. Colonel Houssong did not inform me how and where he had got hold of the Nationalist Chinese. "You may trust them," was all he said, "a well-known American general has vouched for them."

Being well aware of the utter corruption which then dominated the Nationalist army, and which contributed greatly to the final collapse of Nationalist China, I reserved my opinion on the matter. As a rule we trusted no Chinese or Indochinese and we also had some misgivings about the judgment of American generals. The Americans had poured into China money and weapons enough to conquer the earth yet they were unable to preserve a single square kilometer of the "Heavenly Empire" that was now gradually turning into a perfect hell.

I had asked Colonel Houssong if our Chinese companions had been informed about "Longhand" in detail.

"I understand what you mean," he had said, "but rest assured. I did not consider it necessary to reveal all. You may tell them as much as possible under the circumstances." My sigh of relief must have been audible for he added reassuringly, "I am sure they will be all right."

"They had better be indeed."

He had laughed and slapped me on the shoulder in a friendly manner. "I know you wouldn't trust Chiang Kai-shek himself, Wagemueller."

"I wouldn't trust Jesus Christ on a mission like this, *mon colonel.* The slightest indiscretion and – "

"Would you prefer to go on your own?"

"Without reservation."

"It would be much more difficult."

"We may have to climb more hills but we won't be jittery all the way."

"Will you be jittery because of them?"

"By your leave, *mon colonel,* I shall make my own security arrangements."

"*Alors*, make them, but return safely."

So we kept our Chinese quintet under close surveillance, and I made sure that they knew as little as possible of our general plan. The Nationalist Chinese officers could study our immediate objective but nothing else. One of them who spoke good French must have noticed our polite but reserved attitude, for he spoke to me shortly after we had crossed the border.

"You are not sure about our capability to lead this expedition, are you?" he asked me with a hint of sadness in his voice.

"Major Kwang," I replied in a firm voice, "I am going to be frank with you. We met only five days ago. We don't know you or where you come from."

"Colonel Houssong knows," he ventured.

"The colonel is in Hanoi, major. We are on the way to hell – and back, let us hope. But let me ask you something. Have you known your companions for a long time?"

"I know only Major Cheng," he replied. "We used to serve in the same battalion. The others we met in the colonel's office."

"You see, major. They are aliens even to you – "

"But the colonel surely knows them."

"The colonel is only a human being, Major Kwang. Human beings are fallible."

"The colonel, the generals, the prime minister," Eisner cut in. "We have been around here for a long time, Major Kwang. We have outlived the average life expectancy of legionnaires, and I think we are still around because we took nothing for granted – never!"

The major smiled politely. "Then you regard every stranger guilty until proven innocent?"

"We regard only one thing, major – our own survival factors," I said. "We learned that a long time ago: to think, to plan, to calculate, to evaluate and act – everything related to survival factors. Friendship, relations, rank, sentiments are all only of secondary importance. We are living on borrowed time and abiding by the law of probability, which is the only law we carefully observe. Had we done otherwise, we would now be dead heroes instead of surviving experts. For that's what we really are, Major Kwang: neither invincible daredevils nor supermen nor heroes – only survival experts. But survival is the most important thing in any war."

"I will do my best to see that all of us survive during the next few days," Kwang said.

"You do that, major," I nodded. "But keep an eye on those whom you do not know."

"With regard to my own survival factor?" he asked with a smile.

"You might call it that," I conceded.

It was nine P.M. Tuesday when we crossed the Chinese frontier eighteen kilometers west of the one time Cao Bang–Tien-pao road. Between us and the road, we knew, ran a guerrilla trail that joined a dirt road three kilometers inland. Here the Chinese maintained a small guardhouse for the militia which patrolled the border section. Farther to the northwest and past the place where we intended to cross the dirt road was a village with a garrison of two hundred troops – whom we wanted to avoid.

Thanks to the moonlight we made good progress but even so the terrain was difficult and it took us almost six hours to cover the eight kilometers to the road. We arrived there shortly before three A.M. Wednesday. I wanted to proceed farther inland without stopping but Sergeant Krebitz called my attention to the numerous truck tire marks, which indicated frequent military traffic along the road. In those days no one but the army possessed heavy vehicles in China but even so the army was very hard pressed on motorized transport, and the troops were often compelled to march extremely long distances because of the lack of trucks. The loss of a few vehicles along the road could be extremely painful for them, especially if some of the trucks were transporting irreplaceable cargo. Krebitz suggested that we should mine the road, which we did at five different points, approximately three hundred paces apart. The pressure switches were set to permit the passage of anything up to one ton, which was about the limit even heavily laden peasant carts would weigh. We had no intention of hurting innocent civilians walking by or carting home their grains.

By five A.M. we were deep in the hills. Daybreak came swiftly and when the sun rose we camped down. Slipping their haversacks and weapons to the ground, the men dropped into the soft grass, weary and exhausted. A general massaging of feet began, a regular feature of every stop. A few troopers began to munch, while others were too spent even for eating. They just stretched out on their burlaps. Breakfast was no problem. Everybody was still carrying cooked rice and minced meat; the men had their canteens full of coffee or tea, except for those who preferred to drink rum. Sergeant Krebitz carried three canteens to have a bit of everything: two dangling from his belt, a third one in his rucksack.

Sitting on a boulder sipping coffee, I surveyed our rugged company. Looking at some troopers one could indeed wonder if our native pajamas would ever deceive the enemy. Maybe from a distance of five hundred meters but not from any closer. They were armed to the teeth with the latest and best equipment France could offer. But, alas, the main point was that we should not look French, and in that respect we certainly succeeded. As a matter of fact we did not look like anything except maybe the forty thieves of Ali Baba.

Except for sentries posted around the camp, the troops were soon sound asleep; their groanings and snorings could have been interpreted as an oncoming armored division ten kilometers away. I had a good rest under the mosquito net which we needed not so much because of mosquitoes as because of flies. Deep in the woods it was cool enough for the mosquitoes to take over the moment the sun dipped below the horizon. Flies and mosquitoes seemed to live in a merry "divide and rule" arrangement, making sure that no one rested in the open during either the day or at night.

We broke camp shortly before noon and soon ran into trouble. *Gruppe Drei* bumped into four stray peasants from a nearby settlement. Carrying the carcass of a wild boar, the villagers were on their way home from a hunting trip. It was a most unfortunate incident and we had no choice but to manacle them and take them on a long, involuntary trip. Our only alternative was to kill them, for not only the success of our mission but our very existence depended on secrecy.

"I thank you for your decision," Major Kwang said with gratitude. "They are innocent people and every one of them with a large family to support."

We roasted and ate the boar during our next stop in a shady ravine that was deep enough to disperse smoke before it reached the open.

After the ravine our going became more difficult. We found no path and the narrow bed of a small river provided the only "road" for about an hour. Although the water level was down, seldom exceeding twenty centimeters in depth, the river bed itself was rough. Strewn with sharp and slimy boulders it offered the worst possible going. Its banks were steep and covered with thorn thickets, but at least we were safe down there and I knew the ravine would take us to the Cao Bang–Tien-pao road where it ran under a small bridge with the guardhouse, our first objective.

Reaching the road around six P.M., Sergeant Krebitz and a reconnaissance party of *Gruppe Drei* went ahead to survey the bridge. Finding only four Chinese soldiers in the guardhouse, they captured it forthwith. Having mined the road on either side, Krebitz blasted the bridge with fifty pounds of gelignite distributed along its wooden pylons, causing a series of small explosions rather than a resounding military one. The dead Chinese soldiers were then dumped in the woods.

It was my intention to move on without delay against our first major objective, Viet Minh camp "A", which lay only about twenty kilometers to the north, along the same road. I hoped that we might be able to reach it without further contact with the Chinese military. Fate, however, decided otherwise, although not to our disadvantage. As we were about to leave the destroyed bridge, we spotted a row of headlights coming downhill on the winding road. It was a small convoy of eight trucks, and we barely had time to deploy along the road, Eisner and Karl taking the eastern, Schulze and Riedl the western slopes, closest to the mined section.

Obviously ignorant of any hostile presence the convoy drove straight onto the mines. The leading vehicle exploded and skidded over the precipice where the bridge had been. Swerving wildly, the second truck careened off the road, hit a boulder, and overturned. The rest of the convoy came to a screaming halt with still more trucks damaged as some of them piled into one another. There were no soldiers in the trucks, only the drivers and a dozen militiamen, who went down the moment we surged onto the road with our guns blazing. The trucks were loaded with rice, salted fish, cane sugar, and cooking fats – most likely to provision the numerous military posts along the frontier. None of the vehicles transported weapons, but the five still-serviceable trucks gave me an idea. I requested Sergeant Krebitz to unload the trucks and turn them around, a job which was carried out with some difficulty on the narrow road. *Gruppe Drei* poured gasoline over the foodstuff – spoiling everything – then we climbed aboard the trucks. I felt it would be safe to take the road straight to the guerrilla base. There were no privately owned vehicles in Mao's empire and especially not transport vehicles: a number of trucks moving on the road would likely be taken for an army convoy.

I was about to signal start when a gesture of Major Kwang made me step back. The moment he stopped in front of me I knew that something unpleasant had happened.

"Two of my companions are gone," he announced grimly, then added with resignation, "I am afraid that you were right about not trusting anyone. I am sorry."

Had we not gotten hold of the trucks, the major's statement would have been the worst possible news. The renegades were either Communist plants or had simply decided to switch sides, doing a meritorious service by "delivering" the hated German detachment (or so they thought) to the Chinese. As it happened, however, they were compelled to proceed on foot while we were motorized, so we still had a good chance to destroy both bases before the garrison at Tien-pao could be alerted.

"You are not to blame," I tried to comfort the unhappy major. "After all they were vouched for, weren't they?"

"I should have watched them," he said apologetically, shaking his head slowly, "but the colonel was so sure. . . ." He wiped his perspiring face with his handkerchief. "Shouldn't we look for them? They cannot be far away yet –"

"Good heavens no!" I exclaimed, mounting the truck. "We have no time to play hide-and-seek. Come aboard, major."

We drove north on the bending gravel road, negotiated a few sharp bends, and came up against a small guardhouse with a sentry in front of it. "This isn't on the colonel's map," Schulze commented, grabbing his gun.

The guard turned, opened the door, and yelled something inside. Another Chinese soldier appeared. Shading his eyes he stared for a moment toward our incoming vehicles, then with a savage yell he dived behind a pile of logs. The sentry's rifle came up, Schulze stepped on the brake, somewhere behind us a short burst of a machine pistol crackled, and the windows of the guardhouse shattered. Sergeant Krebitz threw open the door and jumped, his gun blazing even before he hit the ground. The sentry went down and the militiaman behind the logs cried out in pain, staggered a few steps, then crumpled up. From the guardhouse a shot rang out, followed instantly by two more reports. Two men of *Gruppe Drei* who came running a few steps ahead of Sergeant Krebitz stumbled, made a couple of erratic steps, and fell with blood oozing from neck and chest wounds. Krebitz hurled a grenade into the house, then jumped to the wounded troopers. Sergeant Zeisl came with two medics, examined our unfortunate comrades briefly, and shook his head. "They are both dead," he said gravely.

I glanced at Krebitz. He nodded quietly. Four troopers lifted the corpses and carried them into the woods. Krebitz shouldered a flamethrower, a few other troopers took spades and a can of gasoline and followed. A couple of minutes later a dull explosion came from the woods, the faint "whoooos" of the flamethrower, then thick, oily smoke rose and spiraled upward.

"Attention!" Eisner shouted. The troops froze where they stood. "Salute!"

The hands went up. It was all we could offer our fallen comrades.

Sergeant Krebitz and his troopers returned. Their faces were grim and without a word the men climbed into their vehicle. "It is done," Krebitz said. "We buried what was left over, Hans."

"On your trucks, men!" I commanded.

We drove on.

The Viet Minh base was not exactly on the main road but about two kilometers inland. We had to turn off into a narrow dirt road which we might easily have missed, except for the vigilance of Major Kwang. We encountered no more Chinese either on the main road or on the smaller one, but we stirred up so much dust that the enemy must have seen us coming from miles away. Yet the ruse worked. No one challenged us. We were being accepted as a Chinese army transport column.

The base was a spacious quadrangle, fenced off with barbed wire and featuring a number of wooden barracks and crude tents. It was already dusk and most of the camp inmates were gathering for dinner. I wasted no time at the wooden barrier but careened off the road and into the compound, while Eisner shot the bewildered sentry at the gate between the eyes. I shouted at Schulze to stop at the nearest barrack, which he partly demolished by driving into its plank wall.

The other vehicles roared through the gate and stopped right between the buildings in a cloud of dust. The troops piled out with their guns blazing; more sentries went down and the camp came alive with screaming terrorists. Grenades began to explode. The barracks and tents split apart and collapsed. Forming six assault groups, our troopers swept the place in a violent free-for-all. Within seconds the air was heavy with the smell of cordite: the clatter of machine guns and the death cries of guerrillas came from every corner. Although the Viet Minh did not yet know it, the destruction of this base snuffed out the comforting doctrine of sanctuaries inside Red China.

The flamethrowers went into action. Wood and canvas caught fire. We had to remove our trucks from the compound. Screaming shapes of seminude terrorists ran blindly among the blazing buildings. Only then did we discover that the majority of the Viet Minh carried no weapons. As it turned out, it was a camp for basic training only and no guns had been issued to the trainees. There must have been at least eight hundred Viet Minh recruits at the base, which soon turned into a slaughterhouse with my men literally wading in blood and on top of writhing bodies and blackened corpses. Having realized that the enemy could offer no serious resistance we stopped firing.

Eisner commanded: "*À la baïonnette!*" It was an evening of the bayonets.

When the skirmish ended half an hour later, except for us there was not a soul alive, not a building standing. Colonel Houssong's objective "A" had been erased from the face of earth.

Objective "C", the second Viet Minh establishment within our reach, lay about fourteen kilometers to the southeast, along the same dirt road. Originally it would have taken us days of hard marching to reach both targets, but our good Russian trucks still had gas in their tanks and the road was still clear. I saw no reason why we should not attack the second base in the early morning hours. The faster we moved the sooner we could return home. Because of the two escaped turncoats three more targets situated farther to the north and close to the Tien-pao–Sengen highway had to be ignored, but we were resolved to make our trip profitable by blasting a few additional establishments which lay in our path.

We drove east, bumping and slithering along the narrow road through the woods. There we ran into a platoon of militiamen led by an officer. At least we thought he was an officer, for he was the only one in the group shouldering a submachine gun. Seeing us coming they moved off the road, shading their eyes from the dazzling headlights. The officer raised a hand as though requesting us to stop. It was his last conscious act, for an instant later he doubled up and fell, hit by a salvo from Riedl's submachine gun in the second truck. A short burst of withering fire roared from the other vehicles, shredding belts, uniforms, and flesh, and the platoon went down. They never had a chance – and we hadn't even slowed down.

The sun was rising above the horizon when we arrived in the vicinity of objective "C". Halting briefly on the edge of the woods,

I leveled my field glasses and looked across the grassy flat. About a thousand meters to the southeast a conglomeration of thatched huts, tents, and barracks lay huddled among the paddies. The camp and the village were separated by narrow irrigation ditches. The village consisted of about thirty dwellings, situated at the junction of four dirt roads and a forest trail to the south. We spotted the guerrilla base on the western side of the hamlet. I could count about fifty tents, each capable of accommodating twenty men, and two administration barracks with barred windows. Adjoining it were four barracks in a separate compound for the Chinese militia. I stopped to survey the compound to search for signs of alertness but found none.

"Forward!"

Repeating our successful former coup, we drove straight up to the militia compound and within seconds my men were storming the gatehouse, where after a brief exchange of fire the five guardsmen were killed. Again surprise was total and we encountered no organized resistance. My rugged company descended on their quarters, rushing from window to window, pouring steel and grenades into the barracks, spraying the tents with withering salvos. The automaton-like precision of my troops was awesome to behold. Five troopers sprayed a barrack with machine-gun fire and raced on, changing magazines as they ran. Another five then lobbed grenades through the windows. Four troopers kicked open the four doors simultaneously and jumped aside to make way for another team working with flamethrowers. No orders, no shouting, no confusion – it was expert teamwork which never lasted longer than thirty seconds. Although here the enemy did possess weapons, they never had a chance to use them with any effect.

In the camp and among the huts hell erupted. Every tent, every barrack spilled out terrorists and militiamen. Dodging bullets and bayonets they ran for cover. A few of them even tried to stop and fight back but were killed instantly. Like a human avalanche our troopers cascaded onward, shooting, slashing, and bayoneting their bewildered adversaries. From the trucks the light machine guns blazed. Scythed by the merciless hail of slugs, the enemy toppled like grain.

Sergeants Krebitz and Riedl discovered a number of underground depots which were stocked with food and ammunition. The grenades set fire to them, killing those Chinese and guerrillas who had taken shelter there. The shooting jolted the inhabitants of the village and there was an even greater commotion when the population began to flee to the nearby hills. Hens, dogs, goats, and cattle panicked and through the melee raced people, many of them naked and in abject terror, intent only on escape. About two hundred guerrillas and militiamen managed to break out of the compound and were running across the paddies, heading for the woods eight hundred yards away. Bracing their machine guns against the truck sideboards, Schulze's detachment raked the fleeing mass of flesh out in the field.

The fire spread to the village and soon black smoke blanketed the place. Briefly I spotted Riedl leading a skirmish line, driving into the churning dust and the smoke of blazing huts, pausing only to switch magazines. From behind a barn emerged Corporal Altreiter and six troopers herding a dozen Chinese officers at gunpoint.

"Are you promenading or something?" Karl challenged him.

"We might want to question them," Altreiter replied.

"To hell with questions. Wipe them out, Horst," Eisner shouted.

Altreiter shrugged. "You do it, Bernard," he said quietly. "I am not gunning down prisoners."

"Put them over there and under guard," I commanded, pointing toward the paddies. "We will decide about them later."

Bracing their rifles against a fence, our sharpshooters were busy picking off the escaping enemy. Although the foremost escapees had already covered the better part of the distance between the camp and the hills, those who were caught in our telescopic sights crumpled up one after another. Then, acting on Eisner's order, *Gruppe Drei* began to fire mortar shells into the patch of land between the runners and the forest. Some of the guerrillas ran into the explosions and were torn to pieces, others veered off, recoiled, and stopped just in time to receive the full impact of the next salvo sent a hundred yards shorter in anticipation of just such a halt by the fugitives.

Leaving the Viet Minh establishment a corpse-strewn inferno, we moved on, destroying two more bridges and mining the roads behind us. Fortunately for us the Chinese communication system must have been very primitive in the area. Twenty kilometers farther, toward the frontier, we overran yet another militia guardhouse near a stone bridge. We killed everyone within, but that was as far as our trucks would go. Two of them had run out of gas.

We gave the group of Chinese officers enough food to last during their long walk home and turned them loose. We never bothered with questioning them. Until the very last moment they thought they would be shot. One of them spoke to Major Kwang, then turned toward me bowing twice. I thought he would lose his balance and topple over. He rattled off a long sing-song sentence. "He is very thankful to you that you won't execute them," he interpreted.

"Why should I execute them?" I replied with a shrug. "It won't topple the Mao régime."

Sergeant Krebitz destroyed the vehicles and the company continued on foot, carrying two of our comrades on improvised stretchers. Encouraged by the easy victory we did not enter the woods but kept to the winding dirt road, resolved to wipe out whoever might try to stop us. The frontier was only fourteen kilometers distant.

By noon we were safely back in French territory, having completed an eighty-kilometer foray into Red China in record time. From the first French blockhouse I radioed to Colonel Houssong. He could not believe that we were already back.

"What did you do, Wagemueller, fly?" he asked puzzled.

"We rode a couple of trucks, *mon colonel*," I replied matter-of-factly. "We stopped before customs though."

"Any casualties?"

"Nine dead, *mon colonel*." There was a pause. I knew what the Colonel was thinking. I added: "Not a trace of them is left."

"I am sorry for that, Wagemueller, but we had no other choice, had we?"

"No, *mon colonel*. There was no other solution."

Altogether our expedition was rather more a moral than a material success. As we later learned from intelligence reports, we did manage to kill 1,350 terrorists and 60 militiamen but the material damage we caused was relatively light. The main enemy supply depots were located farther to the north, close to the Tienpao highway and beyond our reach. The foodstuff and weapons that we destroyed at the second base would have supported a battalion for six weeks.

The loss of eight trucks was the most painful blow to the Chinese. Eisner was right when he asserted that the loss of over a thousand men was but a drop in the ocean for the enemy. It did not really matter. We all knew that we were fighting at hopeless odds. To check our fast-breeding adversaries we needed poison gas and atomic bombs. The French will to conquer had long since ceased to exist. But we were not French but Germans. We must be beaten ten times before we admit a single defeat. And even then our will to win persists.

A month later we learned that our well-planted mines had demolished four more trucks and a new Soviet tank. Three cheers for Sergeant Krebitz and *Gruppe Drei.* One of the trucks was transporting new trusses for a demolished bridge; the blast delayed reconstruction by three months.

Consequently the Chinese dismantled over twenty Viet Minh establishments across the border and moved them to the Siang river in the north. Ammunition dumps were moved even farther to an area which the enemy considered safe. Thereafter we could rightly assert that our blitz into China had indeed caused the enemy more damage than the destruction of a few bases, guardhouses, bridges, and vehicles. The removal of the camps from the frontier areas added more problems to the already overburdened Chinese supply system. Hard-pressed Viet Minh battalions in the northern provinces of Indochina could no longer dash across the border, replenish their supplies, and return the day after to fight some more. When they needed weapons or ammo, the guerrillas had to march a long way for it.

9

The End of a Garrison

ALMOST two months had gone by and, thanks to the benevolent consent of Colonel Houssong, Suoi was still with the battalion. I think the colonel must have believed that Suoi was someone's mistress but he could not quite decide who the lucky party might be, for we all spoke of her with equal enthusiasm. Actually, there was nothing of the sort between the girl and us. On the contrary, we regarded her as a sort of ward of the battalion and her welfare was of paramount importance to us.

Schulze had been as good as his word. He did find the bank where Suoi's father had had his account, but there was no need to "blast" the manager, who himself had been a victim of terrorist perfidy. He had lost a little daughter when her school bus hit a Viet Minh road mine. The manager was most sympathetic and, after talking to the girl for a while, he accepted her signature and permitted her to dispose of her father's estate. His only condition was that Suoi should not withdraw more than fifty thousand piasters per week for the first twelve weeks. He was obliged to impose that restriction in case other relatives should come forward, although he believed like Suoi that there was none. He also had to place a public notice in the principal papers to make Suoi's claim known.

Suoi was a wealthy girl by local standards. Her father's estate consisted of over two million piasters in cash, apart from interests in mills and granaries. Schulze and Riedl established her in a nice little apartment within the army housing area. Suoi's place soon turned into a sort of "club" for social gatherings. Suoi did not seem to mind our frequent visits and showered her lovely smiles on all of us without special distinction. From the very beginning Suoi was indeed an asset for us. She certainly altered our previous way of life. For one thing, we quit spending our off days in the stinking bars of Hanoi, and we also cut down on drinking and swearing.

Suoi made some friends, one of whom, Mireille, was a French-Indochinese girl with a beautiful figure. She even moved in with Suoi, who disliked living alone – "like an old lady" as she put it. Mireille was a secretary at a French shipping company, and she also had friends. Soon our private club provided company for all of us.

Suoi must have felt that one girl could never entertain five battle-hardened legionnaires, two of whom were in obvious rivalry. The timely coming of the other girls prevented an impending showdown and preserved peace. As a matter of fact we "never had it so good" in all our years in the country. We equipped the club with a record player, a movie projector, an espresso machine, and a drink mixer. Everyone supplied something; Riedl the discs, Schulze the films, Karl the drinks, Eisner the sandwiches – and I supplied the time off for pleasure.

One evening we invited Colonel Houssong, and he came, bringing along his wife and Yvette, and we had a wonderful time. Afterwards, Madame Houssong and Yvette became regular visitors at Suoi's place, and we often met there with the colonel and Lieutenant Derosier to discuss various military operations. While the others danced we studied maps in another room or held a "staff conference" in a homey atmosphere, as the colonel used to say.

But our days of relaxation were always numbered. For every week we spent within the city boundaries we had to spend a month in the guerrilla-infested remote areas. The enemy was becoming preponderant everywhere and we were less than a thousand men altogether. We could only hit and destroy, cause the Viet Minh painful losses, but never hold anything we gained. When we relieved a beleaguered garrison or cleared a district from hundreds of terrorists, the French sent in the Territorial troops who could fight bravely and go down gloriously but without preserving an inch of land. One day some "big brains" in the High Command conceived the idea of bringing pressure on the terrorists by deporting their relatives into distant "protective establishments" or, as they called them, *Camps de Régroupement* (a polite way of saying concentration camp) for safekeeping. It was an ill-begotten idea and a magnificent folly which plainly revealed to what extent the French misunderstood the psychological aspects of the Indochina war. The guerrillas, actually *relieved* at having their own families out of harm's way, slaughtered the "disloyal" citizens more ferociously than before. The Viet Minh also knew that their international Communist associates would raise enough hell in the world's press to ensure the welfare of the "innocent civilians" in the French camps. The guerrillas became more enterprising. If the French wanted to frustrate the terrorists by holding their families, they should have used the hostages as we did. Riding them on trucks fitted with loudspeakers. None of the hostages had been killed and none of our vehicles destroyed.

"You know that we cannot do that, Wagemueller," Colonel Houssong told me with resignation. "I agree with you. Our *conduit de la guerre* in Indochina is wrong to the core. By removing the terrorist families, we are only giving the enemy *carte blanche* for aggression. But we just cannot revert to your practices here. We may be inclined to overlook them, but we must never encourage them. Your methods might pass occasionally and locally, but they would never survive for a week on any large scale. I know that your Heinrich Himmler would have settled the Viet Minh problem a long time ago with Zyclon-B (poison gas used by the Nazis in the extermination camps) and the crematorium but France is supposed to be a democracy. The terrorists are firmly entrenched in the world's opinion as resolute heroes who are fighting a modern military power with bows and spears, striving only for independence and human rights. No one has ever protested against any Viet Minh outrage, although I could show them a list of thirty thousand civilians slaughtered by the

Communists in cold blood. All the same when *we* execute a terrorist with the blood of a hundred people on his hands, the execution is headlined even in America, let alone Europe and its Communist press, as another French war crime. Whenever we touch a filthy killer, there are demonstrations and protests. They would even call us Nazis, Wagemueller. You should hear some of Moscow's broadcasts."

"I have heard many of them," I replied with a smile of irony. "Come to think of it, *mon colonel*, we should have fought together in the last war. Just imagine France, Britain, Germany, and America fighting Stalin. It would have been like driving our tanks on a highway right to Vladivostock on the Pacific coast, stopping only to cool the engines."

"Maybe," he compromised, "but at the end Hitler would have gone berserk all the same, Wagemueller."

I smiled. "A berserk Hitler would have been more reasonable than a sane Stalin, *mon colonel*. Hitler never wanted war in the west. I know that. But I concede that he committed a grave mistake when he attacked Poland. He should have arranged a free passage across Poland – into Russia. He could have talked the Polish army into fighting alongside the Wehrmacht."

"It is always easy to see the better ways ten years after the event. I only hope that French and Germans will never fight each other again."

"I think we will all be much too preoccupied in another direction, *mon colonel*. And not in the too distant future," I replied.

"True!" he nodded. "They stop at no frontiers."

Shortly afterwards we departed on an expedition to Muong Hou Nua, a small town northwest of Hanoi and only twenty miles from China. The entire district was controlled by the terrorists to such an extent that the Viet Minh had openly established various Communist institutions and had introduced their "socialist reforms" – expropriations, land reform, and mass extermination of the wealthy class. In reality these reforms meant principally exterminations; property owners, government officials, teachers, missionaries, and merchants had to die. The terrorist control had been gradually extended to other localities: Phuong Saly, Muong You, Bun Tai, Lai Chau, as far as Dien Bien Phu, where a strong French garrison blocked their further expansion. Refugees from the area reported several wholesale massacres and the murder of at least five thousand "class enemies," often supervised by Chinese officers or civilian "experts" – the advisers of the Viet Minh. For Chinese "volunteers" the frontiers were wide open. Intelligence reported several Viet Minh camps around Muong Hou Nua and even the establishment of a permanent Chinese command post *inside* French territory.

Returning the favor, we overran a Chinese observation post and wireless station at Chen-yüan, killing twelve officers and thirty troops in a short but desperate combat. The shooting had taken place on Chinese territory, but after the battle Pfirstenhammer removed the Chinese border marker and set it up again two hundred yards farther inside China. We then photographed the Chinese machine gun emplacements and the corpses around them with the marker in plain sight in the background; everything appeared to have taken place *inside* French territory – therefore the Chinese had committed a bona-fide aggression which we repelled.

Karl had a great deal of *le cran* – nerve, or more commonly, guts – and his coup had an echo befitting a comic strip. The Chinese had no idea where their borders really ran. Several months after the incident, reconnaissance photos showed the border marker still standing where Pfirstenhammer had placed it. Instead of returning the marker to its original place, the Chinese constructed new gun emplacements four hundred yards *behind* the marker. For all we know, we may have acquired a few hundred acres of good land for what is presently Laos. We should have claimed an agency fee for the real estate.

During the foray we managed to decimate several Viet Minh units and destroy some of their supply dumps. We could never enter Muong Hou Nua or go into any enemy-controlled population centers. To do that we would have needed at least a brigade with tanks, artillery, and air support. All the same, we reached our limited objectives, destroyed them, and returned to Dien Bien Phu with the loss of only fifty-nine men. Although we constantly received replacements for our losses, no recruits, not even veteran Germans, could make up for the skill and experience of those whom we lost. No one in Indochina became an expert headhunter until he had spent a year or more in the jungle. Until then, a recruit was a liability rather than an asset to our battalion.

At the beginning of the fifties the Foreign Legion had to tackle another menace: desertion! Already planning a general offensive against the French, the Viet Minh embarked on an intensive propaganda campaign to weaken the ranks of the already faltering Legion. Liberty and a free passage home was offered to all deserters. In addition the Viet Minh promised a generous cash reward for war material, vehicles, weapons, or just valuable information. The propaganda campaign was directed chiefly toward those legionnaires whose homelands were under Soviet occupation: Poles, Czechs, Rumanians, Hungarians, and Germans from the Soviet Zone or Austria were regarded as potentially responsive. But men from any countries where the French authority had no power to retaliate were also sensitive targets.

The men deserted not because of cowardice but simply because they were utterly disgusted by the way the French conducted the war and sacrificed regiment after regiment for no gain whatsoever. Soldiers of a victorious army seldom desert, and the Foreign Legion was an army suffering from years of constant reverses and routs. And it was not the fault of the ranks either. "The white-gloved slobs" (as Pfirstenhammer habitually referred to our generals) considered themselves born Napoleons with nothing left for them to learn except maybe new card games. The entire general staff should have been kicked out (with the exception of General Salan, whom we all respected greatly) and the corporals and sergeants promoted to generals. Then the Legion would have "started to roll."

The Viet Minh magnanimity had results. The troops began to vanish, at first singly, then in groups; occasionally entire platoons deserted to the enemy. Let it be said to the Viet Minh's credit that they *did* honor their promises. The deserters were free to leave Indochina, either for Hong Kong or for Europe, via Peking and Moscow. Weapons and other war material which the Communists could have simply seized were duly paid for; thus an escapee was not only at liberty to return home but he could return home with ample cash. The Viet Minh paid in hard currencies. It was an ingenious coup. I know of two Swedes who went over with a truckload of automatic weapons, ammunition, and medical supplies – "made in USA." They received nearly ten thousand

United States dollars *cash* from the guerrillas. Where on earth the Viet Minh could obtain all that hard money was a mystery that only the Kremlin could have cleared up. The two Swedes, I know for sure, arrived in Hong Kong safely, where they established a business in silk which is still prospering.

So far as we knew, none of the East European deserters were ever prosecuted when they arrived home. (Communists have good international connections.) On the contrary, they were sending cards and photos to us for months afterwards, telling us their stories. The Viet Minh made sure that copies of their letters reached the still-hesitant ones.

The French retained control of the important cities and valleys but in the country disaster followed disaster. Had we obeyed the codes of *La Conduite de la Guerre*, we would not have survived for a year. I daresay, without bragging, that amidst the general debacle, my battalion emerged as victor from every engagement. We did it with minimal losses, and we did it by playing the same game as the terrorists. If Mao's doctrine had worked so well for the enemy, we thought, it had to work for us too.

It *did* work!

While the battalion was on a foray against a Viet Minh supply train reportedly moving south, we received an urgent radio message: A French stockade, sixty miles west of Hoi Xuan and forty-six miles north of where we were, was under intensive terrorist attack. The commanding officer reported several breaches in the perimeter defenses and that he was destroying confidential papers and codes.

Riedl, who had brought the message to me, remarked grimly, "If he is already destroying code books, then we won't be of much help. It will take us three to four days to reach the stockade." All the same we sent a message to the commander, asking him to stand fast. Without delay we headed back to base, where we could get the relief on the road.

We left Hanoi in a small convoy of trucks and jeeps, our customary way of leaving the city, to travel as far as it was reasonably safe to go on wheels. For some time I had been aware that our garrison was under constant enemy surveillance; when we moved, the Viet Minh knew about it. Therefore our measures of deception began from the moment we rolled through the gate. When our destination was somewhere southwest of Viet Tri, we departed toward the northwest; never taking the direct route but skirting or traversing the town, performing diversionary turns while the men in the last vehicle were constantly on watch for motor scooters, cycles, or even cars that seemed to follow the convoy. When a vehicle appeared suspicious we requested the nearest military checkpoint to stop and entertain our unwelcome escort for some time.

On that particular day, Schulze requested our driver to stop the jeep at Suoi's place. "I won't be a minute!" he excused himself and raced up the stairs. Five minutes later he returned, hand in hand with the girl. "She's always wanted to come along," he stated flatly, and before I could open my mouth, he helped her aboard and off we raced after the convoy.

"The headhunters plus one," he stated flatly. I glanced at Eisner, who seemed not the least concerned.

"Did you know about this, er . . . arrangement of Erich's?" I asked him.

"Sure," he replied, "the whole battalion knew about it – except you."

Suoi was probably the smartest-looking "legionnaire" in the entire outfit. She was wearing custom-tailored battle fatigues complete with belt, a pair of miniaturized paratroop boots, tropical helmet, and a small shoulder bag. Obviously Schulze and Suoi had been plotting the coup for some time. During the past few weeks the girl had told me occasionally that she wanted to come along on our next expedition, but I had never taken her seriously. She had said that she did not feel like sitting at home for weeks, that she wanted to do something useful. "After all," she said, "the battalion has adopted me!"

Now there she was, braids, ribbons, battle fatigues and all, casting bewitching smiles and fluttering eyelashes at me, pleading in a tone of mock consternation, "I hope you don't mind my coming?"

I felt like answering, "Like hell I don't mind," for I had enough problems without the additional worry about Suoi's welfare, but said instead, "Well, Suoi, we are not going by jeep all the way, you know."

"Oh, I know that," she replied quickly. "I grew up in the hills and I am not afraid of walking."

"She wanted to come," Erich insisted. "She wanted to help us."

"And naturally you complied."

"What else could he do?" Eisner cut in. "Suoi's eyes would melt a tank turret."

"I will take care of her, don't worry," Erich reassured me.

"You are crazy . . . taking a young girl on a murder trip."

"Hell! How about all those girls with the Viet Minh, Hans?"

"They are trained guerrillas, Erich. Your Suoi can't even fire a bloody gun."

Schulze's eyes kindled. "Are you so sure? . . . Hans, you will be surprised."

"Are you telling me – "

"Wait and see, commander sir!"

I saw all right. The convoy stopped at a river to let the engines cool. As the men settled down to eat, Erich walked up to the embankment and erected a small pyramid of empty tin cans. Taking a submachine gun from the jeep, he handed it to Suoi. "Now watch the show." He winked at me.

With four short bursts, Suoi demolished the pyramid, sending the cans topsy-turvy into the river. Only two of them remained standing.

"*Voilà!*" Erich exclaimed, casting a triumphant glance at me. He took the gun from the girl and handed her a rifle. "Now get the remaining ones, Suoi."

Holding the rifle in the best professional manner, she took aim and fired twice. One of the cans went flying, the other one bounced and toppled over – a glancing shot. A third bullet then struck home and flung the tin into the river. The troops cheered openly. There was amusement in Eisner's eyes and Riedl chuckled. "So much for our defenseless little ward," he said.

Suoi turned halfway toward me, holding the rifle in a casual manner. She was blushing but held her chin up; her eyelashes flickered in what Karl used to call "a starry look of the first magnitude." She said, "Do you think I can take care of myself, commander?"

"Where did you learn to shoot?"

"On the army range on Sunday afternoons," she replied

smiling. She took a spare magazine from Erich, reloaded expertly, put the gun at "safe," and handed it over to a trooper.

"Do you want to see her with a pistol, or hand grenades maybe?" Erich inquired grinning.

"Can she drive a tank too?"

"Not yet," he laughed, "but she is an apt pupil, Hans."

I ran a finger under my nose to repress a smile. "Did the colonel know about your little exercises?"

"Of course. He had to sign her pass to enter the range."

"The colonel was very nice," Suoi interposed. "He gave me a pistol."

"A what?"

From her shoulder bag she pulled a small holster. Out of it came a light, ivory-handled, Italian Beretta automatic. "Pretty, isn't it?" she asked. "I was afraid of putting it on. I thought you might consider it childish."

I stepped up to her and snapped the holster onto her belt-rings. "Wear it then, general! When you have to shoot you don't have time to look for it in your bag."

I had my first feelings of foreboding from the moment I noticed the absence of the Tricolor and the sullen stillness that hovered over the entire compound. Even from the small hill where we stood the stockade presented an appalling spectacle. The multiple coils of barbed wire which circled the perimeter showed wide breaches; the palisade was blasted at several places and heavy logs lay scattered around the gaping holes. Every building appeared damaged. We spotted the burned skeletons of a dozen vehicles and a large number of corpses.

"They've had it!" Eisner remarked grimly and lowered his field glasses. "But they keep on building forts." He turned briskly. "Krebitz!"

Sergeant Krebitz stepped forward. "Off the road everybody!" Eisner commanded. "Troops single file . . . distance twenty yards. We are cutting through the woods."

He turned to Suoi and said quite harshly, "You will stay right here, behind me. Understood?"

"*Oui!*" she nodded, blushing slightly. "You don't have to shout."

A truly feminine way of taking an order, I thought, repressing a chuckle.

We wasted no time discussing the situation. The garrison had been exterminated, and since the enemy had not been pursued, we expected to find the dirt road and every regular path around the stockade booby-trapped and mined. The enemy had had ample time to prepare traps, as they had done on many occasions in the past. The only sensible thing for us to do was to leave the road, avoid the paths, and cut a new trail to the stockade while *Gruppe Drei* searched for traps on the regular approaches. Every step in the area could mean sudden death. Where the Viet Minh experts had been at work, every inch of a trail had to be surveyed – a lengthy procedure.

Among the prominent Viet Minh deserters who had come over to our side was a squat little man, Ghia Xuey, now the honorary "commander" of *Gruppe Drei*, working hand in hand with Sergeant Krebitz. Xuey had been a guerrilla company commander until a tragic mishap induced him to switch sides in 1950. During a raid and the ensuing roundup of French "collaborators," a neighboring Viet Minh detachment had executed Xuey's family along with a group of other "traitors" in a village near Thanhhoa. Xuey could not reveal his painful secret, for the others would no longer have trusted him. With a resolution that only an Oriental mind can muster, he buried his grief deep within and even celebrated the victory with the assassins of his parents, wife, and three children. He bided his time for revenge. One evening when the culprits were asleep, Xuey stabbed the commissar, slit the throat of the propagandist, then set up a machine gun twenty yards from the sleepers and emptied the magazine into the lot. He surrendered to the French at Nam Dinh and offered his services against his former comrades. Xuey was, of course, welcome and most generously treated. It had taken us four months of constant persuasion and ample paperwork for Colonel Houssong before Counter-Intelligence finally consented to Xuey's reassignment to our battalion. Xuey himself preferred to work with us, a diversion from the dreary training routine at the Special Forces camp. He said that he no longer believed that the ideas of Marx and Lenin should be spread by any means, including murder. "True Communists do not kill," he stated bitterly. "They are supposed to build life where there was none. People who murder in the name of Communism are nothing but ordinary bandits and should be dealt with accordingly."

Xuey was worth his weight in gold. He moved in the jungle like a panther. Nothing escaped his searching eyes; no crushed grass, no awkwardly lying bough or bent twig. He noticed marks on the ground, however faint, and he could read a trail as ordinary people read books. We were immensely glad to have him with and not against us. His incredible abilities in the jungle made me shiver at the mere thought of having a guerrilla with similar talents tracking us!

With Xuey's help we succeeded in destroying over two thousand terrorists, and I could not recall the number of my own men whose lives had been saved by Xuey's alert eyes. He recognized a trap in the most innocent disguise; he knew well enough what to look for. He was and always remained a bitter man. In all our months together I never saw him smile. The loss of everyone he loved, and at the hands of those whom he had most trusted, had turned him into a ruthless agent of death.

"Take good care of him," Colonel Houssong said when he introduced Xuey to us. "He is worth a Viet Minh brigade!" The colonel was right.

After four years in the jungle we were fairly competent trailblazers. We had developed a system that permitted a relatively rapid advance through dense forest which usually consisted of a wild variety of thorny brushes, weeds, and creepers. The foremost six men advanced cutting a path wide enough for them to pass; close behind them ten men enlarged the path as they went, and the next six men then polished off the passage. Immediately behind the trailblazers marched two cartographers whose job was to mark the newly cut trail on the map and to control its direction with the aid of magnetic compasses. Otherwise the trailblazers could have gone around in circles without ever noticing it. Moving in the jungle resembles flying in the clouds. When the average visibility shrinks to less than twenty yards, man will lose his sense of direction. Strangely enough the larger tracts of unbroken forests are usually less dense than the smaller patches of a few hundred yards or more. Where the trees grow sparsely, sunshine penetrates more effectively, inducing the growth of creepers and bushes. Thick overhead foliage shuts out the sunlight entirely and rainwater partially. This retards the growth of vegetation on the ground level.

We arrived at the perimeter wires safely while *Gruppe Drei* was still halfway up the hill searching for road mines and traps. Xuey, who had gone off to survey one of the trails, suddenly called us. "Keep right behind me," he cautioned, "and don't touch anything, not even a twig."

He walked about a hundred yards into the woods, then lifted a hand for us to stop. Lowering himself to his knees in front of a small bough that bent casually over the footpath, he carefully removed some leaves to expose a thin wire. I noticed that the upper point of the bough was delicately hooked into another branch. The wire ran from the center of the second branch. A glimpse was enough to know what it was.

"A bamboo bomb!"

"Very deadly," Xuey nodded. His comment was superfluous. We all knew what those hellish bombs could do. From his pocket, Xuey extracted a ball of thin cord and, working with great prudence, tied the loose end to the bough. Then rising slowly, he motioned us to retrace our steps. He followed us, gently playing out the cord as he went. When we were about eighty yards from the bough, he stopped and told us to take cover.

Sheltered behind a tree Xuey pulled hard on the cord. Instantly something large and heavy came crashing down from the trees. There was a shattering explosion, and a shower of splinters tore through the underbrush. The bomb had been suspended above the path and the small bough was the trigger.

Xuey walked up the trail and returned with a pair of hardwood pegs, about three inches long and sharpened at both ends. Holding them wrapped in a large leaf, he pointed out some dark brown substance that covered the points. "Cadaver poison!" Eisner said, taking the pegs from Xuey, who nodded agreement. Eisner observed the pegs briefly, then handed them to me. I gave them to a trooper, instructing him to preserve the pegs carefully.

"Do you have any idea who is behind this?" I asked Xuey.

He replied without hesitation, "Nam Hoa would keep even his mortar shells buried in cadavers. He believes the splinters will kill even those who are only slightly wounded."

"Nam Hoa is supposed to be farther south in the hills around the Phu Son mountain."

"We had better check on that," Schulze interposed. "He could have returned north to be closer to the Chinese dumps."

I suggested that we should move into the stockade.

Constantly on the alert for booby traps we entered the compound and beheld a scene of utter rout. Around the gate corpses of a dozen Legionnaires lay in grotesquely twisted attitudes; there were bodies whichever way we turned. Large patches of blood stained the ground that in turn was pockmarked with the craters of mortar explosions. None of the victims made the slightest movement to indicate a spark of life. Closer inspection disclosed that the throat of every victim had been slit. There was no need to search for survivors. When the terrorists could work at leisure they always did a thorough job. I sent a couple of troopers to examine the partly demolished gatehouse. When they reported it clear, I led Suoi in there and told her to sit down on a cot. "You are staying right here until we have finished searching the compound. The yard is probably full of mines, and besides it isn't a very pleasant sight."

Out in the compound the men were busy. From under two of the corpses the demolition squad extracted a pair of primed grenades arranged in such fashion that any casual moving or turning of the bodies would have triggered an explosion. It was an old Russian partisan trick, but one which nevertheless still claimed many ignorant or forgetful victims. We tried our best to preserve the corpses of our comrades for a decent burial but many of them could not be touched with any degree of safety. These had to be turned over by men stretched out on the ground, sheltered behind a pair of sandbags and using long poles or ropes. Of them we could gather and bury only bits of flesh and bones – a very unpleasant undertaking.

By noon, Xuey and Sergeant Krebitz had uncovered thirty booby traps and mines inside the stockade. More were forthcoming during the afternoon. We marked the cleared areas with cords laid on the ground to form corridors in which it was safe to walk. Booby-trapped corpses were marked with pebbles. The pools of blood were already congealed or absorbed by the gravel.

The men must have been dead for over a day. The scene was truly disheartening but such debacles could no longer shock us. We had seen similar slaughters only too often.

At the command post we discovered more corpses, among them that of the commanding officer, First Lieutenant Roger Martinet, whom I had known since 1948. He lay on the wooden steps of the pile-supported porch. Save for his pants, he was naked, and he had a large, jagged hole in his breast about which a cluster of flies were buzzing. The steps, the porch, and the walls were splintered with shell fragments, some of which must have hit Martinet in the chest. Eisner found another primed grenade in the pocket of the lieutenant and this was exploded outside the compound.

Another ingenious instrument of death was hidden by the closed door of the command post. The guerrillas had placed an antipersonnel mine on the inside floor with a strong, biforked branch wedged between the door handle and the pressure switch of the mine. If one of us had pressed the handle, the entire building would have gone up in the blast. But that single closed door looked wrong to us from the moment we saw it, for all the other doors and windows hung wide open or torn loose. Men with less experience could have easily fallen for it. Similar ruses accounted for our calling most of the Viet Minh tricks naïve. Most of them derived from wartime Russian ruses, which we knew well after our years in Russia: one opened a door and the house exploded; turned a water tap, moved a casually placed object, removed a book from a shelf, righted an awkwardly hanging picture on the wall, or pushed down a piano key – a bomb went off.

Sergeant Krebitz entered through a window and removed the mine.

By early afternoon the number of disarmed or exploded booby traps increased to fifty. We combed the stockade yard by yard. From the desk of the commander, Sergeant Krebitz extracted four bombs. It was a very delicate job to get at the charges. Krebitz had to remove the rear panels for the drawers could not be touched.

All the corpses had been stripped to underwear. The guerrillas always collected shirts, belts, and footwear, in addition to watches, pens, lighters, and weapons. Beside Martinet sprawled two officers. Both had been shot at close range; a third victim, a North African sergeant, had been shot and stabbed in the abdomen.

"I guess this carnage is payment for our visit to Man-hao," Schulze remarked ironically. "Will the French *ever* learn how to fight the Viet Minh, Bernard?"

In the communication room we found the corpse of the signal officer, Lieutenant Mazzoni, and that of a sergeant. The wireless equipment and the telephone exchange were missing and the connecting wires hung as if they had been ripped from the wall. I was puzzled that the guerrillas had taken the heavy radio equipment while leaving behind the converter unit. The set was not a battery-operated one but depended on the electric current generated by a diesel engine. The engine itself was far too heavy for removal, so the terrorists had settled for breaking it up.

The yard behind the command post was littered with over a hundred corpses. Some of the men had been killed by mortar splinters, others had died in hand-to-hand combat. Near the mess hall we discovered another dead officer.

A Viet Minh unit strong enough to exterminate a garrison of three hundred well-armed legionnaires must have consisted of at least six hundred men. Nam Hoa was known to have commanded a group of about two hundred guerrillas, but he could have ganged up with a few local units who were equipped with mortars. We counted over a hundred spots where mortar shells had exploded. Coming from far inland, Nam Hoa could not have possessed such powerful artillery.

"There is only one man in the district who commands so many mortars," Xuey explained. "Trengh. He also commands three hundred men. Maybe even more. His village is about twelve miles from here, on the far side of the hills." He showed us the direction.

We had heard of Trengh before. He had been a Hanoi police officer who, conspiring with the Viet Minh in 1949, had engineered a daring terrorist raid on a police station and had assisted the guerrillas in freeing fifty prisoners. With that coup to his credit, Trengh deserted to the Viet Minh. Ever since then his head carried a reward of 75,000 piasters dead or alive. The French had also posted a reward of 100,000 piasters for Nam Hoa, not a very tempting reward for such an important guerrilla leader. Such financial "courtesies" were mutual. Every member of my battalion had been similarly "price-tagged" dead or alive by the Viet Minh or by the Chinese.

At the entrance to the canteen we counted sixteen European legionnaires and a young corporal. The corporal's eyes were open, gazing into the sun; under his hand lay a pistol which the enemy had overlooked. The magazine of the pistol was empty. The mess hall looked as though a hurricane had gone through it. Chairs, benches, tables were overturned or wrecked. Broken glass littered the floor. The smell of blood and decomposition was strong. More men lay under the debris, behind the counter and the overturned tables which they had used for cover. The walls and doors were riddled by hundreds of bullets. There must have been desperate combat inside the building, with the adversaries shooting it out at close range. My men removed twenty or more bodies from the mess hall alone, among them many Europeans. More corpses sprawled outside the building in and about a gaping hole in the wall. Still wearing their white aprons, two of the six cooks had been pressed head first into their ovens. Since, by rule, all open fires had to be extinguished while under attack, the corpses were not burned. Even so we found it a macabre bit of Red humor. The debacle culminated in the sleeping quarters, where the remaining troops had been mercilessly slaughtered. Eighty men altogether. The barracks had been stripped bare. Blankets, sheets, even some of the mattresses had been carried away. The underground ammunition depots were empty.

We stood in sullen silence, watching the demolition men as they moved from corpse to corpse looking for bombs. The bodies which had been checked were carried out to join the long lines of corpses laid out outside the palisade. Eisner dispatched two hundred men to dig a huge grave for the fallen garrison. None of the corpses wore identity tags. The brave men would probably rest as "unknown soldiers." Eighteen trucks and jeeps in the parking lot were burned-out steel skeletons; four 75 field howitzers were still hitched to four of the GMCs – wrecked, but even so we could see that none of the great guns had ever been fired.

The wind wheel, which used to pump water from the well, had been knocked down. The pump mechanism was demolished. The well itself appeared intact and flashlights revealed water thirty feet below. Sergeant Krebitz examined the well, searching for corpses, but found none. I became even more suspicious, for whenever the Viet Minh seemed to spare something important, it did so on purpose. We became doubly alert.

Had the terrorists poisoned the well?

Bidding us wait, Xuey left for a nearby river and brought back a few frogs and a fish, which he then settled in a can of water drawn from the well. Ten minutes later the creatures were still alive and obviously not affected by any poison. "The well is not poisoned," Xuey stated, "but there might be something else to look for." He examined the surrounding ground, then suddenly called our attention to some brownish stains which Sergeant Krebitz thought was human excrement. Moments later Pfirstenhammer found a pair of buckets with a length of rope attached. The buckets were covered with refuse. We examined the ground between the latrines and the well and spotted more bits of filth. The rest of the story was easy to conclude. The enemy had spoiled the well with refuse. Another Viet Minh joke!

I decided that the next macabre joke should be played by us. I remembered having seen a small sack of arsenic in the partly destroyed food storage. The cooks had probably used it to fight rats and other pests. I sent a man to fetch the bag.

"We will preserve those poisonous pegs," I told Eisner. "We will also take a water sample from the well and photograph the whole area, the buckets, the refuse on the ground . . . just in case the Reds accuse us of starting chemical warfare."

They all turned toward me sharply. "What do you mean by chemical warfare?" Riedl queried with a puzzled expression.

I lifted the bag of poison. "This stuff here, Helmut. For if we find the camp of those bastards, I am going to fill *their* water with rat poison, morphine, and whatever else Sergeant Zeisl might have in excess. We will see how the Viet Minh appreciate that."

"How about making a few cans of mustard gas?" Pfirstenhammer asked, lighting his pipe. "Its formula is very simple." He rattled off the ingredients. "When we return to Hanoi, I will look for the basic chemicals and next time we can mix for the Reds a real cocktail, Hans."

10

With Bayonets and Arsenic

WE computed the possible enemy losses by fixing the number of spots where blood had been found but with no corpse to account for it. Karl and Erich were able to establish eighty-two positive and about the same number of likely places where guerrillas might have fallen. More should have fallen outside the stockade, while storming the compound. Schulze calculated over two hundred Viet Minh casualties, including the wounded.

Schulze had other computations as well. "Do you know what?" he exclaimed suddenly, glancing up from his notes. "The terrorists carried away their dead and wounded, which means that at least two hundred or more men transported nothing but corpses and the wounded." Before he came to the point, I already grasped the implications of what he was saying.

"How many people do you think were necessary to remove *all* the weapons, the ammunition, the food stores, blankets, and God knows what else, apart from carrying their own equipment?"

"Over a thousand! Thirteen hundred might be a close bet."

"Precisely!" Erich agreed. "Nevertheless we know that no Viet Minh unit of such proportions is operating anywhere in the province or Xuey would know about them. I think we had better start looking for additional clues."

"What clues?" Karl asked.

"Footprints! Those of women and children from ten years upward. The guerrillas alone could never have taken everything that has been removed." Shading his eyes he surveyed the neighboring hills. "I think somewhere in those hills we are going to find a guerrilla graveyard and the place where the population of a whole village camped out while waiting for the terrorists to seize the fort."

I could only agree with Schulze's reasoning. None of the corpses had been stripped naked – a frequent terrorist practice – probably because of the presence of women and children in the stockade.

"Well, gentlemen," Erich concluded, "neither women nor children can walk very far laden with crates and sacks. I think we will discover the responsible party in a not too distant settlement, and the Viet Minh camp won't be far from it either."

"Trengh's village!" Xuey added. "That is where we should look."

I radioed a brief report to Hanoi, suggesting the dispatch of engineers to rebuild the stockade. I waited only for the signal of acknowledgment, then sent the coded signal "unit under enemy attack" and cut the set before any instructions could come through.

"The colonel is going to be mad. We are pulling that on him much too frequently," Eisner said.

"Do you want to sit here?"

"Not me. I prefer the woods."

"Well, I know what Hanoi's answer would have been."

Pfirstenhammer grinned. "Stay put until the new garrison arrives," he said.

I nodded. "Exactly."

That was the very last thing I wanted to do. The headhunters seldom rested. We would come, do the job, and vanish. Our strength lay in mobility; keeping the enemy uncertain and unsafe was our principal maxim.

Schulze was right about the guerrilla cemetery and the civilian helpers. Barely two miles from the compound Xuey discovered the burial site of the dead terrorists. Their common grave was a shallow one and it took us only an hour to exhume and count the corpses. There were one hundred and twenty-one bodies in the grave, but as Schulze pointed out many of the severely wounded would perish in the coming days from lack of proper medical facilities in the jungle. Not far from the burial site we found the place where a large number of noncombatants had camped down for at least three days. The soft soil showed hundreds of footprints and a ravine was soiled with human excrement.

The village of Nuo Hoy, whose population we suspected had participated in the looting, lay twelve miles to the west, amidst densely forested hills. It was plausible to suppose that the sheer quantity of the stolen material had made it imperative for the enemy to establish several secret dumps. They could not have possibly stored everything in their camp, not with any degree of safety. Natural caves and tunnels, either in the hills or beneath the village, were the likely places to look for.

Pondering over the map, we reasoned that the camp itself should be located within a limited area, since to sustain several hundred men the enemy needed plenty of water. A small stream fed by a creek from the mountains flowed through the suspected village. The creek was the only natural source of water in the hilly area. The terrorist camp ought to be somewhere along that creek. We settled for investigating the neighborhood of the village, without revealing ourselves to the enemy. Naturally we could not follow the existing trails that were probably mined and kept under constant surveillance. Although it meant a detour of thirty miles, the alternative route had more appeal for me. It was prudent to suppose that the stockade was still under enemy observation and that Viet Minh lookouts were watching our activities.

We left the compound late in the afternoon when it was still light enough for the snoopers to see us moving in the opposite direction, away from them and our true destination. As soon as darkness prevented further observation we entered the woods and camped down for the night. For all intents and purposes, our battalion had vanished from the sight of the enemy. Now we were on equal terms with the Viet Minh and even had a slight advantage, for we knew where we wanted to strike next but they had no idea where we were.

Shortly after sunrise we set out for the hills. Our trailblazers needed four days to cut a path through the virgin woods and arrive within two miles of the village. Xuey, Schenk, and four men departed on a long reconnaissance trip into the hills south of the settlement, where I suspected the guerrillas had had their camp along the creek. The sky was overcast and it appeared as if a storm was in the making. We established ourselves a mile inside the woods, close to a brook but high enough not to be washed away by a sudden downpour. It began to rain shortly afterwards and poured for almost a day without stopping. Cooking was out of the question, save for an occasional cup of tea or a soup made of extracts. The men were able to prepare these in their canteens by burning spirit cubes under the protection of their burlaps. We were carrying no tents except for a few canvas sheets to protect our radio gear, maps, and sensitive equipment.

The rain came down so hard that it penetrated the overhead foliage like bullets, and we had to seek shelter among the trees and under thick branches. Wild torrents of water rushed down from every direction and emptied into the brook, which became a thundering river. Several times we had to move to safer spots but even so the men were soon in deep mud and could not even sit down properly. The roaring of the rain as it hammered on the leaves around us was so intense that we had to shout to make ourselves understood. By evening our small canteens of rum had been consumed. With it went our only source of warmth. A period of constant shivering now began. The troops swallowed aspirin and sulfathiazole pills to head off illness.

Suoi fared better. When the rain started, she put on a long sleek nylon raincoat with a hood. Now she sat on the rucksacks, her head resting in Erich's lap. He was holding a sandwich for her to bite.

"An idyllic spectacle," Eisner commented. But I had to concede that she put up with all our hardships bravely. And I wondered how Xuey, Sergeant Schenk, and the party were faring out in the hills, for they carried not even burlaps.

Toward morning the rain abated. The clouds drifted off and the sun began to shine. The temperature rose rapidly. By eleven o'clock the forest had turned into a steambath. Stripped to the waist, the troops were strolling off left and right, searching for small patches of sunlight to dry their damp clothes and to warm their chilled bones. The day was spent cleaning weapons, greasing footwear, and learning Indochinese. Ever since Suoi joined our battalion, linguistic studies had gained popularity among the troops. Suoi was a charming and patient teacher and from the moment she took charge of our language courses progress was certain.

The reconnaissance party brought back good news. Sergeant Schenk had discovered the Viet Minh camp and had made a diagram of the area. There was a small cascade in the hills which supplied the enemy camp with water. From a cliff above the cascade, Schenk and Xuey observed the camp for over two hours. Xuey was certain that it sheltered both Nam Hoa and Trengh, along with approximately five hundred terrorists. The camp, Schenk explained, was so cleverly arranged that it was almost impossible to move a large body of troops against it. Save for the one cliff, which could accommodate not more than ten men at a time, there were no other places where troops or automatic weapons could be deployed. The dense vegetation prohibited the use of machine guns elsewhere, and to enter the camp one had to pass along a narrow ravine which the Viet Minh covered with machine guns.

But if the location of the camp prohibited the use of troops and weapons, it certainly invited our bag of rat poison. The creek that fed the Viet Minh water tank could be approached unseen from above. I decided to leave the village alone for the time being but occupy the surrounding hills and trails with a couple of strong detachments. The majority of the troops were to remain with Eisner, Riedl, and Pfirstenhammer to conclude the first phase of the operation – the envelopment of the whole area. Selecting only fifty men, Schulze and I planned to establish a camp close to the guerrilla base, within easy reach of the cascade.

Starting out before daybreak, we broke up into separate groups and proceeded with the occupation of the hills. Suoi insisted on joining Schulze and me and after a brief argument, I bowed to the majority vote. We crossed the stream and the road three miles west of the village, following the trail which Xuey and Schenk had already surveyed. Leaving Suoi with the men in a secluded depression, Xuey, Schenk, Schulze, and I proceeded to the cliff and settled down near the precipice, where jutting boulders covered with shrubs permitted us to survey the enemy base at leisure.

The creek came from high above in the hills. Cold and clear, it flowed past where we were hidden and dropped steeply between the rocks, forming a small cascade a hundred feet below. Near the cascade stood a large water tank made of tin. A circular lid covered the top and it had several taps at the bottom. A system of hollow bamboo served as pipes to convey water from a smaller arm of the cascade to the tank. The tube could be swiveled to and from the water and it was now disconnected. Using canvas bags we dissolved the sack of arsenic in water and added our supply of morphine, digitalis, and a few other drugs to the mixture. Sergeant Zeisl was sure that our cocktail could kill a herd of elephants.

Our major problem was how to convey the preparation to the small branch of the cascade that fed the tank. It would have been of little use to drop the poison into the cascade for only a fraction of it would have reached the branch and consequently the tank. Schulze came up with the idea of using a hollow bamboo to funnel down the poison. There was no bamboo around and Sergeant Schenk had to fetch some from a thicket two miles away.

We occupied the only accessible position in the neighborhood, but the camp was so cleverly hidden among the trees that even we could see only four or five huts. Nearest the tank stood the cooking house, where fires burned in carefully shielded earthen ovens. The overhead foliage was extremely dense, and instead of rising, the smoke dispersed before it reached the treetops. Air reconnaissance could never spot the base, which seemed fairly well established and contained all the necessary components of a permanent base. The mess hut housed a long row of tables made from the sides of ammunition crates which had been nailed to poles driven into the ground. The benches had been contrived in a similar fashion. Along the creek we noticed a spacious natural pool which served as a bath. Farther downstream a couple of empty crates stood in the water, weighed down with boulders; they served as washing stands.

We kept the camp under observation all morning, and I have to admit that I witnessed a great deal of training and discipline, ranging from what were obviously political classes to hand-to-hand combat exercises and grenade throwing. The commissars seemed to keep a rigorous schedule. A roll call took place only a hundred yards from where we lay and I was able to count the guerrillas. There were 322 altogether, among them 58 women. The women, too, were armed and participated in the same routines as the men. But 322 was below the number of terrorists I expected to find in the camp. Schulze reminded me of those who might be lying wounded in the huts. A number of terrorists could also be under way, or in the village. Nam Hoa was present. Xuey spotted him at the pool taking a bath. The local terrorist "fuehrer," Trengh, was absent.

"He will return," Xuey said assuredly. "If not today, then tomorrow, but he will return. This is his camp. Nam Hoa is only a guest here."

Several times the guerrillas came to fetch water from the tank but never to fill it. Dusk was falling and it seemed as if we were to spend a night on the cliff. Then, to my great relief, two men came and mounted the platform on which the tank stood and removed the cover.

"This is it!" Schulze whispered, gesturing us to get ready with the bags. Sergeant Schenk, who was watching the action below the cliff from a narrow parapet, now glanced up and nodded. The pipe had been connected. Schulze steadied the hollow bamboo; Xuey and I kept the bags ready.

Erich signaled.

We emptied the preparation into the brook and sank back relieved. The job was done! We began our careful withdrawal. There was no need for us to spend the night on the cliff. "We shall return in the morning for the burial ceremony," Schenk remarked.

Shortly before sunrise, Schulze and Schenk set out once again for the cascade. They returned after nearly three hours. Still a hundred yards from me. Erich raised his fist with his thumb turned down. "Total rout!" he exulted, gasping for air.

"How's the camp?"

"The plague could not have done a better job."

"The guerrillas killed four of their own cooks, thinking that they were the responsible ones," Schenk reported excitedly.

"Are they all dead?"

"You bet they are," Schulze said. "A few of them are probably still breathing but they wouldn't last long. We finished off a couple of machine gunners in the ravine but they were already on the way to hell anyway."

Assembling the troops we marched to the ravine with fixed bayonets. Schulze found two more gun emplacements littered with dead and dying guerrillas. We bayoneted them and pushed on.

"Do you think it is safe to enter the camp?" I asked Schulze when the base came into sight.

"It is a morgue, Hans," he assured me.

"I want no shooting!" I warned the troops. "The village is only two miles away and some guerrilla detachments are absent. I want them to return to home sweet home."

We found about sixty of the terrorists still alive. Some of them lay in their bunks, others on the ground, writhing and moaning. Only about fifteen Viet Minh had been unaffected by the drugs. They were busy tending the sick ones when we overran them. The body of Nam Hoa sprawled in front of the command post in a pool of partly digested food which he had vomited before he died. We made a photo of him for later reference and to collect the reward. Many of the victims had vomited where they fell before death seized them.

"Suoi," I said to the girl as I led her into the commander's hut, "you can help us now. Look through all the papers which you think could be important for us and please put them into this bag." I handed her a small canvas bag.

"*Oui!*" she nodded and began to work immediately.

I wanted to get her inside; the spectacle of bayoneting the dying and captured enemy was not a pleasant one. I posted a man in the door. "Keep her busy until we finish the job."

"I guess we should have left her with Eisner," Erich remarked when he joined me on the porch.

"We should have left her in Hanoi!" I growled.

Searching the huts, Sergeant Schenk discovered three girls. They had not been affected by the poison but were much too terrified to stand up, let alone to use their pistols. Schenk escorted them to the mess hut. "Sit down here and don't move!" he told them harshly. "Otherwise I will cut your slender throats. . . . And don't utter a sound either."

With Xuey's assistance I interrogated them immediately. The

girls spoke some French but not enough to understand the implications of my questions. According to them, Trengh and his one hundred and sixty guerrillas had departed two days before our arrival. They had taken a part of the stolen wares to another dump fifteen miles away. More items had been hidden in the village.

"Where is that other dump?" I asked, telling Xuey to interpret my question as sternly as possible. The girls did not know the place.

"We have never been there," one of them muttered.

"You are lying!" I shouted in her native tongue. The girls shrank away from my outburst and huddled together terrified. One of them began to sob. I knew I had to apply the squeeze right then.

"Sergeant Schenk!" I called Victor. "Tickle them a little with the bayonets."

Schenk and two of the troopers stepped forward with their bayonets extended, the points touching the girls' throats.

"Have you seen what happened to your sick comrades?" I asked slowly, stressing my words. "I am asking you once more where that other dump is. If you don't tell us, you will die."

The blades, still spattered with blood, were a macabre sight. "Please, no," the smallest girl cried, burying her face in her hands, "please don't kill us. We are very young."

"You weren't so young when you joined the terrorists."

"We had to," she mumbled, "we had to go with them."

"When is Trengh coming back?"

"If we tell you, Trengh will kill us all . . . our families, too."

"If you tell us, Trengh won't kill anybody anymore. When is he coming back?"

"Tonight!" she whispered.

"I want to know –"

"Leave them alone!" A cry from behind interrupted me. Followed by Erich, Suoi came running toward me. She pushed aside the bayonets and stood between us and the girls with her eyes blazing. "You . . . you cannot do this. . . . You wouldn't dare . . . you. . . ." She was so aroused that she could barely form her words and I couldn't resist teasing her.

"Oh, yes, Suoi – if necessary I *would* dare."

"Not as long as I am here – commander!"

I cast a glance of resignation toward Erich, who lifted and dropped his shoulders with a grin and waved the troopers aside.

"I guess this is the end of my interrogation," I remarked in German. "Maybe you and Suoi can take over."

I glanced at the captive girls, a frightened bunch of little rabbits; the oldest one of them was probably less than twenty years of age.

"Why did you join those bandits?" Suoi spoke to them softly. "Do you think it is right for young girls to kill people?"

"We did not kill anyone. We were only tending the wounded."

"Are you nurses?" I cut in.

They nodded.

"All right. You will show us the way to the other dump and we will let you go home." They began to cry again and explained something to Suoi between a series of small hysterical sobs.

"They cannot go home," Suoi translated for me. "The Viet Minh will kill them."

"That's too bad, Suoi."

"You are too bad," she replied, shaking her head. "You are much too hard and have no heart."

"There is a war going on around here. Wars are very bad – not me, Suoi."

"But if they betray the guerrilla camp to you, the guerrillas will kill them all. Can't you understand? You might as well kill them right here."

"All right, all right," I cut her short. "Take care of them, Suoi. I have other things to attend to. We will talk about the dump later. In the meantime the girls can care for our own wounded."

"We haven't got any," Schulze stated, obviously pleased with my decision about the girls.

"We aren't home yet, Erich," I reminded him of something that every one of us should always keep in mind.

We soon discovered not only a large quantity of matériel stolen from the garrison but also hundreds of Soviet-made guns, pistols, and mortars, along with similar weapons manufactured in China. There were Degtyarev light machine guns, Spaghin and Sudaiev submachine guns, Goriunov machine guns which can fire two hundred and fifty bullets per minute to a distance of one thousand meters. There were also Browning automatic rifles, French Mitra Mats, and even MAS rifles produced in 1937.

"What shall we do with all the stuff?" Erich inquired, waving an arm about the depot.

"Don't worry. The villagers will carry everything back to the stockade. They know the way."

The troops spent the day preparing a reception for Trengh and his terrorists. Fifty men with fifty machine guns, which we uncrated in the huts, were deployed to cover the entrance of the camp and the ravine behind it. Xuey, Sergeant Schenk, and one platoon occupied the vacant gun emplacements of the Viet Minh. The barrels of their machine guns had been carefully muffled with blankets and rags to deaden sound. Those in the village were still unaware of our presence in the hills and of the destruction of the terrorist base.

The girls had told me the truth. Around six o'clock in the afternoon Eisner radioed the coming of a Viet Minh unit, riding cycles on the road. "Let them pass," I flashed back. "We have a reception ready for them."

Trengh and his guerrillas arrived at sundown. Xuey waved boldly to them as they passed the first gun emplacement, now manned by Schenk and six troops. The guerrillas waved back and the group proceeded through the ravine and entered the camp.

I waited just long enough for them to come out in the open, then ordered fire. The machine guns opened up simultaneously and fired for less than ten seconds. Their chatter was very dull, resembling the popping of champagne corks. During that ten seconds five hundred bullets were poured into the group. The terrorists didn't know what hit them.

I left a detachment to guard the camp and turned my attention to the village, where shock and consternation was immense, even though we harmed no one. Most of the dead guerrillas were from there. I considered it enough punishment for the people. There was hardly a hut without someone missing. A grim lesson of a cruel war.

From the concealed cellars and tunnels we recovered everything that had been snatched from the stockade. Taking a hundred troops, Eisner escorted a large group of complaining, crying villagers to the camp to bring down more army wares. He allowed the people to bury their dead. The camp was then destroyed with explosive charges.

Taking the three captive girls, Riedl and Pfirstenhammer departed for the other guerrilla dump – supposedly fifteen miles, but it turned out to be over twenty-two miles away. Escorting the villagers – some four hundred people altogether – laden with stores, we headed back toward the stockade.

A new garrison greeted us when we arrived. Trucks, helicopters, and armored cars crowded the yards, while engineers were busy repairing the damaged buildings and the outer defenses. The perimeter was being improved with minefields and concrete pillboxes near the palisade. A system of covered trenches was to connect the bunkers with the stockade.

"What did I tell you?" Eisner exclaimed when, descending from the hills, we beheld the brisk activity for the first time. "The French are the greatest builders of forts." Then he added with a chuckle, "In about five years' time those pillboxes and minefields may have destroyed as many terrorists as we have dispatched in the past five days!"

With the goods properly delivered, we sent the civilians home and settled down to enjoy a well-deserved rest. Riedl and Karl returned two days later. In the secret dump, which consisted of a maze of natural caves and tunnels, they discovered a quantity of Soviet weapons.

"How did you blast the place if it was all rocks?" Schulze asked. He was busy preparing our report on the past week.

"Like hell we blasted it!" Karl exclaimed. "We just mined the lot and left everything in order. Who wants to blow up bare hills, *Mensch?* Sooner or later other guerrillas will come to fetch the stuff. They move a crate and the whole works blow sky-high – with the Viet Minh riding the smoke."

"A good idea," Erich complimented.

"My ideas are always good," Karl stated modestly.

The girls were still with them. "I sent them off near the village," Riedl explained, "but they kept coming back to us. They seemed scared to death of their own people."

"They prefer to come to Hanoi," Karl added. "We couldn't just dump them in the woods, could we?" He walked off to the canteen and returned with a large bowl of rice and meat. "Here! Take it." He handed the bowl to the smallest girl. "Eat! *Mangez . . . essen . . . niam, niam.* Her name is Noy," he explained to us. "The other two are called Chi and Thi – if I spell it well. Chi is not a local girl. She is from Szechwan, China."

"We can use them, can't we, Hans?" Riedl seemed to be suggesting rather than asking a question. "They are trained nurses with hospital experience."

"We can always use a couple of good nurses," Schulze put in.

"Sure!" Riedl agreed and began to cite the advantages of having the girls along. They know the woods. They can march like men. They are nurses. They can prepare better food than we are cooking ourselves. Heading off my decision he added hopefully, "They will be an asset to the battalion, Hans."

"I have heard that already."

"Besides, Suoi won't be all alone."

"Neither will you, I presume."

Karl grinned. "It could be kind of fun to have them along."

"I gather that. But suppose *they* don't like your proposal?"

"But they do!" Pfirstenhammer exulted. He turned toward the trio who sat on the crates, munching without a worry on earth. "You do want to come with us, don't you?"

The girls looked up and giggled, "*Ja, ja,*" the one called Noy replied in German. "*Kayl unt Helmut sint gutte manne*" – "Karl and Helmut are good men."

"What did I say?" Karl beamed. "In six months' time they will even speak German, won't you Noy?"

"*Jahfoll . . . ja, ja,*" she answered what one could decipher into "*Jawohl!*" and giggled. "Yes, yes . . . we like learning, much learning. Kayl said we can come with you. He will fix up Commander."

"He will fix me up, eh? That's what Karl said?"

"*Ja, ja,*" she nodded, "can we come?"

"Of course you can come," Suoi answered on my behalf.

Being outnumbered ten to one, I surrendered.

"*Voilà!*" Erich chuckled. "The battalion plus four."

11

Ambushed

We spent four magnificent days in the stockade, sleeping in soft beds; eating cooked meals consisting of meat, vegetables, and salads; sitting at tables, drinking wine, playing cards; reading, relaxing. Then a wireless message arrived marked "Urgent!"

"Commence with plan TRANSIT in the areas 502 and 511. Intelligence reports massive terrorist supplies moving south to reinforce Viet Minh units in the Delta zone. Advance on point 1123 and interrupt enemy convoys and troops. Send detailed situation report."

Advance on point 1123 – Muong Son, a Communist stronghold. Our short "holiday" was over.

I had my misgivings about such detailed wireless dispatches whether they were coded or not. I had often requested a change of code but all in vain. In the German Army we had changed field codes every other day. The Foreign Legion used the same keys for months in a row. Recent events made me suspect that the "ears" of the Viet Minh were wide open both in Hanoi and in the provinces. Besides, we had discovered quite a few Chinese radio listening posts in the frontier areas and Eisner swore that some of them were manned by Russian signal experts. I would not have been surprised if the enemy had known the key to our code.

While in the stockade, we learned that the guerrillas had begun the attack there only two days after the magazines of the fort had been replenished with supplies and only after the departure of the tanks and copters that had escorted the incoming convoy. Moreover, the attack came when our battalion was on its way toward an alleged Viet Minh trail in Laos and was bypassing the stockade – which was within easy marching distance. The prompt terrorist attack on the garrison had diverted us from the trail and the suspected enemy supplies moving south. Had the guerrillas attacked a day later, we would not have turned back toward the stockade but would have moved on to disrupt the enemy convoys deeper inland.

Was it only a coincidence or the result of deliberate and clever planning? Was there something very important moving south which the enemy wanted to preserve by providing a diversion for us? Had some of their spies been very active in Hanoi? Had they managed to break the army code? Three days later I received my answer to that question.

We were camped out on a barren ridge, waiting for dawn, when suddenly we came under intense enemy fire which persisted for over an hour. Shouting savagely, several hundred guerrillas emerged from the forest below. Still firing furiously, those on the flanks streamed across the entire width of the hill and began to ascend. Silhouetted against the moonlit rocks, they came charging up the rugged slope. There were too many boulders to shelter behind. The machine guns could not stop them. The enemy advanced, hopping from boulder to boulder, gaining ground rapidly. The night roared with machine gun clatter and the explosion of grenades; shrieks, yells, and curses rose from below, echoing among the rocks.

"Hell, Hans!" Schulze yelled, as he knelt against a boulder, sweeping the slope with his submachine gun, "there is a whole bloody brigade of them!"

"It isn't as bad as that, Erich, keep firing!" I shouted back. I glanced at Suoi and the nurses, who were sheltered behind a large stone; they appeared more fascinated than scared.

"Take them higher up!" I called to Schulze and pointed at a cluster of boulders twenty feet above us. Erich nodded and sprang to the girls. "Up there!" he commanded briskly. "Lay low." He helped them climb into a small natural opening and dumped three submachine guns after them. "If they come as far as here, then shoot!" The next instant he was back firing savagely into the oncoming crowd.

Before the enemy troops were halfway up the hill I could see that we were heavily outnumbered, but I did not consider our situation too difficult; we had the advantage of being better trained, better equipped, and we also held the superior position. The Viet Minh had missed a better chance: They should have attacked us when we were still coming uphill.

The ridge where we deployed was a sort of natural fort formed by large jagged boulders, but it was circular and could be attacked from every side. As we lay prone on the slabs, the enemy proceeded to do exactly what I anticipated – make a concentric assault. With some pessimism, Schulze could have yelled "a division" instead of only a brigade, there were so many of them coming at us.

Traversing the machine guns slowly from side to side, the gunners managed to slow down the enemy but still they advanced, hopping from stone to stone. My men were preparing a defense perimeter with Sergeants Krebitz and Schenk, Corporal Altreiter, and even Kurt Zeisl, our medical officer, shouting orders, running from position to position to bolster the men. We were compressed in a limited area, maybe two hundred yards across, and I could but thank our good fortune that the guerrillas were not carrying mortars.

On each side bullets dealt death. The foremost terrorists fell but others came hurtling on, regardless of losses, in what was obviously a human wave assault. Their advance platoons established themselves barely fifty yards below the ridge, where a depression offered them shelter. I had no doubt that the enemy had known where to look for us and thought we could be trapped and finished off on the coverless ridge. It could not have been just another "coincidence"; rather it was a planned and timely delivered action.

The moon suddenly vanished behind a passing cloud and the short period of darkness was greeted by vicious shrieks and yells in the terrorist ranks. Under the cover of darkness the enemy surged forward. We could do little to stop them.

"*À la baïonnette!*" Eisner commanded. "Fix bayonets!" Corporal Altreiter and Sergeant Schenk passed the word. The firing stopped abruptly, giving way to a multitude of sharp, metallic clicks as the bayonets were snapped onto the gun muzzles.

"*Xung! Phong!*" came the Viet Minh battle cry. "Forward! Kill!"

The leading terrorists were but a dozen yards from us, coming on strong. Howling madly and no longer seeking shelter, they charged. Many of them fell, slithering down the slope dead or wounded. Even so, our last volley could not stop the tide. Only then did I notice Chinese militiamen among the Viet Minh – over a hundred miles *inside* French Indochina. Nevertheless for Paris, Peking was "neutral," nonbelligerent; we could not even submit a proper report on our raids into China to be forwarded to Paris. It was against the rules to have been there in the first place.

Indeed the Chinese were nonbelligerent – only bellicose.

"Loose fire! Aim at their guts!" I shouted, bracing myself for the coming melee. More and more of the enemy lurched, spun about, and collapsed, thrashing in agony, but at least a hundred of them reached the plateau, each carrying a rifle or a cutlass.

"Keep shooting!" Schulze yelled. Discarding the empty submachine gun, I drew my automatic and raced up to Riedl, who was already fighting three guerrillas in a desperate hand-to-hand combat. I shot the nearest one through the chest and turned toward the second man, who rushed at me with a broad-bladed cutlass. The terrorist had a submachine gun flung about his chest. Its magazine must have been empty and in the turmoil no one had time to reload. The determination of my adversary was incredible. He saw me lifting my pistol but only howled and kept coming at me. One bullet hit him in the face, the second slug tore out his throat. He stopped, staggered a few steps, and went down.

"Here, Hans!" I heard a yell. A Chinese rifle with Russian bayonet materialized in front of my face. I grabbed the weapon, barely noticing that Sergeant Krebitz handed it to me. "It's loaded!" Krebitz raced off to *Gruppe Drei* on the far side of the plateau. I saw him duck the thrust of a militiaman; an instant later he grabbed his adversary by the chest, kicked him in the groin, and as the terrorist doubled up in pain, Krebitz clubbed him with his rifle butt.

The guerrillas were all around us. They came yelling, howling, brandishing bayonets, spears, and even knives. Shooting became very sporadic. Both sides had fired all their bullets and no one had time to change magazines. It was a day of the bayonets.

Firing the Chinese rifle, I managed to drop four of the closest terrorists, then bayoneted two more as they came over the ledge. Some of my own men were going down; others sprawled among the stones – shot, stabbed, or cut open.

"Watch out for Riedl!" Erich cried, hitting and slicing a guerrilla. Wheeling around I saw a couple of militiamen ready to swamp Helmut. The same instant I felt a searing pain in my head and for a moment my world jarred; but my eyes remained open, I could still see and move my limbs and I was still erect. I did not pay any more attention to it. Rushing on, I managed to drop two of the Chinese but emptied my rifle in the process. The third militiaman leaped at Helmut. He, too, must have spent his bullets, for he raised his rifle club-like.

"Look out!" I warned Riedl and as he turned to meet the charge the sinewy Chinese brought down his weapon at an oblique angle. Had it landed the blow could have sent Riedl spinning into the ravine a hundred feet below, but he ducked in time and the stock only grazed his shoulder. Even so the blow was enough to knock the gun from his hand. Sergeant Schenk uttered a savage yell as he smashed the head of a terrorist with a swinging blow, then stabbed another one with such force that not only the bayonet but also a part of the muzzle entered the wound. Lifting his foot, he kicked his adversary backward to free his bayonet, then rushed to Riedl's side. The militiaman wheeled around and lifted his rifle to ward off the coming thrust. He only managed to divert it. Schenk's blade ripped across his chest and the two went down in a tangle, barely a yard from the precipice. The diversion enabled Riedl to recover his automatic. Still stooping he shot the Chinese behind the ear. Blood, bone, and brain tissue blew across the stones in a savage spray. Sergeant Schenk rose, covering his ringing ears, dumbfounded by the proximity of the blast; his face and hands were sprinkled with blood and bits of flesh.

"Sorry, Victor," Helmut apologized, "I had no choice." From the hand of the still writhing Chinese he kicked free a short curved knife. "He was about to cut your belly open."

A tall, lean guerrilla with protruding teeth materialized in front of me. Howling with his mouth wide open, he pushed his bayonet so far forward that he lost his balance and crashed headlong into Schulze. Erich swore. He reeled, steadied himself, and swung his gun up in a savage blow. The barrel caught the terrorist a terrific wallop across the mouth. He stopped howling as a few of his teeth went down his gullet; staggering back he fell on his knees until a kick from Riedl helped him over the precipice.

The enemy was falling all over the ridge, for numerous as they were, in hand-to-hand fighting my men held the advantage of both weight and muscle power over the smaller guerrillas. A couple of our six-foot-plus comrades were obviously enjoying themselves whacking and tossing aside the enemy troops as though they were mushrooms. Indeed some of the brawny ones fought in what looked like a ring of dead or dying terrorists, heaped high. Still more Viet Minh were climbing upward on the rugged slope. Ignorant of peril and unconcerned about losses, they came flowing over the precipice, swamping the plateau like an army of ants and cutting a swath across the land they invade.

"Drop, everybody!" We heard a vicious yell in German from higher above. "On your belly! Down! Down!" The next instant the clatter of a machine gun erupted from the rocks and a couple of submachine guns joined in simultaneously. Dropping to the ground, I saw militiamen and Viet Minh collapsing in heaps of agonized flesh. Shredding uniforms, staggering under the impact of the heavy slugs, crying, bleeding, twisting, and falling, the enemy went down all over the plateau. Lying on a flat boulder overhead, Sergeant Schenk, Suoi, and the three ex-guerrilla nurses coolly proceeded to clear the place of the enemy, the girls sweeping the ridge and Sergeant Schenk the slope. While we were fighting for our lives with bayonets, rifle butts, and our bare fists, Victor had climbed the rocks and reloaded an MG. The magnificent four were now blazing away at the bewildered enemy.

The guerrilla reinforcements stopped; their ranks faltered and fell back on the slope. On the ridge the struggle came to a sudden and dramatic end. Enemy dead and wounded littered the plateau, but unfortunately our bullets could not distinguish between friend and foe either; a few of our comrades were still struggling with the terrorists, locked in brutal hand-to-hand brawls when the bullets from above began to pour. It was a small consolation that we had no way of knowing who had been hit by our own bullets. But the enemy was beaten. Those who survived that sudden rain of steel were now tumbling down toward the woods, slithering and crawling away to shelter. Schenk and the girls had saved the day. The guns fell silent and we rose.

"Hans, I was right," Riedl yelled. "The nurses *are* an asset for the battalion."

"Hey, men!" Schenk called from above, "are you all dead or asleep down there? Let them have a couple of grenades for good measure."

Still overawed by their unexpected deliverance, the troops now gathered themselves, sprang forward, and began to hurl grenades after the escaping enemy. Explosions shattered the silence. The MGs opened up once more; earth and stone erupted below the ridge as more and more Viet Minh curled and crumpled like broken dolls, rolling down into the ravine. Wiping the sweat from his face, Schulze glanced up and shook his fist at Suoi.

"We will talk about this shooting business of yours – just come down," he called to the girl with joking apprehension mixed with relief.

"I am not coming."

With a few powerful strides, Erich mounted the rocks, caught hold of the girl, and brought her down. "I am going to whack you good and hard, if that's what you want."

"You wouldn't dare!"

No, Erich "wouldn't dare." He only drew her close and held her tightly. And for the first time, at least in our presence, he kissed Suoi. Though surprised for an instant, she responded; the strap of the submachine gun which she was still holding slipped from her hand and the weapon dropped with a clatter. The girls giggled. Riedl and Karl helped them down, glanced at them, then at each other, and broke into a broad grin.

"Shall we join the party?" Karl asked. "At least we won't be the only ones around here." Helmut nodded as he caught hold of Thi and before the girl could do anything about it, he kissed her long and hard. Karl was struggling with Noy for a similar favor.

Sergeant Schenk wiped his lips, turned toward Chi, who stood leaning against a boulder giggling. "You are the smallest one here and I am small too. We seem to match, don't you think so?" he asked. Chi did not understand much of the commentary but she understood what came afterwards.

"What a touching family scene," Eisner commented.

"Are you hurt?" I asked, lowering myself beside him.

"Not that I know of." He glanced at me. "Say, Hans, you're bleeding like a pig."

I touched my scalp. It was matted with blood. "It seems they put a hole in your head," Bernard joked. "We had better call the girls."

I called them. They came, holding hands with their newly acquired sweethearts – every one of them obviously very content with the turn of events.

"I cannot give you a medal but I thank you for what you did," I told them. "You were magnificent." They blushed and stood looking at each other, then at us. Noy stepped closer.

"You are wounded," she said. "Shall I look?"

I sat down on the ground and bent my head obediently. She opened her first aid kit. Eisner sent Suoi and the other girls to help Sergeant Zeisl look after the wounded. Smiling apologetically, Noy began to examine my scalp. Only then did I realize that Noy, too, was a very pretty girl with her faultless oval face, large dark eyes, and long braids neatly woven and held in place by a pair of wide orange ribbons.

"When you are through with me, you are going to change those orange ribbons for some blue ones," I told her. "They are much too conspicuous and we don't want to see your pretty head being shot at by the Viet Minh."

"I change ribbons – why?" she asked, not quite understanding the meaning of my "complicated" sentence.

"Because the terrorists can see your ribbons from far away," I explained, imitating a pair of binoculars with my hands. "The Viet Minh see your ribbons, tatatata – and Noy is dead."

She nodded, a series of quick little nods. "*Oui, monsieur*. I change ribbons."

"Good girl!"

"You have luck," she commented, working on my wound. "Your head was shot by a bullet. It comes little lower and you drop dead." Her way of selecting and assembling words was charming.

"Thanks for the consolation," I grinned, submitting myself to the treatment.

With deft fingers, Noy separated my matted hair and began to bathe the wound with disinfectant. The process brought tears to my eyes, which seemed to amuse my faithful companions.

"Stop grinning like a clown," I snapped at Karl, "and go look for your men. Noy won't be running away."

Sergeant Krebitz came, carrying papers. "Twenty dead and thirty-five wounded," he reported grimly, handing me the list.

"How many serious ones?"

"Seven, Hans. Shot through the lung, in the groin, in the abdomen."

"We are moving out in twenty minutes!"

"I know."

"How about the rest of the wounded?"

"They will be able to march any reasonable distance."

Noy finished bandaging my head. "Tomorrow I see you again," she said quietly. "Your head will be good, one week time."

We walked over to our gravely wounded comrades. One of them, Heinz Auer, a former paratrooper, had already died. The six others were barely conscious.

Although it seemed that, at least for the time being, the guerrillas had had enough, they still occupied a dense patch of forest and I knew we had to march before they could receive reinforcements, or even worse, mortars! Exposed as we were on that barren ridge we would have no chance to withstand a prolonged mortar attack.

Sergeant Zeisl came slowly toward me. He was carrying a small medical container. We all knew what it contained and for what purpose. "Shall I proceed?" Zeisl asked grimly.

I nodded. "Make it quick."

The troops began to gather. Some of them bandaged, others uninjured. No one spoke; all stood in bitter silence. Riedl kneeled down beside a wounded comrade to wipe his perspiring forehead and to shoo off the flies. Zeisl filled a syring with a lethal concentration of morphine. Noy, who was watching thc preparations, and thinking that all we wanted to do was ease the suffering, suddenly bent down for the empty vial which Sergeant Zeisl had discarded. She looked at it, then turned toward me with her eyes wide open.

"Sergeant do wrong!" she exclaimed pointing at Zeisl. "Gives them too much. The men die. He is mistaken."

"He is not mistaken, Noy," Pfirstenhammer drew her aside gently. "We cannot carry them and we cannot leave them here either. Do you understand?"

"I understand," she answered and her eyes began to fill. "You kill them!" She looked around bewildered, looking at Karl, at Eisner, at me. We all averted our eyes. Noy began to sob. "You cruel people . . . you very, very cruel people."

"Come, Noy," said Karl, placing an arm around her shoulders. "You should not look."

"You are worse than the Viet Minh," she cried, "for even *they* help their wounded."

"We cannot help them, Noy. You are a nurse, you should know better."

"You why not call helicopters?"

"It would take hours before the copters could come. Do you think they can live that long? Or that *we* can live that long? The Viet Minh will gather more men, then attack again and again."

"You are not God," she sobbed, "you cannot give or take life."

Karl led her away gently.

Sergeant Zeisl delivered the injections, replaced the needle in a small vial of alcohol, and put it away in his kit. He turned. Facing the six men on the ground, he raised his hand for a last salute.

"Attention!" I commanded. The ring of troops froze.

"Salute!"

And as Sergeant Krebitz proceeded with his gloomy task of collecting identity tags, watches, wallets, and pocketbooks from the men who were leaving us forever, the troops began to hum, then sing in a low tone, the old German soldier's song, "Wacht am Rhein."

I read their names from the list in my hand: Ernst Walder Rudolf Forcher, Leopold Ambichl, Josef Bauer, Josef Edler, Anton Gebauer, and twentyone more. Although the Free World has yet to honor them, they had fought the enemy of all mankind for ten long years and in battlefields ten thousand miles apart. The same enemy in different uniforms, in a different disguise. They had done more to preserve freedom and civilization than many much-decorated generals and celebrated statesmen. Only they received no medals for their deeds. Not even a decent *Memento mori!* They were forgotten and forsaken heroes. We could not give them as much as a decent burial. We placed them in a deep crevasse and blew rocks over the makeshift tomb. A single line in German was inscribed on a jagged boulder: "Deutschland - Poland - Russland - Nord Afrika - Indochina 1939–1951, 27 comrades."

We had no time to count the enemy dead but they must have numbered several hundred. Removing the weapons, grenades, ammunition, and papers of those who had fallen on or immediately below the ridge, we descended the southern slope, still under sporadic enemy fire. But the very boulders which had sheltered the guerrillas before now provided us with cover. Keeping low so as not to silhouette ourselves against the moonlit sky, the battalion descended. Covered by the MGs of *Gruppe Drei* we entered the woods, and followed a path which we sighted and compass-marked from the ridge.

A few hundred yards inside the forest we passed a small clearing, but as we penetrated deeper and deeper, the forest became thicker. The trail led straight toward Muong Son, but that was precisely the place where I no longer wanted to go. The enemy seemed well informed about our destination and that concentration of Viet Minh troops below the ridge was the very last "coincidence" I was willing to digest.

We were moving deep within enemy-controlled territory and far from French fortifications or patrol routes. We could march without fearing mines or even traps; we could even use our flashlights, shielded with green plastic. My idea was to advance as far as possible, then rest for the remaining hours of the night. At dawn I intended to leave the path and to move west, penetrating still deeper into the Viet Minh "hinterland," seeking a favorable spot to vanish into the jungle. As we had often done we would cut our own trail, starting a few hundred yards from the regular path without being connected to it.

We had, in the course of months, cut several secret trails in the guerrilla-held areas. Since our routes had no connection with the existing paths, it was very difficult for the enemy to detect them. Arriving at an existing path we never continued directly opposite but fifty paces to the left, or to the right. In each section my men left a few innocent-looking objects to serve as "markers" – a casually bent bough tied with threads, a discarded tin holding a few cigarettes, an old lighter, or something similar. The disappearance of the marker would tell us immediately that strangers had come across our trails. Naturally no guerrilla would ignore a lighter or a fountain pen on a tree stump.

Having marched for over two hours without finding a suitable place for camping out, Sergeant Zeisl suggested that we should stop because of our wounded comrades. "We will have to remove two bullets tomorrow," he reminded me. (Two of the men were marching with bullets in their flesh.) "They have lost much blood and need a rest."

I decided to camp down where we were. Eisner dispatched advance and rear guards to cover the trail with machine guns. Sooner or later the enemy would catch up with us.

"Change the sentries as frequently as possible, so that everyone can have some sleep," I told Bernard.

At dawn two platoons went up and down the trail to plant mines and primed grenades triggered with boughs or trip wires. Another group advanced a mile to discard cigarette butts, empty tins, and other "evidence" of our presence far beyond the point where we intended to leave the trail. A hundred yards inside the woods the trailblazers began to cut a new path. Very cautiously, careful not to leave tracks or break branches, the troops left the trail. I was confident that the guerrillas would bypass the place. Discovering our planted evidence farther up, they could easily march headlong into our mines.

Around 10 A.M. we stopped at a shallow creek to cook a meal and to attend the wounded. With the help of the girls, Sergeant Zeisl extracted the two bullets and changed the bandages of the others. I thought it was time to give the troops a well-deserved rest.

"We will camp out here until everyone is fit again," I told Eisner. For a moment he looked surprised.

"It might be a week, Hans . . . or even more."

"So what?"

"You are forgetting about action Transit."

"To hell with action Transit," I growled, massaging my aching temples. My head was throbbing like a steam engine and I could imagine how the two men with bullets just extracted from their flesh must have felt. "What if we blast a few wretched Viet Minh convoys? It won't stop the war. They can wait." I swept an arm about the woods. "This is a good place. We have ample shade, water, and we are far from villages and trails. The enemy has no idea where we are. A week later we may hit them like a bolt out of the clear sky." I lowered myself to the ground with my back against a tree and closed my eyes. "We need a rest, Bernard. Especially the wounded ones, including me. I am weary."

Eisner nodded. "I will give the word to build shelters," he said.

"Do that, Bernard – but tell the men not to make much noise."

We were to camp along the creek for eight days. By the afternoon we had a triple row of small huts, made of branches and leaves, on either side of the creek. Suoi and the nurses were presented with a cozy little hut, "furnished" with love and appreciation. It even had beds – thick layers of dry leaves, covered with towels, in place of mattresses – and a table. In order to insure their comfort and privacy, Sergeant Krebitz and a few men from *Gruppe Drei* built a bathing hut for the girls right in the creek. They had become very popular with the troops who kept referring to them only as "our angels," not only because the girls cared for the injured ones with tender zeal and were always ready to help and never complained of hardship or fatigue, but also because their very presence, their cheerfulness and ever-present smiles, seemed to uplift everyone's spirit.

Game appeared to be plentiful in the area. Carrying the silencer-equipped rifles, our *Abwehrkommando* left for short hunting trips every day and brought back deer and wild boar. Xuey and the girls prepared wonderful native meals and taught the men how to cook better meals for themselves. We had no facility for mess-cooking. The men had to take care of their own meals.

One evening, I think it was our third evening in our jungle camp, I sat in my hut writing my journal, when Erich appeared all of a sudden. "Hans," he addressed me in a troubled voice, "do you suppose you can perform a marriage ceremony?"

"Perform a *what?*"

My chin dropped, and so did the pen from my hand. "Marriage," Schulze repeated and I saw he was in earnest. "I want to marry Suoi!"

"That is no news!"

"I want to marry her *now*," he added quickly. "I thought you could do it . . . like a captain of a ship."

"Are you serious, Erich?"

"Hell, of course I am serious. Can you marry us, Hans?"

"I don't think it would do you any good as far as the law goes, Erich."

"We can take care of the legalities later."

I lit a cigarette and offered him one, then taking my canteen, I filled two small cups with rum. "I think we both need a drink, Erich."

We drank, but all the time Erich's eyes remained on my face questioningly.

"What does Suoi think of your idea?" I asked.

"I wouldn't have come to you on my own, Hans. We are in love."

"That is also known," I commented repressing a smile. "But you had better wait until we return to Hanoi."

He wet his lips and wiped the perspiration from his handsome face.

"I will go to pieces before then, Hans," he confessed. "What do you suggest?"

"I suggest that we have another cup of rum."

We drank. "Where is Suoi?" I asked after a while.

"In my hut – crying."

"I hope you did not – "

"No, I didn't!" He cut me short. "That's exactly why I am cracking up, Hans. I am crazy about her."

"I can understand that," I agreed sympathetically. "She is a beautiful girl."

"She takes my hand, I kiss her, and the scent of her hair is enough to send me up the wall."

He lit another cigarette with shaking fingers. I never saw Erich so excited. "There ought to be a missionary around. The men say there is a priest in Muong Son."

"So is the Viet Minh, Erich!"

He ran his hand through his hair and rose slowly. "Hans," he spoke to me, his voice full of emotion, "I've never asked for any special favor in all these years together. I am asking for a favor *now*. We don't know how long we will last, do we, Hans? We cannot think of the future, not even in terms of weeks. The only certain thing we have is our present – this very day. Get me that priest from Muong Son."

There was a pause. He was looking at me penetratingly and I was thinking.

"I suggest that you should return to Suoi now. I will see what I can do about you. But whatever I do will depend on what Xuey thinks of it. He knows Muong Son and Father Bousseau, a French priest there, and only Xuey can make the trip. For anyone else it would be suicidal even to try. The place is teeming with guerrillas." I glanced at him. "I presume you know what it could mean if we lose Xuey?" He answered nothing, only sat there with his face buried in his hands. I went on. "Provided that the priest is still there and he is willing to come, and he is *able* to come, I shall try to get him here."

"Thank you, Hans . . . thank you indeed."

"Don't thank me, Erich. I am not happy about it – and I will be damned if this isn't the bloodiest military expedition I have ever been on."

"I am sorry."

"In a sense I was afraid that this would happen, Erich. Today you, tomorrow maybe Karl or Riedl. After tomorrow it might be Schenk or someone else."

"I am sorry, Hans."

"It's all right. In the meantime be kind to Suoi and remember that she is not a European girl. The Orientals still consider love and marriage something truly sacred and everlasting."

Erich swallowed hard and extended his hand. "I shall remember it, Hans. You have my word."

Schulze left and I spread out my map to spend almost an hour pondering the problem. Muong Son was about eight miles away, as the crow flies, but overland the trip would be much longer. I sent a trooper for Eisner and told him the whole story. He seemed amused, but he only shrugged at my dilemma.

"Well, say something," I urged him. "What would you do in my place?"

"Turn in my uniform and open a marriage bureau, Hans." He chuckled. "You should ask Xuey what *he* thinks of going to Muong Son."

"I should never have brought the girls along."

"Nonsense!" said he. "The boys never did so well before, Hans. They are marching better – no one dares to bitch while the girls keep going without a complaint – and they are fighting better because they know we have to protect our angels – and you know it too."

"All right. You've convinced me. Now let's hear from Xuey about the affair."

The little Indochinese listened to my explanation intently. I was truly embarrassed for requesting his services in such a non-military and unimportant private affair. But Xuey's face showed no emotion whatsoever – neither approval nor disapproval. "I think I can manage it," was his comment. "Do you want me to go right now?"

I nodded. He asked me to write a short note to the priest, which I did, imploring him to trust Ghia Xuey, for I could not disclose the place where he was to come.

Two days later Xuey returned alone. "The priest is dead," he reported. "The Viet Minh shot him seven months ago. I got this book from an old servant of his." From under his shirt he pulled a small leather-bound Bible and placed it on my cot. "I am sorry that I could not oblige Lieutenant Schulze."

"Thank you, Xuey, all the same."

He bowed and withdrew. I sat for a while, thinking of what to do now. Erich was right; none of us knew whether we had a future. He came in shortly afterwards, hand in hand with Suoi. He had already spoken to Xuey and looked very disappointed. I motioned them to sit down.

"What do we do now?" Erich asked.

I reached for the Bible and opened it at random. It was the first time in my adult life that I had held a Bible in my hands. "Well, at least we have a Bible," I stated, trying to smile. "Even a ship's captain must have a Bible if he wants to perform a marriage ceremony."

Schulze's eyes lit up. "Will you do it then?"

"As a very temporary arrangement, Erich. I will do it mainly for Suoi's sake. But it won't be legal."

"Who cares!" He exclaimed. "We will know that we are married and God will know it too."

"God might know it but He won't give you a marriage certificate!"

Suoi blushed and lowered her face. "Suoi," I spoke to her, "do you understand that I cannot marry you legally and that if I do so, you will be married only in our hearts and in our eyes, but not in the eyes of the world?"

"*Oui*, I know," she whispered, her voice barely audible.

"Do you want me to do it?"

"*Oui*, Hans. I want you to do it."

The news spread through the camp like wildfire. And there, out in the wilderness, Sergeant Krebitz's men erected a small altar, covered with a tarpaulin sheet and decked with flowers; on it Riedl placed a wooden crucifix which he had carved the day before, expecting the priest. I placed the open Bible in front of the cross. Noy and the girls came, each carrying a single flower which they tucked gently into Suoi's hair, kissing her on both cheeks. The troops gathered around the makeshift shrine, everyone freshly shaved and wearing a clean shirt. They stood in solemn silence and were deeply touched when Erich and Suoi appeared, Erich with a stance of determination but Suoi blushing and with eyes averted. I motioned them to the altar and said, "Place your hands on the Holy Bible." Obediently they extended their hands, with Erich's hand resting lightly on hers. Strange as it may be, I saw my men, the rugged, tough fighters, who believed in only one power – that of the gun – now standing overawed before an invisible, spiritual force, no one daring to move or to do as much as clear the throat.

"Now, with your hands on the Bible, you shall say aloud, Erich and Suoi, that you will accept each other as man and wife," I said.

"I do!" they whispered.

"For better or worse."

"For better or worse."

"Until death do us part."

"Until death do us part."

It was all I could remember.

I said to them, "I am not a servant of God. I cannot proclaim you man and wife in the name of God. I can speak only for us. We do accept and respect your union and we shall regard you as man and wife. And I believe that if there is a God, He, too, will accept your covenant."

I embraced them both. One after another the troops came to congratulate and to express their good wishes. Everyone was touched. Even Eisner was clearing his throat much too often.

"Blast me," he remarked, "if this was not the holiest of all the weddings I ever saw." He hugged Schulze and kissed him and then Suoi on the forehead.

"Still I suggest that you see one of God's emissaries when we get back to Hanoi. While we take care of the worldly authority," I added jokingly.

Four days later we were on the march again.

In the jungle the battalion was perfectly safe and could make better progress than on the roads or trails where we had to be on the alert for traps and enemy troops. We could, however, safely use remote paths, which sometimes crisscrossed the Viet Minh-controlled areas, far from the French garrisons. The chance of encountering enemy forces in the forest was minimal. In areas under guerrilla control the guerrillas no longer camped in the hills but in the villages, and they moved openly on the roads, dispersing only when reconnaissance planes happened to fly by. In districts from which the Legion had been expelled or had withdrawn for tactical reasons, the rules of the game changed; the Viet Minh occupied the settlements and the abandoned French stockades. Then our battalion assumed the role of the guerrillas with great success. We penetrated into areas which were out of reach for the regular army.

It was my intention to bypass Muong Son ten miles to the north-west. The same evening our trailblazers hit a wide jungle path that seemed to run in approximately the right direction. After a brief survey, Xuey announced that the path had not been used for several weeks, and that it was safe. We proceeded openly and at a good rate, spending the nights in the woods, marching from dawn to about eleven o'clock, then again when the midday heat abated. Late in the afternoon of the third day after leaving our jungle camp, the forest became less dense and we finally arrived at an open area of grassland with a small settlement two miles away. It was not marked on our maps. Xuey observed the place for a long time and insisted that he could see a flag flying from a pole – the flag of the Viet Minh. We deployed on the forest line and Xuey decided to survey the hamlet at dusk. There was nothing we could do but wait.

Taking a submachine gun, Xuey prepared to leave. He wanted to go alone, and when Riedl asked concernedly, "Won't it be too dangerous?" our little Indochinese companion only smiled and said, "Remember that I was one of them." He vanished in the dark field like a cat. Half an hour later we heard the distant baying of dogs.

Xuey returned, soaking wet but satisfied. "There are paddies all around," he reported. "I could not get very close because of the dogs. The guerrillas are all local people, not more than fifty men. But I spotted two trucks."

"What trucks?"

"Loaded trucks," Xuey added. "The Viet Minh must have captured them from the army."

"Now isn't that great!" Eisner exclaimed. "They are trafficking in trucks, happy and unconcerned. Next time we may discover an underground railway line running between Chen-yüan and Muong."

"I wouldn't be surprised," Pfirstenhammer remarked. "The way our reconnaissance works...."

"There is a road but we will have to circle the paddy fields," Xuey explained. Then turning toward the girls he ordered, "Now face the woods, all of you. I want to change clothes."

I switched on my shaded flashlight and examined the map.

"The road is here all right but the village is missing," Riedl commented.

Taking my pen I marked the apparent locale of the village with a small cross. "It is about here."

"Trucks . . . ," Eisner fumed. "I believe the Chinese could build a four-lane highway to the Mekong delta without our intelligence ever noticing a thing."

Because of the dogs we could not enter the village undetected. I made a plan for encircling the settlement and moving in right on the road. It was a bold plan but I thought it would work. Dividing forces with Eisner and Riedl, we set out, following the forest line for a mile, then skirting the paddies until we arrived at the dirt road. It was comfortably dark and the neighborhood deserted. The woods on the southern hills, the route I planned to use later on, extended almost to the road and offered ample concealment.

"What are we going to do about the dogs?" Schulze queried.

"We are going to whistle!" I replied with reserve.

He screwed up his mouth and shrugged. "If you think your whistling will quiet the dogs, Hans. . . ."

"I want to quiet their masters, Erich!" I said, then added, "Can you hum the 'Internationale'?"

"What 'Internationale'?"

"The Communist one!"

I hummed the first bars. Xuey glanced up and broke into a grin. He understood me. "Now we are going to turn into a bunch of real Viet Minh," I told the troops. "We will have to confuse the enemy, if only for the first critical minute and I think the Communist song will do exactly that."

Erich flashed a quick look of approval. "I am with you. *En avant!*"

Splitting troops once again, I sent a hundred men to approach the settlement from the north, between the road and the forest, then we moved on. My group was about four hundred yards from the village when the dogs began to bark. Within seconds the place was alive with barking and baying.

"Whistle!" I passed the word, "whistle for all you're worth."

Behind me the men began to hum, at first hesitantly, seeking the proper tune; then with Xuey's help, they found the melody and whistled "Proletarians of the world unite" as they marched with steady strides. Ahead of us lights appeared; dark shapes, carrying lamps, emerged from the huts.

One hundred yards!

In an open space between the huts fires burned; a group of villagers was busy boiling syrup distilled from cane sugar. They rose and moved closer to the road to have a better look at us.

"*Chieu hoy!*" Xuey yelled the native greeting which was returned by a few discordant, hesitant voices coming from the darkness. "Long live father Ho!"

Sixty yards!

No one was shooting yet. The people were curious but not alarmed. The figures on the road raised their lamps, trying to see into the darkness.

Forty yards! I knew that we had them.

"Who is there?" a heavy voice demanded. A couple of men moved forward with lamps.

"Friends," Xuey replied, "on the way south with ammunition. We are going to liberate Saigon."

The next instant we were upon them.

"Disperse!" I shouted, firing a red Very light over the huts. In a moment, the small group of people was enveloped by my troopers. The women began to scream, the men cursed. Lamps, tools, and weapons clattered to the ground.

"The French! The French!" someone yelled. From the far end of the settlement a short burst of machine-gun fire crackled. We heard a shriek, then silence.

Within seconds my men occupied the huts. Motioning Erich and Karl to follow me, I entered the nearest dwelling where husband, wife, and grandparents were already lined up, facing the wall; half a dozen children sat or rolled whimpering on the floor.

"Over here!" Krebitz called, pointing at the wall where a pistol hung in a holster. He took it down and examined it expertly. "Seven-sixty-two caliber Tokarev TT," he remarked. Emptying the magazine, he dropped eight bullets into a canvas bag which one of his troopers held ready. "The goddamned cutthroats don't even hide their guns anymore," he remarked. With a sullen glance from his blue eyes he stepped to the owner of the hut and turned him around by the shoulder. "Where are your other weapons, you whore's son?"

The guerrilla was a squat little creature with wide nose, square facc, and bold, large eyes with closely grown brows. He reeled, steadied himself by grabbing at a bamboo rafter that supported the roof. His eyes seething with hatred, his fists clenched, he replied defiantly, "You may take our weapons but we shall have new ones before the sun rises."

Without warning, Sergeant Krebitz struck him with the back of his hand. The man toppled over a low bench and crashed to the floor with his lips ripped. "Before the sun rises you will be a dead hero, you scum," Krebitz growled.

"Take them out!" I ordered the troopers. "The kids too." As they were being led out, Pfirstenhammer handed a length of bamboo to a trooper and pointed out the man Sergeant Krebitz had struck. "Give him a dozen strokes for the good of his soul."

Krebitz was already pulling away mats and boxes, searching for trapdoors. Outside the civilians were led to the paddies, where the men had to lie down with their hands extended, facing the water; the women and old people were permitted to sit, but also facing the paddies.

From down the road came Riedl. "Anything there?" I asked him.

"Guns and grenades," he replied, "and plenty of them."

"Keep looking."

More people were brought forward and taken to the rice fields. Ransacking the huts, my troopers dumped weapons and ammo on the road. The local terrorists had an incredible selection of weapons ranging from vintage muskets and swords to submachine guns. In one of the huts, Sergeant Schenk seized a bow with twenty-six arrows, every one of them poisoned. The owner was taken to the woods and executed immediately.

Sergeant Krebitz selected weapons and ammunition that we could use, and the rest of the terrorist hardware was taken to the trucks, marked for destruction. "Let's have a look at those trucks," Schulze suggested. "I wonder where they got them?"

We found Eisner already busy examining the vehicles. "Look at this," he said, "Soviet Zises with Chinese plates."

"Don't tell me they came all the way from China."

"I wouldn't be surprised if they did."

"There is no road," Erich interposed.

"Not that we know of," Eisner agreed. "But keep searching. We might find a couple of tanks too."

Beneath one of the dwellings, Pfirstenhammer discovered a

large underground shelter packed with guns and ammo. "Mortar shells," Xuey interpreted the inscription.

"Over one hundred crates, each containing eighteen shells," Karl remarked. "Two thousand rounds."

"You had better get busy," I told Sergeant Krebitz. He nodded and began to work, arranging primers and fuses. I ordered Schenk to march the villagers down the road. "Half a mile will do. We are going to blast the dump along with the trucks."

While Krebitz and *Gruppe Drei* mined the dump and the trucks, Corporal Altreiter and fifty men gathered foodstuffs: rice, bundles of dried fish, fruits, and sugar cane were distributed among the troops. Half an hour later we evacuated the settlement.

"They will see the blast from Peking," Riedl remarked, waving a thumb toward the village.

"Let them!" Pfirstenhammer shrugged.

Schenk and company were waiting on the road with the prisoners. Krebitz glanced at his watch. "In three minutes...."

The minutes ticked by. Then a blinding flash of fire illuminated the sky, followed instantly by a second blitz. The hills thundered and from the village exploding shells spiraled skyward. We could see huts flying in every direction. Moments later the place was engulfed in flames.

"Which is the way to Son La?" I asked one of the natives. Son La was in the opposite direction from where we really wanted to go. Numbly the man showed us the way. "Let them go!" I told the guard. "Except for those who were caught with a weapon." Fifteen men had been caught with weapons on them. They were taken to the paddies and shot.

We continued on the road for a mile. Walking between me and Erich, Suoi was unusually quiet. "Do you feel tired?" I asked her. She shook her head but said nothing.

"It is the village," Erich remarked in German. "It reminded her of her own place."

"We did not kill anyone except the armed terrorists."

"Even so. She thinks that those people, too, have lost everything – their homes, their food, their livestock."

"We are not the Salvation Army!" Eisner interposed. "They ought to learn that no one may play war games and get away with it unpunished."

We spotted our advance guard, stationary on the roadside.

"There is a trail running due west," Sergeant Krebitz reported. "Xuey considers it safe. He is already way ahead with Schenk."

The battalion left the road and took to the hills.

12

Dialogue with an Agitator

A MOST extraordinary event was brought about by a simple routine raid on a "liberated" village where no French troops had set foot for several months. Our search parties had discovered a group of terrorists in a hut, dozing off the aftereffects of rice liquor. We collected their weapons, then bayoneted them where they lay snoring on the bamboo mats.

Summoning a group of villagers, Sergeant Krebitz ordered the corpses taken out and buried in the woods. The headman, sinewy and heavy cheekboned, informed me that all the guerrillas were strangers – none of them belonged to his village. He implored us not to burn down their dwellings for, as he said, "We can do nothing but obey the Viet Minh. The French are far away and the guerrillas can come and go here at will." The man was probably telling the truth, for although many of his people, among them women and children, had gathered about the hut to watch the bodies being taken away, no one cried or lamented over the dead terrorists. Instead the women asked my permission to remove some clothes from the dead, especially their bulky sandals fashioned from segments of old tires. Allowed to do so, they literally stripped the corpses, taking even the torn, blood soaked pajamas.

Their motive was not greed, as Suoi explained to me later. The pajamas would not be washed and put into use, she said. On the contrary, the tribesmen would carefully preserve everything that belonged to the guerrillas. Should another Viet Minh unit occupy the hamlet (as it was expected the moment we departed), they would find the pajamas beflowered and displayed above the house altars, on the walls, with candles burning around them: homage to the dead "patriots." This simple trick would save the people from the vengeance of the terrorists.

But the sixteen drunken "liberators" were not all the enemy the village yielded. Barely through the burial "ceremony" we spotted Riedl's four troopers coming down the trail, driving two gagged prisoners toward us. One of them, a bespectacled, mild-looking character, appeared more like a schoolmaster than a terrorist. The men reported briefly that the two had been caught while trying to escape through the outer perimeter which Helmut and Karl had established a mile down the trail. None of the fugitives had been carrying a weapon but the dignified-looking Viet Minh, about forty-five years of age, had been carrying a number of papers which he had tried to discard in the tall grass when my men challenged him. A glance at the papers was enough to tell me that Riedl's catch was a valuable one; the prisoner turned out to be a certain Kwang Lien-hu, a *Chinese* political officer and adviser to the provincial Agitprop section of the Lao Dong. His companion was a smaller fish, only a district propagandist of the Viet Minh, Kly Nuo Truong. The name had a certain familiar ring but I could not recall where I might have heard it.

I handed Eisner the papers. He studied them briefly, whistled, then he lifted his eyes to the prisoners. Turning slowly, he folded the papers and handed them back to me. "I guess we had better start looking for a golden rope, Hans," he commented quietly.

In many ways we regarded a Viet Minh propagandist as more deadly than a terrorist who was carrying a machine gun. The guerrilla "brain-washers" were the ones who induced the indifferent or uninterested peasant to exchange his hoe for a gun and embark on a rampage of murder. We had standing orders to call in copters for any important Communist functionary whom we captured, but frankly speaking we never really bothered with sending anyone to Hanoi or elsewhere. As long as our General Staff refused to study the basic literature on Communism or guerrilla warfare, interrogation of the Viet Minh prisoners would do little good for the troops in the jungle. I had sent back scores of reports and documents throughout the years, some of them related to vital and often immediate enemy threats which could and should have been averted by a simple countermeasure. Nothing had been done; my reports had been swallowed up by the insatiable desk drawers of the General Staff. The Legion fought and died as usual and, as though nothing had happened, the Viet Minh could even carry on with an attack our HQ had known about a week in advance. So whenever we captured a terrorist leader we interrogated the man, gave him the third degree if necessary to obtain all the information that was important for our own campaign and security, then dispatched him to the only perfect Communist paradise, as Karl had put it – hell!

On that particular occasion, however, Schulze had a different idea and, just for the fun of it, I allowed him to have his way. Erich suggested that instead of executing the party cadres, we should hold a "panel discussion" with them in front of the whole village. We would discuss both ideology and politics. "The Communists have been talking to these people for years," Schulze explained. "Everyone was obliged to listen but no one was ever permitted to ask impolite questions, or to oppose the agitators; the people could only bow to whatever they were told, accepting the party dogmas – criticizing nothing. Now they will have to listen to me too. Let the two *tovariches* partake in a truly democratic dialogue. We will permit them to say whatever they feel like saying, then we shall tell the people what we think of it."

Eisner chuckled. "Are you planning to shoot it out with a provincial agitator? He will crack your arguments in no time, making you the laughingstock of the whole village."

"Nonsense! All they can do is to parrot some hackneyed slogans."

Eisner laughed. "That's what you think, my friend, but they are professionals and whatever they parrot they will parrot it well. String them up and be done with it."

"Nonsense!" Erich waved, dismissing Bernard's suggestion. "Up till now we were killing them all. Now let us talk a bit – it might work."

Riedl agreed. "They aren't going to run away, Bernard, you can hang them later." He turned toward Pfirstenhammer. "What do you think of Schulze's idea, Karl?"

"I am fascinated! Especially about finding out how much Erich knows about Communist ideology."

Schulze ordered the troopers to untie the prisoners and the two were seated on an improvised bench made of empty crates and planks. We seated ourselves in a similar fashion. Erich's "dialogue" was to be a welcome diversion from our dreary routine. The villagers, about one hundred men and women, had been requested to bring mats and sit down. Xuey explained to them briefly what we were up to, an explanation our prisoners acknowledged with a wry smile of contempt. Xuey and Suoi stood by to interpret for us.

I was a bit skeptical about Schulze's ability to argue with a seasoned Communist agitator and doubted if he could present our side of the picture without talking sheer nonsense and receive sneers instead of cheers. But he seemed confident enough, and I thought, why shouldn't he have his fun. Besides, as Karl remarked, should Erich go wrong, we could always deliver the final argument, and he tapped the stock of his submachine gun with a significant grin.

Schulze protested. "Nothing of the sort men, I want to play it absolutely fair."

Karl chuckled. "How can you possibly play it fair when, at the end of your conference, they are going to be shot anyway? The people will think that we killed the prisoners because they won the argument."

"Well, we can spare them for once, can't we?"

Karl glanced at me. "What do you think, Hans?"

"Personally I think the whole business is nothing but a shot in the dark, but since I did not intend to leave here before sundown anyway, we have time. We can also decide about the prisoners later."

Schulze advised Commissar Kwang, "You may say whatever you want, *tovarich* Commissar – nobody is going to hurt you for it, but you will also have to listen to our arguments."

"As you wish," the agitator bowed in mocking compliance. "We are your prisoners and consequently we have no choice."

"Commissar Kwang," Erich shook his head slowly, "I am

telling you that you may speak as freely as if you were in Peking, yet you begin with unfair remarks. Speak to the people. You should not feel embarrassed. Say whatever you feel like saying. Quote Lenin, Stalin, or Mao Tse-tung, condemn the French colonialists, curse us. The people here know you. You have been talking to them before, haven't you?"

"A most extraordinary favor from an imperialist puppet who calls himself an officer," the commissar replied, and as Xuey interpreted his words, Schulze broke into a jovial grin.

"That's much better, Commissar Kwang. Now you are hitting familiar chords." Kwang smiled and turned toward the villagers, whose faces revealed eager interest. They understood that we were permitting the important Viet Minh leader to speak with impunity granted to him in advance, something the Viet Minh would never do.

"The colonialist officer wants me to speak to you," Kwang began slowly, his voice picking up momentum as he went on. "You all know that only an hour ago they murdered sixteen brave patriots, devoted men who have been fighting the white oppressors for many years, so that you may gain your freedom one day. They were killed while they slept, for these brave men here were afraid to face them with a weapon in hand. With blood still dripping from their hands, these aliens are making a mockery of freedom by offering me immunity for whatever I might say against them. They *permit* me to quote Comrade Mao, they *permit* us to condemn the colonialist criminals, so that you may see what a great *freedom* they represent. We don't need the freedom which the white killers *permit* us to have. We shall have our freedom *without* their consent. The colonialist officers are still walking and talking, they can still murder your brothers and sisters – but they are dead men already. Now they are posing as great heroes but they are nothing but frightened rats who sneak in the night to raid your homes, to murder the brave fighters of the people. They know they are losing, therefore they try to make our victory as bitter as possible. The people laugh at them everywhere. The people know who are their true friends, and millions in every part of the country follow Father Ho and Comrade Mao. I have already told you how the brotherly Chinese people defeated colonialists who were a thousand times stronger than the French puppets in your country. We don't have to condemn them. They have condemned themselves a thousand times. When this mockery is over, they will kill me and Comrade Kly, and afterwards they will speak to you again. You should never believe them, for no oppressor is ever telling the truth to the oppressed."

He stopped, bowed slightly, and without looking at Schulze he returned to his place. "We are ready to face our executioners now," he said aloud instead of sitting down, "for we are going to die for the people and when our bodies return to mother earth, for every drop of our blood a hundred avenging fighters will rise."

Schulze stepped forward.

"Commissar Kwang seems to have told you what he wanted to say," he began slowly, ignoring Kwang's dramatic "farewell." "You have heard what he thinks of us colonialist officers. He called us rats, oppressors, dead men. I am addressing him as Commissar Kwang, and not a Communist murderer, which is what his kind really are. He may speak to you freely but I am sure that you have never seen a captured French officer speaking to you with the permission of a Viet Minh commissar. And you will never see one, for the Communists will never permit anyone to speak the truth, or to oppose them in any way. What Lenin, Stalin, and Mao Tse-tung have written down fills enough books to build a dam across the Mekong River. But once their ideology is put into practice, it does not work. It may hypnotize the people but it can never convince them of anything because Communism is the biggest fraud ever conceived by a few wicked men who wanted to get rich through robbery and murder."

"Say, Erich!" Eisner cut in. "Speak in simple terms or you won't have a chance of getting through. If you are going to use words like 'ideology,' 'fraud,' 'hypnotize,' then you might as well speak German for all the good it will do." He paused for a moment, then added: "Just tell them Communism is a big lie and they will get you."

He sat down. "I'll bet they don't even know what Communism means," he said to me. "Ho Chi Minh isn't using the term either."

"I can tell you in front of the agitators – " Erich went on.

"*Merde!*" Bernard interposed again. "They don't know an agitator from Adam."

"Shut up, will you?" Schulze snapped. "Or stand up and speak yourself."

Riedl grinned and the prisoners smiled contentedly. Although we spoke German, they had obviously caught the meaning of our exchange. Eisner, however, accepted the challenge. He strode over to Schulze, cleared his throat, then pointing a straight, accusing finger at the Party men he bellowed: "The Lao Dong say that Ho Chi Minh is bringing freedom and a better life for you people, but it is a big lie! They are Communists, though they do not like to use the word for so many people around the world hate them; they talk of freedom, but they want it no more than you want cholera. When the Viet Minh comes to a village, the big leaders speak to the poor people, for it is only the poor people they can cheat. They point to the land of a rich owner and tell you: Kill the owner and you may have his land. In the big city they tell the poor people: Kill the owner of this large store and you may take the food from his shop without paying for it. But even children know that one cannot have food without paying for it. It was so ever since man was born on earth. They point to the house of a wealthy man and say: Kill the rich man and his house will be yours. But the house will not be yours. It will belong to the Lao Dong secretaries, to the commissars, or to some other big Viet Minh leaders; you just do the killing for them. We know that here, too, you killed the rich landowner and took his land. The Viet Minh lets you have the land for a short time, because the Viet Minh needs food. Without your help they cannot fight the French. But should the French leave your country, your lands will be taken away from you and you will have to work in a colchos." He paused for a moment waiting for Xuey to catch up, then went on. "Do you know what a colchos is? It is the Communist way of sowing and harvesting, a big piece of land where every villager is obliged to work. But the land does not belong to them and what they harvest will not belong to them either. If the Lao Dong party wins, the Communists will tell you what you must do and nothing will be yours – not even your huts."

As Xuey interpreted for Bernard, I noticed breathless interest in the eyes of our audience. I began to hope that we were getting somewhere.

"They say," Bernard went on, "that if the Viet Minh wins the war, you will no longer have to obey the orders of the French colonialists, or the rich landowners. That is *not* a lie. If Ho Chi Minh wins the war, you will have to obey the orders of the Lao Dong party, the Viet Minh commissars and commanders. When you disobey the orders of a French colonialist, or an order of your landlord, you are beaten or put into a jail. But afterwards you are free to go to Saigon or to Hanoi to seek justice from the Big Police, or from the Big Tribunal Judge. And if you were innocent when punished, the rich landlord is going to be punished even though he is a Frenchman. But you all know what happens to people who disobey the orders of the Viet Minh. They are shot down like dogs and cannot seek justice anywhere anymore. The Communists don't like complaints. They prefer cheers and clapping. And if they find out later that you were shot innocently, Ho Chi Minh will give you a big red medal, but *that* won't bring you back to life."

He paused for a while, then concluded his speech, at least for the time being. "They tell you that Father Ho and Comrade Mao are bringing you a better life. What the commissars are not telling you is that last year three million of your Chinese brothers died because they did not have anything to eat. The Russians are sending the Chinese people food, but Stalin is buying food from the big colonialist countries because his own people have nothing to eat either."

Eisner gestured to Schulze to continue and dropped down between Riedl and me, grunting: "I don't say it was perfect but what else could these halfwits understand?"

Commissar Kwang lifted his hand, indicating that he wanted to speak. Erich allowed him to proceed.

"There is always something to learn." Kwang said mildly, speaking to the people. "The colonialist officer said that everything written by comrades Stalin, Mao Tse-tung, or Ho Chi Minh is a lie. But then we should also believe that the Soviet Union does not exist, that Comrade Mao did not liberate China, and the Viet Minh is nothing but a dream."

"It's not a dream but a bloody nightmare," Karl growled, as Kwang went on.

"The Great Proletarian Revolution has already liberated the oppressed people in one third of the world, yet the colonialist officer is saying it is a lie."

"Let us talk about one thing at a time, the Soviet Union, for instance," Schulze suggested. "Otherwise these good people here might become confused, Commissar Kwang. I know that you prefer to talk in a confusing manner – that is an important component of the brainwashing tactic. Have you ever been in the Soviet Union, Commissar Kwang?"

"Yes!" Kwang hissed. "I have been there and I *saw* what the great revolution has done for the people."

"What people?" Schulze asked bluntly.

"For the poor people, of course," said Kwang. "We are not interested in the welfare of the rich."

"What happened to the rich people in Russia?"

"Their wealth was taken from them and they were made to work for a living," propagandist Kly interposed. Kwang nodded in assent.

"Like hell!" Schulze erupted. "Their lives were taken from them and the few survivors were sent to work, not for a living, but in labor camps without pay. Stalin murdered ten million people, if that is what you call great revolution, *Tovarich* Kly."

"Who needs rich parasites?" Kly shrugged. "The people don't need them."

"Propagandist Kly . . . the Viet Minh are murdering every rich person in *this* country. I hope you don't want to say that in Russia it has not been so."

"I've already said that we don't need rich people."

"At least you admit that Communism thrives on murder!" Schulze snapped. "But even primitive people know that nothing can be achieved by murder and robbery – what the Viet Minh is doing."

"The Viet Minh is not the Communist party," Kwang remarked with a smile. "The Viet Minh is the striking fist of all the patriots who want freedom and independence."

"Who are the leaders of the Viet Minh?" Erich asked sharply. "Who are the commanders, the commissars, the propagandists? Are *you* not a Communist, Kwang?"

"It is only natural that the most experienced revolutionaries should lead a national liberation movement."

"Call it by its name, *Tovarich* Kwang. Don't say revolutionary when you want to say Communist. We know that you are trying hard to hoodwink the world by calling your Communist Party the People's Party, Revolutionary Party, Workers Party, and the devil knows what else. Why do you need a disguise? Honest people don't need to hide."

"One day the colonialists will be expelled. Then the people may choose freely what society they wish to build for themselves."

"*Merde!*" Schulze exclaimed. "Can you name one liberated country where the Communists have not seized all power over life and death and have not exterminated all the opposition?"

"Drop the high-flown polemics, Erich!" Eisner warned. "You aren't talking to a panel of professors." He rose and spoke to the villagers. "Commissar Kwang, who is from China, is talking to you about the Soviet Union, trying to explain to the people here what is good for them. The colonialist officer here," he pointed at Schulze, "is trying to tell you that whatever Kwang may say, when the Communist party wins power, the Communists kill everybody who disobeys their orders or desires something else. As you can see, neither Kwang nor Kly has anything to say against it, so it must be true."

"That is what you say and what your newspapers write," Kwang said sarcastically. "But we are your prisoners and in no position to argue with you."

"Is anyone holding a knife at your throat, Commissar Kwang?" Karl cut in. "Are you being beaten or tortured? If not, then speak up, *tovarich* first class. Convince us that your cause is a just cause. We might discard our weapons right here and join the Lao Dong."

"This is Erich's party, Karl. Let him enjoy it," Riedl remarked.

"Tell us just one thing your great revolution has so far achieved, apart from drowning the people in their own blood," Schulze continued. "Has your Ho Chi Minh improved the lives of the proletariat in this country? Have these people in this village, Kwang, received anything from your movement? Have you dug a well? An irrigation canal? Have you built as much as a public school? No, *Tovarich* Commissar. You have only destroyed those which were here before."

"We have no time to bring about social changes or to build anything. We are obliged to fight. When peace comes, we will start building. But if you want to see what Communism can build, you should go to the Soviet Union and see it there."

Schulze waved an arm to the crowd. "These people here have no money to visit the Soviet Union and enjoy the benefits of Communism *there*. They want to enjoy life *here*!" And as Xuey translated his words, soft laughter echoed from the crowd for the first time; only quiet laughter but it was laughter and I knew that Erich had scored a small point.

"The people here will enjoy life after the liberation," Kwang blurted, now somewhat agitated.

"Liberation," Schulze sneered. "How many countries has Stalin liberated lately? The British colonialists have just liberated India, as you probably know, you zealous deliverers of slaves. Why don't you go and ask the American workers if they would like to be liberated by Stalin? Afterwards you may also ask the Russian workers if they would want to be slaves in America? I fancy the outcome of your inquiry."

"The Russian workers would spit in your face if you insulted them by asking such a filthy imperialist provocation," Kly hissed before Kwang could answer.

"Sure!" Schulze chuckled. "That is exactly what they would do if you ask them on the Red Square, facing the Kremlin. You should take them to West Berlin and ask them there."

My troops were roaring with laughter that now engulfed most of the spectators, including ourselves. The "dialogue" was gradually turning into a "hand-to-hand" combat between Erich and the agitators, but Schulze was holding his own quite actively. "I was in Russia, too, Commissar Kwang," Erich said quietly. "I went there as an enemy, but the people greeted me as these people here would greet Lord Buddha if he came walking down the road." He rose abruptly and faced the villagers with his eyes ablaze. "The agitators are telling you many beautiful lies about the Soviet Union, about China and about Communism. Now let me tell you what the Communists are truly doing in Russia. First they killed all the rich people and seized their property. When there were no more rich people to be robbed and murdered, or to be put into slave camps, Stalin began to exterminate the class enemies; they were not rich people but writers, doctors, engineers, schoolteachers – learned people. If they had property and money, they had worked for it for many years. But everyone who dared to disagree with Stalin was killed or put into prisons. When there were no more class enemies either, Stalin turned upon his own comrades, all old Communists. He killed his own army officers by the thousands. They condemn capitalism but the capitalists have never massacred anyone. Now they say that the capitalist owner of a shoe factory, for instance – let us call him, Ivan Ivanovich – produced only five hundred pairs of shoes every week; the Communist factory makes five thousand. But the shoes which Ivan Ivanovich made were *good* shoes and the worker could wear them for two years. Ivan Ivanovich had to make good shoes, otherwise the people wouldn't buy them and he would go bankrupt. The state-owned factory has no such problems. If your Communist shoes crack open in four weeks, you should not even complain, for if you do, you accuse the State, the Communist Party, and so you are not a loyal citizen but an enemy agent. The Communists won't give you another pair of shoes but a pair of bullets in your head.

"Now the Communists are promising you everything just to help them win the war. When the war is over, says the commissar, they will start building for you. Building maybe, but not schools and hospitals; they will build army barracks and jails. They might build factories too, but to make tanks not tractors. The hoe or the shovel they give you will break in a week. Only the weapons of the Red army will last. The Communists have always been good weapon makers, for the bayonet is the only foundation the Party can stand on. Without bayonets and machine guns neither Stalin nor Mao Tse-tung would survive for a year. If you think that you are being oppressed by the French colonialists, just wait until Ho Chi Minh becomes your master. You will find a policeman behind every hut in your village; brother will betray brother and the son will sell his father."

Kwang was no longer smiling. He sat on the bench, chewing his underlip nervously. The villagers listened in utter silence; their faces betrayed no emotion – only alertness. Some of the elder men were listening so intently that their mouths hung open and their eyes appeared transfixed on Schulze. I was not sure if all that Erich said had reached the people, and if so, how deeply his words had penetrated into their simple minds. I was sure of only one thing, that never before had they witnessed someone challenging the Viet Minh platform openly, in front of people. They had never heard someone denouncing the holiest of the Communist prophets and everything they stood for. No one could ever call a Viet Minh leader a liar and live to tell his story. Besides, no French officer in Indochina had ever bothered to talk to *les sauvages* on equal terms, and certainly not about political or economic issues. The Communists were always permitted to rake in the benefits of their uncontested propaganda.

Schulze challenged the commissar to take his place, if he had anything to say. "I have many things to say," replied Kwang, "provided that you will permit me to speak without interrupting every second sentence." He cleared his throat and stepped forward, and when Sergeant Krebitz offered him a cup of fresh water, Kwang accepted it with a slight bow, drank slowly, as though he was weighing his coming words before speaking them; then he returned the cup and spoke.

"The colonialist officers are entertaining themselves with their own bourgeois propaganda, thinking that the Vietnamese people are deaf and blind, and cannot see beyond their hollow words, which contain much hatred, but not a spark of truth. This young man here," he pointed to Schulze, "who very likely came from a wealthy family and has never known poverty, is a member of the army which burns your villages and murders your brothers and sisters. He was probably tired of killing, at least for a few hours, so he conceived this mock trial of Communism, which he calls a free discussion. He may be thirty years old, yet nevertheless he tries to prove to us that he knows more than Lenin, Stalin, Comrade Mao, and Father Ho ever managed to learn. He has been in this country for only a few years, but he wants to guide your village elders; he wants to prove that Father Ho speaks empty words. He tries to ridicule the Soviet people whom we may thank for the greatest gift of mankind – our freedom from slavery. There are some facts which the colonialist officer seems to ignore. The Soviet people *have* achieved many things which are very difficult to dismiss with a barrage of empty words and wicked lies. He also tries to blame our Comrade Mao for not having built more in two years than the rich capitalist nations built in centuries. In twenty years time the Russian people had built a wonderful new nation but then the capitalists, the country of this officer here, Germany, invaded the Soviet Union and destroyed everything the people had built."

Kwang spoke slowly and with dignity, carefully selecting his words. Schulze did not interrupt him. Kwang spoke for a long time, about the new towns and villages, about the schools, hospitals, roads, and industries which the Russians had built, and which the Chinese people were endeavoring to build now. He spoke of the "largest" power-generating system in the world, the Volga-Don canal, that was to bring electricity to the remotest villages. Obviously he could not recall many glorious deeds from Mao's China for he kept repeating that Russia did this and Russia did that, citing only Soviet examples. He spoke for the better part of an hour and I felt terribly bored. Then mercifully he concluded his polemic with the eloquent slogan: "The Soviet people, with Comrade Stalin to lead them, have accomplished the impossible."

"It is true that Stalin accomplished the impossible," Schulze picked up where Kwang had left off. "Stalin moves mountains and builds an artificial sea as big as your country, the commissar said. But he forgot to mention that Stalin has six million slaves to work for him without pay. When Stalin needs a hundred thousand more workmen, he just gives the word to the Secret Police to increase the weekly output – or should we say input – and soon the enemies of the people are picking up the shovels. When Stalin tells the Russian worker: Ivan, from now on you will work twelve hours every day, Ivan *will* work twelve hours every day. If Stalin said the same thing to a worker in *my* country, or in any free country, he would be given a shovel and told, 'do it yourself, Joseph.'"

Another wave of laughter followed the translation. Schulze waited patiently for a while, then went on. "This is how Stalin is building the Soviet paradise and this is how Mao Tse-tung is going to build his own empire. The rich people, the exploiters, the slave drivers will no longer be called landlords, mandarins, moneylenders; they will be called party secretaries, commissars, district propagandists, and militiamen. But you people will be toiling harder than you are toiling now."

He turned and walked up to the two propagandists. "When we began to talk, Commissar Kwang said that we were going to shoot him at the end. You should not believe us, he said. I am saying now that you are free to believe whatever you want and we are not going to shoot these Communist liars either. They aren't worth the cost of the bullets."

He grabbed the prisoners by their arms and led them through the ring of people who silently moved aside. Reaching the road he gave them a gentle slap on the back and shoved them forward.

"Go, Commissar Kwang and Propagandist Kly. Fool more people – for the more people you fool, the sooner will the people see you for what you are: cheats, arrogant liars, remorseless killers . . . traitors to your own country, traitors to mankind. You are as guilty as sin but we are doing something you would never do to innocent people – we let you go. You are free men. Go!"

We departed shortly before sundown. What impression we left behind we never learned. But if we left an impression, I felt it was not an adverse one.

Two months later the Viet Minh executed thirty people in that village.

"The poor devils," Pfirstenhammer remarked, when we received the news of the massacre. "They must have remembered some of Erich's arguments and dared to repeat them openly."

13

Those Innocent Noncombatants

A group of villagers, some of them women, working in the paddies – a familiar spectacle as peaceful as it is picturesque. . . . A painter of rural scenery would be overjoyed at the eyecatching sequence: the white-clad figures in the knee-deep, shimmering pond; the sun rising above the green jungle background; a pair of water buffalo squatting in the mire, only their horns and noses visible; a low wooden hut roofed with palm fronds and erected on piles to provide the workers with a shelter against a sudden downpour. It was a spectacle that we beheld almost daily during our dreary years in Indochina; a spectacle very tranquil – outwardly so – and ready to lull the inexperienced soldier into a false belief of security.

It happened once at the beginning of our service that a similar group of unaggressive villagers had greeted our reconnaissance patrol in the most cordial manner and offered the troops fruits, cane sugar, and cooked rice with curried fish in exchange for salt and tobacco. After some friendly bargaining a deal was struck and the platoon invited to share a modest meal with the natives in their village. The platoon leader sergeant (a veteran of the Russian campaign but still a greenhorn in Indochina) gladly obliged.

Twenty-two cheerful troopers entered the village – a skilfully camouflaged Viet Minh stronghold. Only six of them escaped the trap. The rest of the platoon had to stay behind, no longer as guests but as bullet-ridden corpses, among them the trusting sergeant.

It happened to us once. Once!

Afterwards, whenever we encountered a single peasant in a rural trail, we always considered him a potential Viet Minh observer. The alternative that he might be a genuine noncombatant came afterwards. We would check such an individual and if nothing incriminating was found on or about his person he would be allowed to proceed – with a couple of our marksmen trailing him secretly for at least a mile.

Sometimes the traveler would continue on his way as leisurely as before; sometimes the man would hurry up the moment he thought he was safely out of sight and rifle range – most likely to notify the nearest guerrilla cell. Speed meant urgency and for urgency we had but one interpretation: The Viet Minh must be informed of our presence in the neighborhood. If a man speeded up after our checking, then he would die.

When we emerged from the woods the peasants showed no concern. They only glanced up, then went on with their work; their conical straw hats concealed whatever emotion their faces might have shown. No one could tell if they were friendly, neutral, or hostile, but we were not interested in their political sentiments – only in such material possessions as illegal firearms. We learned long ago not to bestow too much confidence on the natives. Boys of sixteen, sixty-year-old matrons, Buddhist monks, or French-nominated administrative officials we regarded with equal skepticism.

Now I found nothing extraordinary about those villagers except the fact that all the men were in their prime. We would always pay particular attention to young men laboring in the fields in what was strictly Viet Minh-controlled territory, where most young men had been recruited by the guerrillas either as full-time or chance "freedom fighters" – depending on how hard-pressed the Viet Minh was for manpower in a particular area.

Remaining out of sight, my troops deployed near the paddies

to keep every individual covered by a dozen guns. It may seem excessive that heavily armed troops should bother with elaborate defensive measures while facing but a few unarmed peasants. But to those who are familiar with the implications of guerrilla warfare no precaution appears superfluous. It often happened that a group of "innocent noncombatants" had turned into well-armed terrorists the moment the troops slackened their vigilance.

Numerical inferiority would deter the fanatical terrorists no more than the thought of certain death would deter the Japanese *kamikaze*. Properly indoctrinated Communists (and especially the primitive, illiterate ones) will do what the Party says. We found that the most wicked and dangerous guerrillas were the so-called "peasant-cum-guerrillas", including women and children from ten years up. We had had scores of engagements with such naïve, untrained, and inexperienced "noncombatants", who would always win, even when licked and exterminated to the last man. When the Viet Minh was unable to claim any success by the force of arms, the commissars always secured at least a political victory. Their formula was a simple one. Had their peasant-cum-guerrillas managed to rout a French garrison, the Communist victory was widely publicized. But when the Legion squashed them somewhere, the fallen terrorists were stripped of military equipment, their corpses were rearranged (often with arms and legs bound with ropes), then photographed and displayed to friend and foe alike as the "innocent victims of a French massacre".

To increase the dramatic effect of such "colonialist carnages" the corpses of women and children who had died of diseases or natural causes would sometimes be put on display alongside the bodies of the dead guerrillas. We found evidence that the Viet Minh had exposed over two hundred corpses in a village that had been demolished by the Air Force. That particular "French monstrosity" had been widely publicized. In reality, for several days preceding the raid the village had been devoid of human presence, and all the bombers wrecked were the empty huts. The "innocent victims" had in fact been the victims of a typhus epidemic that decimated the population weeks before the air raid. Blinded by hatred and devoid of all human sentiment, the local Viet Minh commissar had ordered his men to exhume the corpses, sprinkle them with cattle blood, blow some of them to bits with grenades, dump them all over the devastated village, then credit two hundred "innocent victims" to the French. And since there had indeed been an officially recorded attack on the village (the close results of which could not be established) the reconnaissance and fighter-bomber crews were severely reprimanded, demoted, or relocated because of their "senseless slaughter of civilians."

A few months after that infamy, Bernard Eisner and Pfirstenhammer captured the commissar responsible, who, after some tender persuasion, told us the true story and even signed a written statement. Needless to say, our evidence was never given any publicity and thus could not exonerate the condemned airmen. In our days only the French "crimes" received blaring headlines. The Viet Minh atrocities (far more numerous and excessive) were given a few back-page lines once in a while. But history repeats itself. Nowadays the American GI enjoys a similar treatment. The Communists cannot lose.

Erich Schulze, Sergeant Krebitz and I removed our boots and waded into the stagnant water, taking only *Gruppe Drei*. We may have caused the peasants a few sinister thoughts but we certainly delighted the local leeches which could suck a man dry as well as strangle him to death, according to Erich. The people now stopped working; they rose and observed our approach for a while, then began to press closer together.

"*Chieu hoi.*"

Some of them returned our greeting. Others stood in sullen silence, the women a good ten yards behind the men. A good-looking lean fellow in his early thirties stepped forward, ran his tongue over his betel-stained lips, then spoke. "My name is Van Ho Tien and I can speak French," he announced casually. "My companions know no French." He paused for a moment, then added with a tinge of mockery in his voice, "What do you wish to know, Officer?"

"I haven't asked you any question, have I?" I answered jokingly and offered him a cigarette, which he accepted with a slight bow.

"Oh, the army always wants to know something," he said.

"Maybe you want to know if we've seen the Viet Minh lately, but we have not seen them for many weeks."

"And that's the standard answer number one around here, isn't it?" Erich cut in with a broad grin on his face. "We saw nothing we heard nothing, we know nothing. You must be quite happy, they say God provides for the ignorant ones. Now come, come, Monsieur Van Ho Tien, when was the last time the Viet Minh visited your village?"

"We are very few people and our village is unimportant to the Viet Minh."

"Lucky for you," commented Erich. "Where is your village anyway?"

Van Ho waved a casual hand toward the low hills a few miles distant. "There beyond, two hours' walk from here, officer." Then he quickly added, "But we have no road." This sudden addition of his sounded so funny that we all broke into laughter.

"How are you coming and going then," Schulze chuckled, "thumbing rides on army copters?"

"Oh, I didn't mean that," said Van Ho, "we have a few narrow trails."

"Very precipitous and slippery at places, I presume," Riedl interposed. "Maybe even mined here and there?"

"No!" Van Ho protested, taking Riedl's teasing remark in earnest. "We have no mines, no weapons – nothing we have." He appeared to dislike the direction our conversation had taken. "Our village is very tiny, very filthy, and very poor with many sick people in it. There is nothing to see." We laughed again and Van Ho's face reddened as he realized the childish quality of his remark.

"Don't worry, Monsieur Van Ho Tien," Erich tapped him lightly on the shoulder. "We don't want to visit your village. It seems to be out of our way."

I checked the location of Van Ho's village on Schulze's map, a very special one, which due to his meticulous recording of various significant landmarks revealed a great deal more information than the regular army maps. The village was marked on it all right, with the numbers 12/15 indicating the number of dwellings. But placed alongside the numbers a tiny red star caught my attention and I asked Erich about it.

"I recorded the village from air reconnaissance of the area," he explained. "Here the star means that peculiar movements were observed in and about the hamlet which could be associated with guerrilla activities but not proven."

"I see. . . ."

I wheeled back toward Van Ho and now asked him bluntly, "Are there any Viet Minh cadres in your village?"

"Our village is very small," he repeated after what I thought was a slight hesitation. "Only fourteen dwellings with forty men. The Viet Minh knows that we could be of little help to them and they leave us alone. We hope the French, too, will leave us alone."

"And we hope we can oblige," Schulze retorted. "Believe me, the last thing on earth we care to see is a local village."

Van Ho smiled. "We know that our villages are much too backward for you to enjoy. You live in big cities like Paris, Marseilles, or Lyon."

"Or Berlin," commented Riedl.

Van Ho seemed surprised. "Berlin is in Germany, so I have learned," he blurted out.

"You learned it where?" Erich asked.

I thought it was a most extraordinary encounter – a local rice-picker in the middle of nowhere knowing about Berlin. So after all the natives were not so *sauvage* as the French insisted they were.

"When I was a child I attended the missionary school at Yen Bay," Van Ho explained. "The missionaries taught us many wisdoms, including geography." He paused for a second, then asked with some restraint, "Are you the Germans of the Foreign Legion?" His barely perceptible hesitation before saying "Germans" brought another grin to Erich's face.

"I bet he wanted to say 'Nazis'," he remarked in German and I saw that Van Ho looked up sharply when he heard that word. It must have been familiar with him. "*Bien sûr*," Schulze answered. "We *are* the Germans, the Nazi wolves, the man-eaters, the angels of death, the unceasing fighters."

"I haven't said that you are wolves and man-eaters," the man protested, showing fright for the first time.

"Why not? That's what we are," Schulze teased him. "Have they not told you so?"

"Who should have told us?"

"The commissars."

"We are not guerrillas," Van Ho protested vehemently.

"I have not said you were."

There was a pause and a sense of restlessness in the group "May I ask you something?" Van Ho spoke finally.

"Go ahead," I said.

"Why are you fighting?" he asked.

"Your people won't let us retire," Krebitz told him with a chuckle.

"It is your own choosing, for this is not your war," Van Ho insisted.

"Correct," Schulze agreed. "This is not our war. It is everyone's war – France's, England's, America's, and maybe even Sweden's, or Japan's, but they have yet to realize it."

Van Ho shook his head. "I do not understand your mentality. Truly I do not."

"We are complicated people," said Krebitz. "No one seems to understand our problems."

"Maybe you are very warlike," nodded Van Ho. "The SS –" He cut off as soon as that word slipped out.

"That's right!" Erich roared. "SS tradition, *mon ami*, sheer SS tradition. By the way *where* did you learn about the SS, Monsieur Van Ho Tien, also in the missionary school?"

"I read some books about the war."

"What did you read about the SS?"

"They were much feared during the war."

"You are being very polite," Schulze chuckled. "You ought to have read a lot more about the SS than that." Then shouldering his submachine gun he added, "You are a clever man, Monsieur Van Ho Tien. I think you deserve a better job than picking rice – or," he concluded, stressing his words, "maybe you do have a better job and work in the paddies only part time." He strolled over to the pile-supported shelter, lifted some bags casually, examined a few nearby baskets, then turned. "What do you think of the Viet Minh, Monsieur Van Ho?"

"I feel neither love nor hatred for them. We live far away from the war and we are happy that it is so."

"It cannot be as idyllic as that. Your village is in the center of a very important Viet Minh-dominated province, isn't that so?"

I realized that Erich was playing hide-and-seek with the man and began to wonder what might have awakened his suspicion.

"How about your feelings for the French colonialists?" Schulze pressed on.

"Do you want me to be frank with you, officer?" Van Ho asked with a sour smile.

"*Naturellement*," Erich nodded. "We can take any amount of truth, however painful, and no one will start shooting."

"We have lived here for centuries. The French came to our country only recently. We regard them as passing visitors who will depart one day like the Japanese departed."

"But how about us Germans?" Schulze persisted.

"We think you are capable of only one human feeling, officer, and that is hatred," Van Ho exhaled with defiance.

"Well, aren't we being complimented?" Krebitz remarked. "What do you think we should learn in this bloody country? Love for our treacherous, slimy, poison-spitting, lying fellow human beings?"

"Who told you that we can only hate?" Schulze went on, ignoring Rudolf's outburst.

"The books," Van Ho stated.

"Printed in Moscow? Or in Peking?"

"No, officer," Van Ho shook his head. "I can read neither Russian nor Chinese – only French. And the books which I read about you were all printed in France . . . the country you are fighting for. They call you murderous wolves yet you are serving them. Why?"

"They pay well," Riedl cut in.

"Are you fighting only for money?" Van Ho wondered. "Even the Viet Minh has more money than the French."

"*Bien sûr*," said Erich. "We know that lately Giap has a pile of American dollars to get rid of. Maybe you can arrange a better deal for us with the Viet Minh."

"You will have to find the Viet Minh yourselves," the man evaded Erich's flimsy trap.

"Monsieur Van Ho," Schulze said with quiet persuasion, "your village must have been visited by some Viet Minh commissars."

"There is no village which the commissars have not visited, officer. They go everywhere. Some people listen to them, others won't."

"I am willing to grant you that, but as far as your former remark goes, we do not hate your people. We hate only the Communists – and with good reason."

"Our people are not Communists," Van Ho exclaimed. "The majority of them do not even know what the word stands for."

"It is something you should tell to Ho Chi Minh. *He* does not seem to be aware of it." Erich turned his face toward me and added in German, "Hans, if this one here isn't a political commissar himself, I'll eat my gun – barrel, stock, ammo, and all. The crop in their baskets is dry. They haven't cut it today." Erich was always a keen observer.

Van Ho spoke. "May we return to our work?" he said, obviously disturbed by our low-keyed conversation. Erich slowly turned toward him and asked, "Would you mind if we look around a bit before you leave?"

"No, we won't mind. You will do that anyway. Whenever the army comes by our place we are submitted to searches and other indignities." He raised his arms to accommodate my troopers, who frisked him expertly. There was visible consternation among the women. "Are you going to search them, too?" Van Ho asked with barely concealed hostility.

"Don't worry," Schulze said reassuringly, "no one is going to paw them. We have a couple of female assistants."

He was about to send a trooper to fetch Suoi and the nurses when Krebitz stopped him. "Hell, why should they tromp all over the ponds, Erich? We should send the wenches to the road."

"You're right," Erich nodded. "That's what we should do."

The peasants carried nothing suspicious, nothing forbidden. We combed through the area; examined the shelter, the bags, the baskets, the underpart of the platform, the roof – nothing incriminating was discovered.

"What do you think of them?" I asked Xuey, who had kept silent during our entire dialogue with Van Ho Tien, but was listening with eager interest in his narrow, dark eyes.

"They belong to the local Viet Minh cell and they do have

weapons," Xuey stated with firm conviction. "No people of their age would be picking rice – not in this province."

"That's what I figured, Xuey."

"We can't plug them on that evidence," Krebitz commented.

"I guess we can't."

"You may return to your work." I dismissed Van Ho and his companions. "And keep out of the war."

"The French must be very frightened in our country," he said, now vastly relieved.

"Maybe they are," Riedl replied, shouldering his gun. "*We* aren't."

"You should return home. Our people could take care of themselves."

"Once we are gone your people won't have to bother. The Viet Minh will take care of everything," Krebitz said.

"Why should that bother you, sergeant?"

Rudolf shot a sharp glance at Van Ho. "What bothers me is that you seem to know my badges well enough but you keep addressing the others only as 'officer'. I wonder why is that so?"

Van Ho declined to offer an explanation, and I decided it was time to proceed.

"Sergeant Krebitz!" I called. "We are moving out." I winked at him and he winked back. "Assemble!"

The villagers watched us leave, then they slowly dispersed and began to work as if nothing had happened. Our trial number one ended. Now came test number two.

Balancing on the slippery logs that bridged the irrigation canals, we returned to the dirt road and marched off skirting the paddies. At a quiet command of Krebitz our sharpshooters dropped into the roadside shrubs; from the moisture-proof holsters emerged their precious rifles with their telescopic sights, silencers, and hair-trigger mechanism. The battalion moved on. Soon there was a good four hundred yards between us and the workers and my men began to wonder. Maybe we were wrong about the villagers. Even Xuey could err.

Distance five hundred yards. Our advance guard was entering the woods.

"*À terre!*" someone yelled. "Take cover!" From the paddies came the vicious clatter of a heavy machine gun. Yet the moment we took cover the shooting abruptly stopped. Focusing my field glasses I spotted half a dozen shapes scurrying across the ponds. Three of them staggered and fell, then a fourth one spun about and dropped out of sight. Our marksmen were still at work. The last of the fugitives collapsed only a few steps from the forest sanctuary on the far side of the paddies.

Near the low platform which we had so carefully examined now stood a small boat with a mounted machine gun; two corpses sprawled on the platform and two more hung from the boat with head and shoulders submerged in the murky water.

We backtracked on the road to meet our *Abwehrkommando* and by the time we arrived the men had already cleaned their weapons; the sensitive scopes were capped and the muzzles plugged with small rubber corks taken from empty medicine vials. When they saw me coming they rose but I motioned them back.

"You made short of work of them," I commented with a gesture toward the paddies.

"Child's play," Corporal Walther replied, and the men acknowledged my appreciation with a smile. "There is nothing about Germans and silencers in Mao's library on guerrilla warfare, so what could the poor devils do?"

"Carry on!"

They sat back to enjoy their cigarettes; a peculiar bunch of men, as cool and indifferent as they were unerring. Their sole task being the killing, they were utterly disinterested in the gory details and would seldom bother to pay a second glance at their victims. The postmortem undertakings were left for Sergeant Krebitz and his *Gruppe Drei.*

Into the paddies again. The guerrillas lay where they had fallen. Now every one of them was armed with rifles and Mitras, including the women. A number of yellow watertight bags floating around the platform explained where the weapons had come from. They had been kept submerged in the bottom mire until the enemy thought the time was ripe for a sneak attack.

"Poor all-too-clever Monsieur Van Ho Tien," Erich commented over the corpse of the little Indochinese. "You had known so much yet you knew so little." He turned toward me and added, "He could have been of great service to his country – somewhere else."

I examined the corpses; head, face, and neck wounds and no misses. The machine gun, a Soviet Goriunov, was a clumsy weapon but accurate up to a thousand yards. It had fired only fifteen rounds before its crew died, and to appreciate the skill of our experts one should remember that to fire fifteen rounds had consumed only 1.4 seconds.

How could the enemy produce the Goriunov (weighing nearly seventy pounds) while under constant surveillance remained an enigma. "We saw some brisk comings and goings with baskets and sacks between the shelter and the woods," Corporal Walther explained to me later on. "Then came the boat seemingly laden with empty baskets. All of a sudden there was the gun spitting fire and we blazed away."

One of the machine gun crew was a young woman, the wife of a gunner. Later we learned that they left behind two children, now orphans, because of a senseless raid that was doomed from the very beginning. One needs more than a European mind to understand the Oriental mentality.

Sergeant Krebitz quickly dismantled the machine gun and scattered its parts all over the paddies. The ammunition we trampled into the bottom mud.

Forward!

Three hours later we arrived at Van Ho's village. Its dwellings were vacant, the road and the yards deserted; the hamlet gave every sign of a hurried evacuation. We searched the huts and the hillside and discovered a complex tunnel system still under construction. The slopes of the hill contained a labyrinth of dug-in positions for mortars and machine guns which were connected by caves and tunnels to provide living quarters and storage space for weapons, food, and ammunition. There were several levels of tunnels, many of them with multiple exits, and some suitable for smaller field artillery pieces. The fortification complex was to be a major Viet Minh storage and training center.

The muddy trail revealed many footprints of men and beasts heading for the hills. In front of one hut a trooper discovered Chinese cartridges trampled into the mud. From one of the cellars came a broken mortar. I ordered the tunnels blasted and the huts demolished, which job Sergeant Krebitz accomplished in three hours. Then leaving behind *Gruppe Drei* to set a trap, we moved on in full view for the benefit of all guerrilla spies who cared to look.

Soon after we left the population emerged from the woods and crowded in on the narrow trail; men, women, and children driving heavily laden carts, pushing wheelbarrows and bikes burdened with crates and sacks. *Gruppe Drei* rushed forward and captured the milling crowd before they could utter a cry. Krebitz's booty was a rich one – weapons and ammunition enough to sustain a Viet Minh company for at least a month of prolonged fighting.

Acting on my orders, Sergeant Krebitz spared only women, children, and old people. The entire male population consisting of about fifty men was executed. The destruction of enemy manpower had always been our principal aim in Indochina, and we had no alternative. The Viet Minh could always excavate new tunnels, could always obtain new weapons and ammunition from across the frontier, but not even Ho Chi Minh could manufacture trained guerrillas.

With guns blazing our troops marched up and down the trail shooting up bullocks, pigs, hens, weapons, and other guerrilla hardware until destruction was complete. Another lesson of war told in the language of the Viet Minh.

Whizzz . . . whammmm. . . . A cry of agony; a trooper staggers, his hands grasping a tree for support; then he folds up and lies moaning in the grass. From his abdomen projects the shaft of a three-foot arrow spilling blood and partly digested food onto his clutching hands and tunic. The troops scatter to take shelter. There is not much they can do but squat low and scan the sinister jungle. Bows make no report. There is no telltale smoke or muzzle flash to draw one's attention. But we know that the sniper is not very far away. One cannot shoot far in the jungle.

My men execute the only protective measure available to them; canteens, map cases, and ammo bags come up in front to protect their chests; rifles and submachine guns are held high so that their stocks may deflect projectiles coming for their throats. The bulky rucksacks offer ample protection against a shot in the back. Those who are sheltering behind trees hold their rucksacks in front of their abdomens, and no one moves.

Ignoring the danger, Sergeant Zeisl creeps up to the wounded trooper.

Whizzz. . . .

Zeisl freezes and we look on petrified. The arrow crashes into the thorny thicket, ripping the leaves only a few yards from where Zeisl embraces mother earth. A merciful miss. Taking the chance that the sniper cannot let loose another arrow immediately, I spring forward with Schulze on my heels to cover ten yards in a flash, and drop beside Zeisl.

Whizzzzz . . . Whammmm. . . . The sniper is not alone.

Zeisl examines the wounded man and shakes his head grimly. "The point is probably poisoned," he whispers, "but even without the poison he cannot survive without immediate surgery." A few minutes later the life of our comrade shivers away.

Whammm. . . . Another projectile zooms in to find its mark; a careless trooper has lowered his rucksack to light a cigarette; the arrow plunges into his breast and he falls sideways thrashing in agony. It is a sequence out of the Middle Ages.

"I think one of them is over there," Schulze says pointing at a small elevation. Whizzz . . . whizzz . . . the arrows whine. Whammmm. . . .

One projectile plunges into the soft soil only three paces from where I shelter. The other comes to a quivering halt in Erich's rucksack. The invisible enemy is not joking and he is an excellent marksman. But he made a mistake – he missed! The arrows are coming in at sharp angles and we know where to look for the snipers. Instantly a dozen glasses scan the treetops; a solitary shot cracks, then a submachine gun opens up spraying the thicket. The leaves of a solitary tree rustle. The branches crackle and part; a frail brown body falls from above, tearing the boughs: the sniper – at least one of them. With a dull thud the body hits the ground, rolls over, and lies still, blood oozing from a bullet wound below his left eye. Of the submachine gun salvo we find no trace; the solitary hit came from the rifle of one of our sharpshooters.

A loincloth and a crude leather belt with a curved knife is all the sniper wears. His bow must have got caught in the branches. We look at the guerrilla – if he can be called a guerrilla – in astonishment; he is nothing but a caveman who dared to challenge the atomic age. Yet he managed to kill two of us.

Whizzz. . . .

We duck instinctively. The jungle begins to spit arrows. Another man dies with his throat torn agape. The bushes erupt. Rifles and submachine guns open up, raking the treetops, the hillside undergrowth; Sergeant Krebitz with *Gruppe Drei* withdraws to fan out on the flanks and envelop the small hill where the snipers hide. After an hour's siege five snipers are dead and a sixth one is captured by Riedl's troops. Sergeant Zeisl examines the seized arrows. "They are poisoned with buffalo dung," he comments, "cheap and effective but not for game hunting."

"You mean that they use dung only against men?"

"Exactly."

The captured tribesman is brought forward; an evil-looking young lad of maybe fifteen years of age with a heavily pockmarked face. When I ask him why he fights for the Communists he just stares at me. The word has no meaning for him. He does not know what the Viet Minh stands for. Who is Ho Chi Minh? Now his face erupts in a broad smile. Ho Chi Minh is the great tribal chief who says that all white-faced men should be killed. Why? Because they come to raze the tribal villages, to rape the women, and to bring loathsome diseases to them. White men, and especially white men in uniform, are evil, Ho says. They must be destroyed on sight.

The versatility of Communist propaganda is truly amazing. Without the slightest ideological effort they manage to coax these primitive warriors into *kamikaze* sorties against the Foreign Legion. Bows and arrows versus machine guns.

"Rape, of all things," Schulze fumes and I know what's on his mind. Deprived as they are my troops would sooner rape a female gibbon that some of those tribal wenches with their betel-stained gums and withered skin infected with tropical ulcers and festering insect bites.

With a stinging blow Krebitz sends the prisoner lurching forward. "On to your village, you scum of humanity," he roars. "You don't even know for whom you murder, you *Schweinhund.*" He digs his bayonet into the lad's ribs. "Make it straight there, or I will spill your filthy guts right here."

The prisoner takes us to his village, which we find hidden in a deep valley. It consists of about fifty huts erected on piles, together with a long house which the unmarried men occupy. Soon a search is under way to collect bows and arrows – only a symbolic gesture, for the tribesmen will have new ones made before the day is up. We assemble the people and tell them what their fellow tribesmen have done.

"We are not waging war on tribal people," I tell them and Xuey interprets for me. "We want to hurt none of you and we desire none of your women. We bring you no illness, for as you can see yourselves our skin is clean and healthy. It is your own skin which is riddled with sores. Ho Chi Minh is telling you lies. You have nothing we can use or want to take. We come here to bring you medicines so that you may become healthy again." I, too, allowed myself a small lie for the sake of better understanding. "But because you shot our men now you will suffer punishment."

The captured sniper is executed. This time I choose hanging him – a death more demonstrative than shooting or bayoneting. For the benefit of the sullen spectators Sergeant Krebitz makes sure that the sniper has a long trip. There is no drop arranged and the lad suffocates to death displaying all the usual struggle for almost a quarter of an hour. A cruel necessity.

The dwellings of the fallen ones are destroyed, along with all the food and livestock found therein. Although we have not eaten meat for some time I forbid my troops to seize as much as a hen. As a punishment for the community I also order the destruction of half their household livestock and the confiscation of all salt and tobacco. Bullocks, cows, poultry, and even four working elephants are herded outside the village to be slaughtered, but because of pity evoked by my childhood memories of visiting the zoo, I spare the elephants. They are taken away and turned loose in the jungle. The rest of the animals are destroyed and burned on three large bonfires.

The consternation is great. The lesson is harsh but it could have been worse. Were they not primitive. Stone-Age people I would order every other man shot instead of every other buffalo or cow.

"You keep out of the war and ignore Ho Chi Minh," I remind them before we leave, "and don't ever use poisoned arrows against our men unless you want us to return and kill every one of you. If you want to fight us, then fight like true warriors and not like venomous snakes. We can honor brave warriors but we squash poisonous snakes and destroy their nest."

Later on we traversed the same tribal area on several occasions unmolested by the natives. Primitive as they were the tribesmen understood our message. It was a plain one.

The Viet Minh "section" which we encountered upon entering a small locality near Lac An put up a vicious fight. The guerrillas were shooting from every hut and every ditch, including a narrow irrigation canal which passed through the settlement. We had no choice but to demolish the huts one after another, using flamethrowers, mortars, and grenades, causing heavy civilian casualties in the process.

There were many civilians in the village but only a few genuine noncombatants; even women and elder boys were armed and those who could not handle a gun helped the Viet Minh by snapping off haphazard, harassing shots in our direction, often causing chance casualties. Twelve-year-old boys and aged matrons assisted the terrorists by filling empty magazines for them. The result of this indiscriminate involvement of civilians by the Viet Minh was massacre. Before the battle began in earnest I had ordered my troops to spare women and children. Fifteen minutes and scores of casualties later I was compelled to reverse my previous stand and order them to shoot on sight everyone but children of tender age. Otherwise we would have perished.

Our flamethrowers went into action and soon the village was an inferno. The people who fled blinded and deafened into the open ran straight into a stream of bullets delivered and received on both sides. Fifteen yards from where I sheltered a little girl of about five ran screaming into a hail of tracers which severed her left leg below the knee. Our machine gunner had stopped firing the moment he sighted the child but shooting at the rate of six hundred slugs per minute the fraction of a second sufficed to release a dozen more bullets, which hit the child. Ignoring the firing, one of our medics, Corporal Dieter Lang, rushed to the whimpering child and tried to carry her to a safer place. The moment he started back he was hit by a volley which the guerrillas fired. Soldier and child died on the spot. The enemy was less than sixty yards from Lang with nothing to obstruct their view. They saw well what they were shooting at: an unarmed men with the Red Cross emblem plainly visible on his tunic who was rescuing a wounded child – one of theirs!

We spotted the hut from which the bullets had come. A corporal and half a dozen troops sallied forth to liquidate the strong point. Under cover of machine gun fire the corporal burst through the doorway, but where a moment before a dozen guns were firing the troopers found only an old woman who squatted in the corner cuddling a small boy. Wasting no time the corporal yanked her to her feet with a harsh, "Where are the Viet Minh, grandma?" He must have scared the matron for obediently she pointed at a narrow opening in the rear wall and replied in broken French: "There left Viet Minh." The men piled through the hole and found themselves in a small yard. From behind a pile of logs roared a number of guns; one trooper went down and the rest of the platoon dived for cover. Concentrating on the enemy no one paid any attention to "grandma", whose withered bony arm suddenly flipped through the dark opening to toss a hand grenade at the legionnaires. The expulsion demolished a part of her hut but "grandma" did not seem to mind that; she and her grandson survived unhurt; our comrades perished.

From the back of the yard a bunch of screaming guerrillas pounced on dead and wounded; rifle butts cracked skulls, knives ripped tunics and flesh, and soon the corpses were stripped of weapons and valuables. "Grandma" insisted on keeping a wristwatch, a ring, and twenty thousand piasters found in the pocket of the corporal, for – as she claimed aloud – it was she who had done the killing. The ghoulish apparitions were still bargaining over the corpses when I arrived and dispatched them with a salvo of anger and disgust that emptied the magazine of my submachine gun.

When six hours later the battle finally ended the village was a heap of blackened rubble with dead people and animals littering every yard of its expanse. We counted over one hundred Viet Minh and more than two hundred civilian casualties, among them fifty children. From tunnels and cellars my troops extracted over two tons of weapons and ammunition.

Two weeks after the event photographs of the ruined village with a pile of civilian corpses artfully displayed appeared in the Communist press under the headline: "Massacre of the Innocents." Corpses in the closeups and those in the foreground of the wideangle shots had had their arms and ankles bound to create the impression that they had been brutally murdered instead of killed in armed action. A solitary closeup displayed the body of "grenade-tossing grandma" with fifteen of my bullet holes marked on her corpse with superimposed arrows. The caption read: "Not even a sixty-two-year-old woman was spared."

Twenty miles from the town of Bac Kan we overran and captured a group of fifteen terrorists, every one of them armed with Chinese rifles and none of them older than sixteen. Moments before they were brave soldiers of Father Ho – now they are only whimpering kids, shaking with fear, hollow and shrunken in a ring of towering troopers. I questioned the young prisoners in detail and found them well indoctrinated and versed in ideological issues. They wanted to be "patriots"; fortunately they did not succeed in killing any of my men.

They all belonged to the same locality; kids toying with lethal weapons. I hated their guts but somehow they reminded me of our *Hitler Jugend*, the twelve-to-fifteen-year-old schoolboys sent off untrained with their bazookas to perish beneath the treads of the Pattons and T-34s in 1945. And because they did remind me of those German kids I decided to spare their lives and give them only the whacking of a lifetime, something their fathers ought to have done. But what else could a Communist father teach his offspring but how to degrade, deprive, hate, and exterminate everyone who dared to oppose the doctrines of Marx and Lenin.

We stripped the assassin-candidates and beat them until they could take no more, then we sent them home. They probably crawled most of the way but were still better off than they would have been bayoneted and dumped in the roadside bushes.

Having fired their rifles and wounded four of my men, the small group of "peasant-cum-guerrillas" quickly vanished from sight. They had probably resorted to one of the favorite guerrilla tricks: to submerge in the swamp and stay underwater breathing through hollow sections of cane until it was dark enough for them to withdraw into the woods.

Dusk was still a good hour away. I ordered my men to surround that section of swampland from where the attack had come. The enemy might breathe through canes but he cannot breathe fire and smoke. So we dumped two hundred gallons of diesel oil into the swamp, then set fire to it. Soon the cane thicket burned down to the water level and thick, oily smoke covered the surface. The first batch of snipers surfaced and tried to bolt for the shores, screaming in agony until they got hit or turned into human torches.

We dispatched thirty guerrillas in that action; half of them were women and young boys below the age of sixteen. Innocent noncombatants! Victims of the Foreign Legion!

Women, children, and elderly people were always innocent victims if counted as corpses lying in a devastated settlement. But what is the real position of the so-called noncombatants in an irregular war such as the one in Indochina?

In Communist-controlled areas there is no such thing as neutrals. Every civilian capable of using his or her arms and legs is compelled to assist the liberation movement, either during armed engagements or by transporting supplies or by doing construction work for the guerrillas. In Communist-oriented localities every civilian capable of holding a weapon assists the terrorists during combat, something quite logical for they are, after all, close relatives of active terrorists. Women and older children toss grenades or load mortars; old people help the fighters by loading empty magazines for them. When a sixty-year-old matron increases the fighting effectiveness of a guerrilla gunner by loading spare magazines for his submachine gun, she cannot really be considered a noncombatant.

Some data from my own experience in Indochina:

The majority of all booby traps set by the Viet Minh were manufactured and planted by noncombatants. Concealed weapons and bombs were transported by women, children, and elderly persons. Punji stakes, poisoned arrows, and spear guns were manufactured exclusively by noncombatants, often young children. Such weapons claimed over two thousand French lives during my service in Indochina.

Lookout, reconnaissance, liaison, and similar services of the Viet Minh were manned almost entirely by children, based on the assumption that army patrols seldom pay any attention to kids playing in a pond or passing through a field, while adult males would certainly be stopped, searched, and questioned.

1949

Karl Pfirstenhammer captured a group of fifteen women (many of them elderly) and twenty children (some of them not yet ten years old) while they were engaged in the "peaceful activity" of planting punji traps and crudely made bombs along a regular army trail. These "noncombatants" were transported into Camps of *Régroupement* near Saigon.

An army surgeon and four medics, among them a French nurse from Rouen, had been lured into a "friendly" village by a "bereaved mother" to attend "a seriously ill child." The ambulance was ambushed by the Viet Minh. Its occupants were brutally murdered. The terrorists then made off with a quantity of surgical equipment and medicines.

Seven drugged Legionnaires were garrotted in a Hanoi public house by Viet Minh terrorists.

1950

An old woman street peddler sold a dozen poisoned pineapple sticks to members of a passing platoon. Five legionnaires died and several more had to be hospitalized. The woman was recognized and arrested a couple of months later, but the subsequent military tribunal dismissed her case for "lack of evidence." A few weeks after her release the "witch of Ap Thui Loc" managed to murder a lieutenant of the Paratroops with poisoned squash made of crushed sugar cane. Apprehended by the Paras she was taken to the woods and summarily executed.

A fifteen-year-old girl appeared "responsive" to the friendly approach of a young corporal who encountered her in a Hanoi market and offered to help with her bags and boxes. After a few rendezvous the girl invited the corporal home to meet her family. He accompanied her into a dark side street where two of the girl's brothers waited in ambush. Stabbed to death, the corporal's body was dumped in front of the local police station carrying a placard: "This is only one colonialist dog but many more will follow."

A twelve-year-old boy peddler sold an antique Japanese sword to an air force captain. When back at his quarters the captain showed the weapon to members of his family, the booby-trapped bottom of the hilt exploded, severely wounding him, his wife, and their seven-year-old son.

1951

A North African platoon encountered a group of women distilling syrup from sugar cane. Asking for directions, the platoon was sent off on a treacherous trail ending in a swamp. Nine soldiers choked to death; others still struggling were pushed under by "innocent noncombatants" using long bamboo poles.

Two ten-year-old boys were caught by Rudolf Krebitz carrying a bagful of written information on French motorized transports and troop deployments around the Chinese frontier near Cao Bang.

1952

A young boy shot and killed two legionnaires in Lao Kays using a crude spear gun similar in principle to those used by scuba divers. A fifteen-year-old lad slipped a venomous snake into the vehicle of a French colonel. Both the colonel and his aide were bitten by the reptile but survived because of timely treatment. Caught while trying to flee, the young culprit was clubbed to death by Moroccan *tirailleurs* before the military police could intervene.

The murderous activities of such "innocent noncombatants"

could be cited over and over, but those who have not been actually on the spot would never comprehend them. European or American women, for instance, have simply no conception that their Asiatic counterparts can spray machine gun bullets as freely as other women use hair spray before an evening out, and that children over there are not playing with plastic Roy Rogers guns but with plastic high explosives, destroying life and property as freely as American kids might destroy sand castles.

A convoy of carts loaded with pots, pans, homemade furniture, rice, fruits, and vegetables is heading for the markets of Hanoi. Some of the carts are driven by aged peasants with suntanned, wrinkled faces and white beards commanding respect; other vehicles are occupied by entire families. The convoy has come a long way and has already passed two army roadblocks. It travels within a "pacified" area controlled by the gendarmes, where we have no jurisdiction whatsoever.

We were resting in the riverside meadow to pass the hottest hours of the day. The shady trees offered some relief from the burning heat. The convoy of carts rolled in. While the drivers watered the animals, the families descended; the women began to kindle fires and the children took to the canal. Accompanied by Schulze and Krebitz, I strolled over to the convoy and asked to see their leader. He turned out to be a mild-looking, bespectacled, middle-aged man with a gentle smile on his bearded face.

"We have a *laissez-passer* from the army," he said with some irritation in his voice. He showed me the document which permitted the convoy to proceed to Hanoi. "Checked and allowed to proceed," a pink rubber stamp read. "Examined and cleared."

Having nothing else to do, I decided to check them once more. Sergeant Krebitz assigned four men to each cart, an act which drew vehement protests from the convoy leader.

"Make sure that nothing is damaged," I told Sergeant Krebitz, who replied with a grin, "We will handle their grenades as if they were Easter eggs."

"We carry no grenades," the convoy leader protested.

"Then why worry?" Schulze shrugged. "We will have a quick little look about, then you proceed."

"You have no right to do that."

"Indochina is a lawless country."

"I know that," the man blurted, his face red with impotent rage. "We want to move on."

"You have just stopped to have a rest. . . . Relax."

"I am going to hand a petition to your superior."

"You do that. His name is Colonel Simon Houssong and you will find him at Viet Tri. I am First Lieutenant Hans Wagemueller. And now, if you don't mind, please tell your people to descend."

"You have no right to – "

"I have heard that before." I cut him short and ordered my men to proceed.

The specialists of *Gruppe Drei* knew well where to look for possible contraband and soon I heard a telltale "My God" as one of the troopers hauled a large watermelon from a cart and dumped it on the ground with the comment, "It is over heavy!" With an enigmatic smile on his face, Xuey stepped forward to have a look; the next instant three of the travelers bolted for the woods.

"Hold them!" Riedl shouted, but it was too late for us to stop the fugitives and we could not open fire amidst the milling throng of civilians. The trio vanished from sight.

"Now how about this little interlude?" I said to the convoy leader.

"How about this little too-heavy watermelon here?" Sergeant Krebitz intoned. "The one who eats it will get chronic indigestion."

Leaving the bearded leader under armed guard, I walked over to look at the melon. It was hollow. In the hollow we found an oilcloth package containing a revolver, fifty cartridges, and six hand grenades.

The search continued. Hollow vegetables contained more grenades. Time bombs with corrosion fuses were camouflaged as cabbages; dismantled rifles and a submachine gun were among our haul. Eighteen carts which transported no illegal cargo were allowed to proceed. The rest of the convoy went back to the army checkpoint under armed escort.

"Make sure that nothing happens to these poor innocent civilians," I told Krebitz who rode shotgun on the cart of the convoy leader. "We have about as many atrocities to our credit as we can take."

The Viet Minh company was marching casually along the narrow causeway which ran between an expanse of rice paddies parallel to the forest line. The enemy was obviously ignorant of our presence in the shrubbery. The men of *Gruppe Drei* had spotted them in the drifting mist long before they entered the relatively coverless flatland; about a hundred guerrillas marching in two lines on either side of the road, "Idiots' Row" as our sharpshooters used to refer to such formations. Sergeant Krebitz, who with a platoon of machine gunners had gone forward to occupy a patch of thickets near the trail, now reported that the Viet Minh detachment was a band of green recruits rather than a fighting force. Only the foremost platoon of twenty terrorists were armed with automatic weapons. The rear guard of six veteran guerrillas carried vintage rifles. The rest of the "section" was unarmed. "I am delighted," Sergeant Krebitz commented over the radio. "This is going to be duck shooting, Hans."

"You should spare the recruits," Xuey addressed me suddenly.

"And break our game rule about the golden reserves of Father Ho?"

"They would die innocently, for they are no more Communist than you are, Commander, and have probably joined the Viet Minh only upon the threat of instant death. They don't have weapons because they are not trusted yet."

"Maybe the company hasn't got enough weapons."

Xuey tapped my binoculars. "Have a look at the center of the column, Commander. There are eight men carrying crates, and those crates contain weapons."

Xuey was probably right about the recruits. "Spare the lives of the unarmed ones," he pleaded again. "Their families will need them."

"They should have told that to the Viet Minh, Xuey."

"No one can reason with the Viet Minh – you know that."

"All right, I will try to spare the recruits."

"Thank you, Commander."

I called Krebitz again, asking him if he was well enough deployed to eliminate the armed platoon without causing casualties among the unarmed men. "My God," he exclaimed, "are you having a sunstroke or something, Hans?"

"What do you mean, Rudolf?"

"I mean your good heart. Since when are you so concerned about the welfare of the Viet Minh?"

"Those recruits are not Viet Minh yet. Xuey asked me to give them a chance."

"As you wish," he grunted. "We will shoot the bad guys and let the not-so-bad guys live."

"How about their rear guard?"

"The *Abwehr* will take care of them."

"Proceed then," I said, reminding him to aim low, as we would be moving ahead on the right flank and consequently some of our own troops might stroll into *Gruppe Drei*'s line of fire. "I will keep that in mind," Krebitz reassured me.

"Don't wait for my order to open fire. When you see them properly, let them have it."

The sun was mounting higher and the mist over the paddies began to lift. Soon the enemy emerged into the open. Apart from an occasional cry of the paddy birds there was not a sound, so when the MGs of *Gruppe Drei* opened up, their sharp staccato shattered the silence like a bolt out of the clear sky. Instantly the guerrilla detachment scattered and I had no way of knowing how many of the armed terrorists were killed. The Viet Minh rear guard – Schulze saw it – went spinning and tumbling down into the paddies, but a part of the platoon must have escaped, for a sporadic fire of enemy submachine guns could be heard from the road. However, the survivors were soon spotted and eliminated one after another, until the remnants of the platoon, half a dozen muddy and bewildered guerrillas, finally realized the hopelessness of their position and surrendered. The recruits followed suit. Covered with mire and most of them soaking wet, they scrambled to their feet holding their hands up, some of them still on the road, others in the knee-deep muck yelling for mercy. Most of them were almost children.

"Giap must be hard up for manpower," Schulze commented, observing the miserable lot.

"That may be," said Xuey, "but I think the Viet Minh has only discovered the advantage of recruiting small boys, Commander."

"What advantage?"

"Young boys are rather easy to camouflage for one thing,"

Xuey explained. "When the army comes into a village a thirteen-year-old boy may conceal his gun and become a harmless child." Now I understood Xuey's reasoning and it made sense.

Gruppe Drei collected the enemy weapons. The guerrillas were separated from the recruits, many of whom were weeping openly. By then we had established a deadly reputation in the northern provinces and the commissars usually referred to us only as "the deathmakers" or "the beasts who spare none." I advised Xuey to speak to the recruits, which he gladly did.

"Return home," I told them, "and say a prayer of gratitude to your god, whoever he may be. Thank your god that we captured you unarmed. Otherwise you would be dead men now."

They left, still shaken but overjoyed at being alive. We watched them hurrying down the trail, calling to each other, whistling and chattering excitedly. When the last of them melted into the distant woods I turned my attention to the veteran guerrillas.

"Do you want to question them?" Krebitz asked.

I shrugged. "What for? They were only escorting the recruits to a predetermined point where another platoon would have taken charge of them."

"We might intercept those too."

"To hell with them."

"And what about them?" He jerked a thumb toward the pathetic group of prisoners.

"To hell with them too!"

"Shoot them for a change," Riedl suggested. "Your butchery with the bayonet makes me sick."

"Why not?" Krebitz shrugged. "After all they are supplying their own bullets."

The prisoners were executed and we moved on.

A dreary routine.

14

Action and Vengeance

By the summer of 1951 the Viet Minh had every reason to rejoice. Communism was progressing steadily in Indochina and the "freedom fighters" of Ho Chi Minh were in control of seventy percent of the rural areas. In the heavily garrisoned cities their influence was increasing; consequently the terrorist activities increased as well and soon became a serious problem.

The Communist strategy was a simple one. The Viet Minh mobilized the impoverished peasantry under the slogan "Kill the land-owner and seize his land," a rallying cry that appealed to the basest instinct of the scum. A call to murder, rape, and loot always rallies the scum of any country. For them, the Party offered a People's Democracy – a Communist state which the have-nots were quite willing to accept. The majority of the Party members did not have the faintest idea what Communism meant but they understood the catch phrase "You have nothing to lose but your chains."

The intelligentsia were being hoodwinked more tactfully through their patriotic sentiments and there was little talk about Marx, Lenin, or Communism. For the educated classes the bait was "independence." Regardless of their political beliefs, the majority of the population did agree on one issue: Indochina should rid herself of colonial overlords. In the rural areas the Viet Minh could enforce its "reforms" at will. Government officials, policemen, teachers, wealthy peasants, and merchants (anyone possessing more than about four head of cattle or owned a well-stocked shop was considered rich) had been liquidated. Their property had been seized and distributed among the people, at least for the time being. Those who had hesitated or *refused* to accept property acquired through murder and robbery were terrorized into submission. The moment a peasant accepted and began to cultivate illegally acquired property he was in the hands of the Viet Minh and could but dread the return of the legal authority.

A few months previously Ho Chi Minh had established his Workers Party – the Lao Dong – which was in fact the Communist party with the word "Communist" tactfully omitted. Ho Chi Minh still needed the support of the urban middle class. To them the mere word "Communism" was abhorrent, but they were, nevertheless, ardent supporters of the cause of independence.

At about that time we had an interesting "discussion" with a group of newspaper editors who were rather sceptical about the French endeavors and the general outlook of the war in Indochina. The newsmen had heard about the ex-Nazis of the Foreign Legion and they wasted no time in coming to talk to us. When I asked one of them why the editors wouldn't interview the commanding general, the editor replied in good humor: "I suspect that whatever the general might say could be obtained *printed* in Paris, without taking the trouble of coming all the way to Indochina."

I told them in no uncertain terms that we were fighting for a lost cause. They appeared somewhat surprised, since they had already consulted some high-ranking authority and had heard only the sunny side of the story. For us, it was quite understandable that our generals should be over-optimistic. After all they had been losing every battle since Napoleon and their most recent heroes of the First World War would have achieved little without the massive American assistance they received to bolster the brave but leaderless French soldiers (whose stamina we esteemed as much as we despised their generals). However resourceful and brave, the German troops could have achieved little without their Guderian, Manstein, or Rommel. When ordered into an attack at the wrong time and at the wrong place the bravest troops could only fight and go down fighting but without achievement. The French generals permitted too many of their troops to die. In our eyes, they were grown-up children who liked to play with tanks and cannons and, unfortunately, with human lives. Their little war games have resulted in the unnecessary death of millions of brave Frenchmen during the past eighty years; magnificent soldiers who could have won many victories if they had had capable and daring generals to lead them. After all, the race was the same as it had been in the time of Napoleon and lions will never beget rabbits! It was the *élan vital* – the "conquering will" – that was missing and not the *cran* – the guts.

"It is your conviction that we have irrevocably lost the war?" one of the newsmen asked. "No, not irrevocably," I corrected him, "but the way the war is now being conducted it can only end in total defeat."

"I see. . . ."

I had the notion that someday, not in the very distant future, our interview was going to backfire on us, but we were long since past worrying about consequences.

"What should we do to *win* the war?"

"Withdraw the Territorials from Indochina entirely and reinforce the Paratroops, *monsieur*. Then bring over ten German divisions," Eisner interposed with a broad grin. "That's what you should do. German divisions, German weapons, German generals. . . . Not the ones they have today, of course. Ten *old* German divisions and the French Paras could pacify Indochina, or hell itself, without jet planes, rockets, and napalm."

The editors chuckled. "With Adolf Hitler in command?" someone asked, obviously amusing himself. It did not bother us. The newspapermen wanted to hear our opinion, and we gave them what they wanted.

"For all his shortcomings, no one could accuse Hitler of cowardice, something we may seldom say of the present leaders of the so-called Free World," I said coolly. "Hitler would never take insults, slaps in the face, or political nonsense; not from the equally powerful, let alone moral, economic, and military midgets like the Viet Minh."

My words wiped the amusement from their faces. I went on: "I know that anyone may kick a dead lion but do you really think that Ho Chi Minh could have played his Viet Minh games with Hitler for five years?"

"Yes, we have heard of some of your, er, accomplishments," an editor remarked. "How are you doing now?"

"We are only a single battalion, *monsieur*. We cannot perform miracles; but I think the world knows only too well what the German Army was able to accomplish, if only for a couple of years, alone against the world. I don't think the Viet Minh would have frustrated the Wehrmacht."

"Suppose you were given command in Indochina and had your German divisions. Would it solve the local problems?"

"The local problems are very complex," I replied. "To solve them, one should mobilize top politicians and economists, not army divisions. But if I had a free hand, the Viet Minh would not last for six months. *That* I guarantee you."

"Are you not over-confident?" a voice from the group asked.

"There is no situation which a superior power cannot solve by appropriate means."

"And what do you mean by appropriate means?"

"The most rigorous measures if necessary. We met guerrillas before in Russia. When they gave us too much trouble within a specific area, we carted off the entire male population to Germany. Two days later there was no terrorist movement in the district. There is always a last solution."

"Including extermination camps with gas chambers?"

"If you came here only to wisecrack, gentlemen, we might as well discontinue. You requested me to state facts and present my own unadulterated views – which is precisely what I am endeavoring to do."

"Please go on – we meant no offense," an elderly editor said apologetically. "Your determination is fascinating."

"Historical facts cannot be altered, nor can they be whitewashed," I went on. "We Germans can be very joyful and happy people around a table drinking beer, or in a bowling alley, or in our homes, but when it comes to fighting all our feelings become subjugated to our will to conquer. We were taught to be concerned with results only. The means by which we achieve victory are not important to us. Had we been here, instead of the French, we might have turned Indochina into a country of women and children only, but the Viet Minh would have been liquidated a long time ago."

"Would you care telling us – not being a Frenchman yourself, and this also applies to your companions – why are you so concerned about Indochina and about the outcome of this war in general?"

"This liberation movement is not just a local phenomenon but the beginning of a prolonged struggle which one may rightly call a struggle for survival. The Viet Minh is only a single division of a brutal international force that has many other divisions ready for starting similar wars in any part of the world. This is not a local affair and it should worry every civilized nation of the world."

"You don't consider Russia civilized?" a newsman asked.

"The Russian standard of civilization exposed itself wonderfully when the Red Army occupied the former Axis partners, Rumania, Hungary, and the part of Germany which is now the Soviet Zone, in 1945. . . ."

"How about China? China can claim a four-thousand-year-old civilization."

"That may be, gentlemen . . . but today, China is nothing more than a Red dunghill, and Communism can turn the angel of mercy into an angel exterminator. I believe that we are all aware of that."

"Was Nazism any better?" a voice interposed.

"Suit yourself, *monsieur*," I replied, ignoring the challenge. "If you came here to discuss Nazism we should switch subjects."

"Let us keep to our proper subject," the editor in front of me suggested, then glanced into his notebook and added: "Do you believe that world opinion would have permitted you to employ – let us be frank now – such typically Nazi methods as the deportation of the male population?"

"As far as *we* are concerned, gentlemen, we are fighting against a deadly enemy and not against public opinion. The United Nations is only one of your postwar jokes. A club of senile old men who are trying to play the role of the strict schoolmaster toward nations with a population of ten million souls. To scold anything bigger than that, your United Nations is as impotent as the League of Nations was when it endeavored to censure Mussolini for his aggression against Abyssinia."

"You have, I believe, already completed your five years of service. You are staying on voluntarily. If you know that the Viet Minh cannot be defeated by conventional means, then why are you still fighting them?"

"Why does man fight locusts?" I asked in return and drew a soft chuckle from the group. "We believe that the more terrorists we manage to kill here, the less our sons and grandsons will have to fight against in World War Three!"

No one interrupted me, so I went on. "They say that Nazism was a grave menace to mankind. I see no point in contesting that belief. But would anyone tell me what the Western Allies accomplished in 1945? They liberated a number of captive nations from the Nazi yoke but only at the price of casting a dozen free nations into Soviet slavery. Was it such a wise deal? At least the German-occupied countries could look forward to the day of liberation. What can the people of the Soviet-occupied countries look forward to? Who will liberate *them*? Only death! In ten years' time the Communists will conquer more land than the Nazis ever controlled – and that with the benevolent assistance of the free democracies. In one respect the Communists are right to assert that the free democracies are governed by capitalists and that a capitalist never looks beyond the very next day. For him only the immediate profit matters, the distant consequence never. The free democracies will trade with the Reds, they will back down when pressed, compromise on every principal issue; they will feed the enemy and supply them with everything they need to conquer the world. This is precisely why the Third World War is inevitable."

"What should we have done," a question came from the back row, "kept on fighting in 1945?"

"There was a great chance in 1948 right after the Berlin blockade, *monsieur*. Berlin should have been evacuated. The so-called Free World had enough money and material to build another Berlin in the west and thus wrench a supreme lever of political and military blackmail from Stalin's hands. Industries and stockpiles should have been removed, public works and buildings blown up. Then Berlin should have been handed over to the Communists the way it was in May 1945. I agree that sentiments would have suffered but the German people have lost a great deal more than Berlin. Afterwards the Free World should have built its own Iron Curtain: a fortified line along the entire Red frontier with the world, as we know it, ending at the wall. No diplomatic contacts, no mail, no telephone, no trains or planes going through. Communism should have been totally and mercilessly isolated from the rest of mankind."

"How about the Communists in the Western countries?" I was interrupted. "There are about two million of them in France alone!"

"I would give them a free ticket to the far side of the wall, gentlemen, for, apart from their political aspirations, they are outright military and economic intelligence agents for Moscow. Should the Kremlin request their assistance, the French Communists for instance would never hesitate to map French targets for a Soviet missile attack against France. Besides, it is much too comfortable to be a Communist in a free country, earning good wages, driving a car, having the right to protest, to strike, to change jobs. The Communists should go where their loyalty belongs, the Soviet paradise."

"But they are citizens. They have their constitutional rights like anyone else."

"You also have a sentence of death, already signed in the Kremlin," I replied coolly. "Only the day of the execution has not yet been fixed."

My conclusion provoked a small revolution in the conference room.

"I agree with him!" someone exclaimed.

"Lunacy!" someone else yelled. "They should be disbanded!" – "They should receive every support." – "Shame upon France!" – "Shame upon those who are ready to sell France down the drain...."

"You are a ... fanatic!" one of the newsmen exclaimed, with a look of astonishment and hostility on his lean face.

"I know that you wanted to say either 'Nazi fanatic,' or simply 'lunatic,' *monsieur*," I remarked with a smile and rose slowly. "Go ahead. We are Nazis if one has to be a Nazi to think in terms of years and not only in terms of days. And if one of us had not become a Nazi under Hitler, he would have turned into a Nazi right here in Indochina. You may also consider us crazy but that was exactly what the British thought of Rudolf Hess when he foretold what would happen if Germany lost the war: Soviet domination of Central Europe, Communist takeovers, rebellions, the dissolution of the British Empire. . . . I can see that some of you are amused. Just wait a dozen more years, gentlemen, and you will no longer be smiling."

I was perfectly aware that the ideas of a "Nazi extremist" must have sounded quite insane to a group of petty bourgeois newsmen who had probably never smelled gunpowder in their lives. Nevertheless they wanted the truth and that's what I gave them. We Germans can believe and follow only determined and powerful leaders. It has nothing to do with Nazism. It is our heritage of centuries. We would have followed Julius Caesar, Attila, Napoleon, or Washington with the same devotion we showed Adolf Hitler. But we think nothing of rich boys who gain a plush chair or a marshal's baton because their parents happen to have plenty of money.

It was evident that the Free World was already looking toward America as the Lord Deliverer and Protector. Surely America is a great country, wealthy and very advanced. But so was the Roman Empire in its own time. Wealth is not a precondition of power and history tells that the richer a nation grows, the weaker it becomes. It was not a wealthier or a more advanced nation that destroyed the Roman Empire. It was the barbarians!

Shortly after the interview we were out again for three weeks of hard trekking along a wide and well-maintained trail. Gia Xuey thought it was one of the principal Viet Minh routes to "Nambo" – southern Indochina. We crisscrossed some three hundred square miles of guerrilla territory, which Ho Chi Minh considered conquered and secured forever.

We succeeded in wiping out that illusion. Within the first ten days my men destroyed two major Viet Minh bases, each of which accommodated two or three guerrilla "sections" (about one hundred men constituted one "section" or company).

Our task was relatively easy, because in the conquered areas the customary guerrilla vigilance appeared to be relaxed. With the nearest French garrison holed up at Luang Prabang, a hundred miles away, the Viet Minh could move and manage its affairs practically unhindered. In the liberated villages the enemy openly displayed the Viet Minh ensign, along with large propaganda posters and banners inscribed with slogans. Small groups of terrorists moved freely within the village and a pair of binoculars always revealed their presence. The loudspeakers, which some propagandists used for mass indoctrination, could be heard from miles away. In their jungle camps, too, the enemy had grown astonishingly careless. Across the wilderness their singing, chattering, and shouting served as "beams" on which our trailblazers could home. Masquerading as guerrillas, Xuey and Noy often infiltrated enemy-held localities and returned with important information. In fact, that little native nurse proved so effective in reconnaissance that I decided to assign her to *Gruppe Drei* – a great distinction. Noy was as resourceful as she was daring. She would casually stroll into a terrorist camp and hold a sentry's attention while Sergeant Krebitz and his men closed in on the unsuspecting enemy. With the sentries eliminated it was always easy to penetrate into the camp proper. We did it either at dawn or at dusk, invariably posing as guerrillas ourselves. The ruse always worked.

Frantically the Viet Minh High Command was trying to suppress our activities in their vital staging areas, hitherto safe from French harassment. Giap concentrated over a thousand guerrillas in an all-out attempt to destroy us, but the more troops he concentrated, the less he could preserve the secrecy of their whereabouts. General Giap found us a hard nut to crack. We were too strong for Viet Minh units of company strength and could in fact easily outgun any guerrilla battalion. The enemy needed at least a brigade to tackle my headhunters. A brigade, however, cannot play hide-and-seek in the jungle. Units consisting of over three thousand men need ample supplies; besides they also make a great deal of noise. Whenever the enemy appeared to be concentrating several battalions in a particular area we either delivered a preemptive strike to grind them up piecemeal or we slipped quietly away towards safer hunting grounds.

The loss of one guerrilla camp must have been particularly painful for the Viet Minh. In it we discovered twelve fully equipped workshops for servicing weapons, manufacturing mines, spear guns (the terrorists were still extensively using this brutal weapon), sandals, bombs. A printing shop and a dressing station were also among the camp facilities. Lathe benches, grinders, power drills and other machines were in the workshops. The power came from five small diesel generators placed in a long underground tunnel to deaden sound. Some of the machines weighed over a ton and had obviously come dismantled from one of the principal cities.

The battalion killed over a hundred guerrillas and captured thirty or forty of them in that camp. The majority of the casualties were irreplaceable specialists: machine tool operators, electricians, weapon makers, five engineers, six printers, two pharmacists, and two doctors. Among the prisoners were six Lao Dong functionaries, including a district secretary and a district Agitprop secretary.

The camp was a marvel of guerrilla ingenuity. The overhead camouflage netting was covered with natural green that matched the surrounding flora. To keep the foliage fresh it had to be replaced every other day, and for that purpose the various sections of the netting could be lowered or raised. Where air reconnaissance observed only unbroken forests, in reality a spacious clearing spread for hundreds of yards, with permanent huts, living quarters, water tanks, mess halls, depots, and workshops.

Strolling about the camp with Schulze I spotted Xuey, who was closely inspecting a section of ground where I saw piles of bamboo spokes neatly arranged under a tarpaulin sheet.

"Anything wrong?" I tapped him lightly on the shoulder.

He looked up and nodded. "Plenty wrong! There were French prisoners working here, sharpening stakes. Dead or alive they should be somewhere around."

"Prisoners?" Schulze exclaimed incredulously. "We searched the whole camp, Xuey – "

"Look at the footprints," Xuey said. He squatted on his heels and drew a finger around the contours of a bare print. "It was made by a very large foot. . . . No local people have feet as large as this one."

A glance at the print was enough to convince me that Xuey was right. "But where on earth could they be?" Erich pondered.

"Somewhere in the woods, maybe underground," Xuey suggested. "We should start looking for them or they may die."

I called for Sergeant Krebitz and he came running. I told him of Xuey's discovery. "Get a hundred men and comb the neighborhood. Don't destroy anything, unless the place has been searched with the utmost care."

The troops surveyed the entire area and combed the woods for five hundred yards but all in vain. There was a trail which Xuey and Krebitz went to investigate as far as a mile and a half, but it ended in a rocky depression among barren hills strewn with boulders and dead trees. The depression seemed to have several exits and it would have taken days to examine them all.

The surveying parties found neither prisoners nor caves and tunnels where prisoners could have been kept confined. I spoke once again with Xuey. "Are you sure that those prints were recent ones?" I asked him.

He looked at me and asked in turn, "Have I ever erred in my judgment, commander?"

"Not that I know of, Xuey," I had to concede.

He nodded contentedly. "I am not mistaken now!"

"But where can they be? They aren't in the camp and if there was another place nearby, we ought to find a path leading to it."

"I was looking for a path," Xuey said. "Sometimes they are very difficult to detect. Often the Viet Minh make no paths at all but use different routes between two bases every day, allowing the grass to recover. Such trails cannot be detected. Only the people who use them know their location."

"What do you suggest we should do?"

"Question the prisoners!" Xuey replied.

There was nothing else I could do. If Xuey was right about the French prisoners, they had to be helped at once.

"Sergeant Schenk!" I turned sharply. "Where are the captured guerrillas?"

He swung the barrel of his submachine gun toward a long, thatched hut. "Over there, commander!"

"Bring them here!"

Eisner and Riedl appeared. "What's going on?" Bernard inquired. I briefed him on the situation and his face darkened. "Then I am afraid they are dead," he remarked grimly. "If any French prisoners had been here, they must have heard us moving around. They would be screaming their heads off by now for help."

"They might be underground."

Sergeant Schenk returned with the prisoners and lined them up facing us. Without preliminaries, Sergeant Krebitz grabbed the district secretary by the shoulder.

"Where are the French prisoners, ratface?" he sneered at the slim, pockmarked terrorist. "Open your goddamned mouth or I'll break every bone in your wretched carcass."

"We have no French prisoners," came the defiant reply.

"You are a liar!" Xuey cut in, stepping closer. "I saw their footprints."

"You are a filthy traitor," the propagandist hissed and spat toward Xuey. "We will get you one day, you colonialist puppet – Gia Xuey. . . . We know you well."

"Indeed?" Eisner stepped in front of the prisoner, drew his bayonet and held it against the man's belly. "Do you happen to know *me* as well?"

"We know you all and we will get you, too, one day."

"You will get us, *too*, eh? Whom have you got already?"

He paused for a moment, then repeated his question in a low, menacing tone, "Where are the French prisoners?"

Silence and a defiant, sardonic smile were all he got as an answer. With a sudden, powerful thrust, Bernard plunged the blade home. The propagandist uttered a bubbling moan, his mouth opened, and his face contorted in pain; with a low, animal grunt he sagged toward Eisner. Bernard pulled his bayonet free and let the man drop.

"I am not a man of jokes," he sneered at the dying terrorist. Stepping up to the party secretary he repeated his question.

"You may kill us all, you Fascist dogs," the guerrilla breathed with hatred oozing from his lips. "Kill us all, and you may also forget about your legionnaires for you will never find them." He uttered a short, hysterical snort. "They will rot away alive!"

"That's what *you* think, *cher ami*," Bernard grinned. "But you are going to tell us where they are. We will find them all right." He lifted the still dripping bayonet.

The party secretary paled but gathered himself and cried, "Go ahead and stab me, too!" But Eisner only smiled at him with narrowed eyes. He wiped the blade on the prisoner's pajama and sheathed it.

"*Your* death is not going to be so easy," he said quietly. "When I am through with you, you will be praying for death to come." He turned to the guards. "Strip the swine!"

"Schenk!"

"*Jawohl!*"

"Take him over there, behind those logs," Bernard pointed to a place some fifty yards from where we stood, "and the others too. . . . Sergeant Krebitz! Please get me a roll of fuse and a couple of primers."

Moments later the naked district secretary lay prostrate on the ground, spread-eagled between four short pegs driven into the ground. His companions were lined up facing their leader.

"Erich," I gestured to Schulze and nodded toward the huts, where Suoi and Chi had appeared carrying a few small boxes. "Take the girls for a ride!"

When we wanted to keep the girls away from some unpleasant spectacle, some of us would take them for a "ride," usually an "assignment" to do an "important job" elsewhere. Schulze hurried off to meet the two. Taking the girls by the shoulders and talking rapidly, he ushered them towards the far side of the camp.

Krebitz returned with the detonators and a roll of fuse. Eisner cut a length of fuse and began to coil it about the prisoner's body. "This is one of Karl Stahnke's ideas which the Gestapo adopted," he explained. "Stahnke swore that it would open the mouth of a stone statue."

He coiled the fuse about the district secretary's leg, his trunk and chest, talking all the while, "So, tovarich . . . you are a cool one, eh? This should warm you up a bit." He ran the fuse down the man's hip, attached the detonator and slipped the charge under the prisoner's scrotum. "It won't kill you but you had better talk now, *cher ami*. By the time the primer blows your balls off, you will have turned into a pink zebra, you hero of Ho Chi

Minh." He lit a cigarette and looked down on the prisoner. "I am asking you once more, where are the French prisoners?"

The guerrilla spat in Eisner's face. Eisner wiped his cheek with his handkerchief and lighted the fuse.

The moment the white-hot fire touched the guerrilla's skin he heaved violently and began to scream in agony. He twisted and arched to escape the searing heat. The fire slowly ate along his leg, leaving a burned, bleeding path of raw flesh in its wake. Seconds later the man's body was bathed in sweat. Krebitz gagged him to muffle his cries.

Eisner turned toward the rest of the party leaders, some of whom already looked more dead than alive. "How do you like it, comrades? The next client will have a real nice slow-burning fuse."

With a persistent low hiss the fire circled the prisoner's chest, burning an inch-wide blistering trail as it advanced; the wretch had almost severed his wrists as he twisted against the restraining rope.

"Speak!" Eisner urged him, snatching the rag from the prisoner's mouth. "In a minute you will turn into a eunuch, *cher ami*. What will your wife or girl friend say?"

"You will . . . all hang . . . you Fascist brigands . . . you . . ." the district secretary gurgled. "Father Ho will . . . avenge . . . us." His eyes rolled up, then slowly closed. He blacked out.

"Put the fuse out!" Riedl stepped forward. "You can't make an unconscious man talk."

"I knew that he was not going to talk," Bernard replied, nodding toward the others. "But they will!"

"Bernard . . . you are a bloody sadist. Put that fuse out."

"Go and join the girls if you cannot stomach it, Helmut."

Without a word, Riedl turned, shouldered his rifle, and left. The fire reached the prisoner's thigh, then the primer exploded with a short, sharp crack. The man's body heaved as a spurt of blood splashed across his thighs, then he fell back and lay still. Eisner pulled his automatic and coolly put a bullet between the district secretary's eyes.

"Riedl is wrong," he remarked, holstering his gun. "I don't enjoy doing this. Remember our twelve comrades in Suoi's village. I am only giving them tit for tat. Strip the next one!" he commanded the troopers.

Before the fuse began to burn he was told what he wanted to know.

Sergeant Schenk cut the prisoner free and pulled him to his feet. The man was shaking in every limb. "I have a family to support," he muttered almost sobbing, "wife and children . . . five children."

"You still have your balls, so don't complain," Eisner snapped. "Show us the way to the French prisoners and I will let you go home."

"You lie!" the guerrilla cried; the next instant he was staggering backward under the impact of Eisner's backhand blow. Bernard stepped forward and grabbed the man by his shirt.

"Never call a German officer a liar, *cher ami*," he sneered with his eyes narrowed and boring into the guerrilla's face. "We always keep *our* part of a bargain." He pushed the man toward the woods. "Forward! *Allez vite!*"

The prisoner led us to a small but well-concealed camp about two miles from the main base. It consisted of only five huts which contained rice, but a nearby spacious natural cave secreted five hundred cases of rifle ammo, seventeen machine guns, and fifty-two satchels of grenades. Not far from the huts the prisoner showed us the entrance of a tunnel. When Karl threw open the bolted lid a repugnant smell of human filth rose from below.

Hairy, haggard faces appeared in the opening, staring into the sudden brightness; thin, skeleton arms and hands tried to shield a dozen hollow eyes.

"*Nous sommes le bataillon allemand,*" Sergeant Schenk shouted, bending down to grasp a pair of hands. "*Ascendez-vous!*"

"Come up! You are free!"

An instance of frozen silence followed, then someone groaned, "*Mon Dieu, c'est la Légion. . . .*" The dark hole exploded. Now everybody began to scream, holler, demand, and plead. Hands shot upward, filling the opening, grasping for help. We pulled them out, one after another, lowering them gently to the ground.

"Goddamit!" Karl swore. "Look at them! Look at the poor bastards. . . . They would have died here like rats."

The troops hauled up twenty-eight prisoners, among them a

lieutenant and an Arab sergeant, both in pitiful shape. Most of the prisoners were suffering from festering sores and untreated wounds. I sent word to Sergeant Zeisl to get ready with warm water, antibiotics, ointments, and bandages.

Cigarettes, water, something to chew, something to drink – the poor devils demanded everything at once, trying to hug us and shake our hands at the same time. We distributed all the cigarettes we had with us, our canteens, our biscuits. Some of the legionnaires began to sob openly. Others laughed or joked, still others just sank to the ground overwhelmed with relief.

"Pull yourselves together," the lieutenant urged them. They slowly rose and we carried or helped them back into the main camp.

"Marceau is my name," the lieutenant shook my hand. "Jean Marceau."

"From the *Régiment Amphibie*?" I asked.

He uttered a short laugh. "Rather *Régiment Sous-terrain*. . . . I am glad to see you."

"How long have you been here?"

"For seven months, *cher ami*," he replied. "Are you the famous one-time SS officer Wagemueller?"

"I do not know whether I am famous or not, but I am an officer of the French Foreign Legion, Lieutenant Marceau; that I do know."

"No offense meant."

"No offense taken. . . . I also know that we haven't settled our bill yet."

"The SS shot my brother in Rouen," Marceau remarked quietly.

"I wasn't the one who did it, Marceau. I haven't been in France."

"I believe you, but it is hard not to remember."

"Now the SS saved your life. Strange, isn't it?"

"Times change." He extended his hand again. "Thank you all the same."

We set the legionnaires up in guerrilla sleeping quarters. Sergeant Schenk and the girls made them as comfortable as possible. The sudden appearance of Suoi and the nurses startled the men and occasioned a small outburst. Clapping and whistling and muttering complimentary remarks, they forgot about their sores and aches.

Sergeant Zeisl and the nurses quickly attended the seriously ill ones. "They won't be able to march for weeks," Zeisl stated after a while. "We had better call in the copters."

"The copters will bring the Viet Minh here from miles around," Karl said.

"If they aren't on the way already," Eisner agreed. "I have been thinking of those huts and the prisoners' bunker. Some guerrillas ought to have been there to stand guard."

"*Bien sûr!*" Lieutenant Marceau cut in. "We could hear them chattering only minutes before you arrived."

"They have gone off to warn the others. We had better get busy here, Hans," said Erich. "I'm going to set up a perimeter right away."

"Do that, Erich. Take four platoons with MGs."

I turned to Karl. "You should deploy along the ravine to cover the trail with flamethrowers."

"I have only four tanks left, Hans."

"Then take more machine guns."

Karl and Erich left and I walked to Corporal Altreiter, who had just set up the wireless aerials. "Report to HQ . . . I request the immediate dispatch of helicopters to evacuate twenty-eight wounded legionnaires liberated from Viet Minh captivity. Eisner will give you the coordinates. Tell HQ that we will guide the copters by straight signals transmitted at one-minute intervals on the usual frequency."

"Say, Hans," Riedl cut in, "how about asking for some supplies. Flamethrower tanks, for instance."

"And booze," Krebitz added, shaking his empty canteen. "We could also use some more tracer ammo."

I turned to Riedl. "Draw up a quick list for Altreiter but make it a short one. Otherwise the copters will never get here. Sergeant Krebitz! Begin with the demolition."

"Don't demolish your prisoners," Lieutenant Marceau interposed. "I am looking forward to seeing the canaille. We still have scores to settle."

"Do you want to . . . entertain them, Marceau?"

"You bet I do," said he. "Do you know what those bastards

did to us? They forced us to eat shit . . . *real* shit, I mean. When I demanded more food for my men, the Viet Minh commander ordered us to chew their excrement. He thought it was funny."

"Don't say –"

"He said it was a great honor for us colonialist pigs to eat the shit of a Viet Minh hero."

"Well, that is a new one!" Eisner exclaimed. "I know a few original Red jokes but that beats them all."

"For us it wasn't so funny," the lieutenant retorted grimly. "Three of our men who refused to comply were dumped head first into the latrine and kept submerged until they choked to death. . . . A very unpleasant way to die."

"Their commander is dead but you can have the rest of them. Have fun," I said.

"Fair enough," Marceau nodded. "I am looking forward to it."

After his sores had been dressed, I led him to the prisoners. Slowly, Marceau walked past the sullen group, recognizing some of them. "Comrade Nguyen Ho and Comrade Muong Ho," he said softly and turned toward me. "You still have a fairly good collection here. I would appreciate it if you could take them to where my men are resting, for soon the comrades are going to have *their* dinner, and no one would want to miss the show."

"A dinner similar to the one they gave you?"

"Oh, no." Marceau shook his head, allowing his eyes to travel from face to face. "We are much too civilized to feed men on shit."

We returned to the Legionnaires, some of whom were busy shaving and washing themselves. (Before our nurses appeared on the scene the suggestion of shaving and washing had been dismissed en masse with a loud "What the hell for" or "We'll do that in Hanoi.")

In the camp, the demolition work was already under way; thuds, cracks, small explosions could be heard everywhere as Sergeant Krebitz and *Gruppe Drei* proceeded to destroy guerrilla equipment. The crates of medical supplies had been carefully opened. Zeisl removed what we needed; the rest of the drugs were then intermixed, the containers resealed, and left in place as though we had entirely overlooked the small underground depot. The Viet Minh was always hard up for drugs and in most instances our undoubtedly mean but deadly ruse would liquidate a large number of terrorists by "delayed action," as Sergeant Krebitz put it. Malaria was always a problem for the Viet Minh and the terrorists readily consumed any drug bearing the label "quinine bisulphate." Entire Viet Minh battalions had been wiped out in this fashion. Sometimes, when we heard that a guerrilla detachment was hard up for food, we permitted a truckload of foodstuffs to fall into their hands. The enemy carried away everything, unaware that we had mixed rat poison, containing strychnine, into the flour and the sugar.

Should one call our ruse "chemical warfare"? After all, twenty-nine of my men had died of wounds caused by poisoned Viet Minh arrows, spears, and stakes.

Lieutenant Marceau indeed arranged a "dinner" for the captive Viet Minh. He forced them to swallow their leaflets and printed propaganda manuals, page by page. When one of them stopped chewing, Marceau poked the man with a bayonet and occasionally topped the meal with a spoonful of printing paint, commenting, "Have some pudding too." Then tearing up and distributing the propaganda material, he shouted, "Chew, you canaille. . . . It is surely better tasting than shit."

The "dinner" lasted for the better part of two hours. The *après-souper* wine was machine oil. When a prisoner resisted, a narrow rubber hose was forced into his mouth and he would either swallow or choke to death. Soon the last of them collapsed. Others still writhed in the grass or were already dead, lying in pools of vomit, black paint oozing from their lips and nostrils.

But we did keep our part of the bargain: the guerrilla who had led us to the underground prison was set free. Eisner even gave him a large sack of foodstuffs with a grunt. "That's for your wife and children. Instead of roaming the countryside with a gun you should stick to the hoe and take care of your family." He gave the terrorist a kick, sending him head over heels toward the trail, then he called Schulze on the walkie-talkie: "There's a pig heading your way. Let him pass."

Lieutenant Marceau was standing over the last dying terrorists. "*Eh, bien,*" he said, dropping the container with the remaining paint. "They are black enough to join their fellow devils in hell."

"How about *this* show?" Eisner said when it was all over. "Only a few more Communist brutalities and we are going to celebrate the birth of the first French SS division in Indochina – composed entirely of grudging democrats." He chuckled. "They might call it AB or BC but it is going to be SS from A to Z." He extended his arm in a mocking Nazi salute. "*Vive la France! Sieg Heil!*"

"*Merde!*" Lieutenant Marceau commented. "One does not have to be an SS man to slaughter *these* pigs. They aren't human."

"You are right! They *aren't* human. That is precisely what we have been saying for five years."

Early in the afternoon the copters emerged from behind the hills. Pfirstenhammer fired very lights to guide them. There was no place to land and the copters had to keep hovering above the trees. The crew lowered the supplies for us, along with a bundle of letters, then hauled the legionnaires aboard. I received a long letter from Lin Carver. In the envelope I found a color picture of her with a small poodle. She still addressed me "My dear Hans" and complained that I wrote so seldom. . . . Dear little Lin, I thought, wondering if I would ever see her again. Sitting on an ammo case, I wrote her a quick note, promising a long letter when we returned to Hanoi.

It was very nice to receive a letter in the middle of nowhere. Colonel Houssong had arranged for our mail to be taken aboard. I asked the lieutenant to mail the letter for me.

"I certainly wish I could stay with you," Marceau said when we shook hands. "You are still giving Ho Chi Minh his money's worth – a heartening thought. . . . You know, in a way you have convinced me that France could still win this bloody war."

"Not with a million Red deputies sitting in your parliament, Lieutenant Marceau," I replied jokingly. "Sooner or later they are going to bust the *République*."

"Not if they push the army too far in the process," he remarked gloomily. "We might give up our colonies but we are not going to give up metropolitan France, *cher ami*. . . . By God we won't. It would be better to die than to see the savages ruling France." He reached for the rope ladder. "Give them hell, they deserve it. . . ."

"*Ciao!*"

"*À bientôt.*"

The copters clattered away and we were alone. "Now let's get out of here," Riedl said, lifting his rucksack and rifle. "The Reds must have spotted those copters from miles around."

I was about to order assembly when I saw Karl emerging from the woods down the trail. "Hans!" he called and gestured toward me with his gun. "Would you come over here for a moment?"

"What's up, Karl?" I asked, somewhat puzzled, but I joined him as he turned back toward the woods.

He replied curtly, "There are a couple of wenches down in a ravine – raped and bayoneted."

"Who did it?"

"I have the ones responsible."

Karl led me to a ravine not far from the huts. Passing some shrubs I saw Sergeant Krebitz holding a submachine gun; a few steps from where he stood sat a small group of troopers. They were already disarmed and their belts taken away. When we appeared they rose and stood in sullen silence.

"There they are!" Karl said pointing toward the nude bodies of five young women who lay in a large pool of blood. I turned to face the culprits.

"All right. Whose idea was it?"

They stood in silence. Five unshaven ragged men, gazing down at the sodden earth, fingering their buttons; none of them looked at Sergeant Krebitz and his party of guards as they began to carry away the ravished corpses. None of them looked at either me or Karl.

"Mueller!" I addressed a small, chubby trooper. "Step out!"

He stepped forward and stood at attention. "Were you the perpetrator of this outrage?" I spoke.

"I . . . I . . . found them, *Herr Oberleutnant*," he stuttered, "the girls – "

"You mean when you found them they were already dead?"

"No, *Herr Oberleutnant* . . . they were . . . alive," he replied, barely audible. Then he looked up and added, "They had guns . . . all of them. . . ."

"Go on, Mueller!"

"So we killed them," he went on hesitantly, "We killed them just like the others . . . all the others." He uttered a short nervous snort and glanced at his companions, looking for a sign of support, as he added. "We always execute the armed terrorists, don't we?"

"You raped them, Mueller!"

"What difference does it make, *Herr Oberleutnant?* They were to die anyway."

"Steiner!"

A second man stepped out. "Do you agree with Mueller that it does not make any difference whether you raped the girls before killing them or not?" I waited for a moment but no answer came. "Speak!"

He made a feeble gesture with his hands. "I guess it was wrong."

"You *guess?* Where did you serve during the war, Steiner?"

"I was a paratrooper, *Herr Oberleutnant* . . . Belgium, Greece, Italy . . . I've been many places and been wounded five times."

"That's meritorious . . . but that's what you learned with the paratroops? Were you raping girls in Belgium too? Or in Greece, in Italy?"

Steiner protested vehemently. "Never! *Herr Oberleutnant* must surely know. . . ."

"I *know!*" I cut him short. "Because you would have been punished very severely, if that's what you wanted to say. What makes you think that it is different here in Indochina?"

"Those guerrilla bitches, *Herr Oberleutnant,*" he ran a nervous hand over his face, "they aren't human."

"They were human enough to satisfy your lust, weren't they?" He did not answer, only stood, wetting his lips with the tip of his tongue.

As a matter of fact we seldom executed woman guerrillas except for a few truly hardened Communist she-devils who had been guilty of hideous crimes. Sometime back in 1949 we had captured one Viet Minh amazon who had found immense pleasure in the torture-murder of captive legionnaires. One of her victims we discovered in a horrible state of mutilation. The naked sergeant's arms and legs had been drawn outward by stakes and burning splinters had been slivered under his skin; finally cutting away the dying man's private parts she had forced them into his mouth. At first the sight was terrifying, then it made us sick. The wrath swelled in us so that we swore to hang every Viet Minh tigress we could lay our hands on.

"Stolz!"

A lean, lanky Saxon stepped forward. With a quick jerk of his head he tossed his long blond hair from his face and froze at attention. During the war Karl Stolz had been a *Panzer* driver and a much-decorated one. He had to his credit vicious engagements from Poland to Paris, from Belgrade to Athens, and from Salerno to the Po valley in Italy. He had lost twenty-six *Panzers* and survived five direct hits. He had been wounded eleven times and spent altogether seven months in various hospitals. During the offensive in northern France, Stolz had driven his *Panzer* into a burning town which the French had barely evacuated. In front of the shell-torn town hall he had spotted a young woman. Lying in a pool of blood and crying for help, she was a pitiful spectacle; her left leg had been torn away by a shell and she was eight months pregnant.

"Save my baby . . . oh, God save my baby," she implored in broken German. "I am dying . . . please save my baby." Stolz stopped his *Panzer*. With his gunners firing furiously and with explosions still raking the street, he rushed to the woman and applied a tourniquet to her bleeding stump. Then with the help of another trooper he dragged her to the tank and lifted her onto the rear armor. With the trooper supporting the woman he had driven his *Panzer* to the hospital half a mile away. Not wasting time at the entrance, Stolz drove his tank through the closed oak gate, stopping a yard short of the cellar entrance. He handed the woman to a frightened surgeon and two nurses, backed out of the garden, and raced off to tackle the French artillery outside the town.

He had been severely reprimanded and reduced in rank for having withdrawn from combat without permission, but the woman and her baby boy survived the war. Stolz saw her again in 1945 after he escaped from an American camp. The Frenchwoman gave him a civilian suit, food, papers, and money enough to reach Marseilles.

Now the same man was standing in front of me, after having participated in the rape and killing of five female Viet Minh.

"Why did you do it, Stolz?" I queried him looking straight into his eyes. He opened and closed his hands in a gesture of uncertainty.

"I don't know," he replied, "maybe the heat did it . . . the jungle . . . this whole *Gott verdammte* war. . . . Maybe it was sheer madness. . . . I am ready to take the consequences."

In a way I could understand him and all the others. Ten years of constant war is not exactly what one can call the education of samaritans. The men were tired and fed up. But raping and looting I never tolerated in our ranks. The men had to be punished. I stepped back to face the lot.

"You have committed a loathsome crime," I spoke to them. "I presume that you were banking on the fact that we have neither a court-martial nor a prison here and that we cannot lose five good fighting men by simply shooting you. You should be shot but it would be a luxury our battalion cannot afford. . . . Sergeant Krebitz!"

"*Herr Oberleutnant.*"

"From now on these five men are going to serve as an advance guard for *Gruppe Drei!*" I said.

Krebitz looked at me, puzzled. "*Gruppe Drei* has no advance guard. We look for traps ourselves."

"From now on you will have an advance guard," I said, stressing my words. "For these men here are going to walk a hundred yards in front of *Gruppe Drei* – on every march, Krebitz!"

"But . . . they don't know much about traps and mines. . . ."

"They had better start learning!"

"*Jawohl, Herr Oberleutnant.*"

"And something else. . . . Should you have a particularly dangerous job in the coming weeks, you will not call for volunteers. You already have your volunteers. We have to spare the lives of the more valuable men."

"*Jawohl!*"

"Dismiss!"

We marched back to the main column.

"Assemble!"

"Companies – single file! Attention!"

"*En avant . . . marche!*" Eisner commanded.

Daylight filtered away imperceptibly; the blue sky changed into grey and the breeze stilled. We stopped at a small cascade to grab a quick shower, then rested until daybreak.

I could not sleep that night. I was thinking of my family, of Lin, of the raped girls – and of what tomorrow might bring.

15

Move Quietly—Kill Quickly!

THREE days later and forty miles away Xuey and Krebitz detected another guerrilla base. It was not a permanent one but even so our raid was a success. Moving in the dead of night, we literally caught the Viet Minh napping. Posing as guerrillas, Xuey, Krebitz, and twelve men from *Gruppe Drei* infiltrated the camp and killed the sentries.

I moved in with fifty troops. The enemy was sound asleep in improvised hammocks stretched between the trees. Except for the low whisper of the wind-driven foliage the only sound we heard was the peaceful snoring of the terrorists. They must have come a long way. They were sleeping soundly. Dispersing into teams of three men each, we bayoneted the sleepers. With loathsome teamwork one trooper switched on his shaded flashlight, the second man thrust home into the heart. The moment the blade plunged in a third member of the team muffled cries and moans under a folded blanket which was pressed tightly against the victim's face. Sometimes a man had to be turned over or uncovered, and the executioners had to work very fast to prevent noise.

My headhunters moved with a precision born of experience, and liquidated some seventy guerrillas without causing as much as a whimper. Only seven girl Viet Minh were spared; their heads were later shaved and then we released them unhurt. The wind, the snoring and the quiet hiss of the blades; a few muffled moans and sighs – it was quite a spectacle. The groups worked like a hospital team around a surgery table, though not saving but extinguishing lives. We had no choice. In hostile territory one must move and kill like a leopard. It was a rule that had existed eons before the great Mao had come to write it all up and claim ownership.

War, whether in the desert or the jungle, is not a new invention; one may bring innovations but one may not alter the rules. A machine gunner who mows down a hundred men in a minute will seldom think of his victims. It never occurs to an artillery man that he kills. He may be working his howitzer in a peaceful meadow, or on the shore of a lake, to trigger death in a burning village many miles away. To shell or to shoot people is an impersonal affair. The executioner has no personal contact with the executed. To kill with the bayonet is not so easy. To kill with the bayonet in cold blood, one has to summon every ounce of hatred from deep within. Bitter recollections from the past, the haunting images of tormented and mutilated comrades, recalled in short flashes, give one the resolution to plunge the blade into the living body of another human being.

In all my years in uniform I have seen thousands of people die. I cannot recall the number of those I killed in combat or executed with my own hands – or killed indirectly by issuing an order to kill. Still, when the occasion arose, I had to repeat mentally, forcing myself into a state of self-hypnosis: You are trying to beat wild tigers into submission. . . . They are not human. . . . You are killing sharks, rats, bacteria. . . . Yet I doubt if I could ever have stabbed a captive tiger. I would lack the all-essential driving force – hatred. The tiger only follows the call of its nature, its instincts. The tiger never kills for pleasure. The Viet Minh kills only to spread terror and to intimidate its victims. For them I could feel no pity. I regarded the Viet Minh as the real prototypes of the Hitlerian subhumans. The most primitive Russian peasant harbored some noble features in his bearded face. At least I thought so. But the faces of those ratlike little Red gnomes in Indochina showed nothing but bestiality. Our hatred towards them knew no bounds. If we had had the means, we would have gassed them by the thousands without the slightest remorse.

Once again it was Xuey who spotted the guerrilla company as it forded the river. We split into three columns and deployed on the neighboring hills. Three hundred yards below the hill which my group occupied, a wide trail ran between the river bank and the woods farther to the east. Obviously the trail was a major enemy route. Between the river and the woods stretched a wide patch of open bushland. We observed a number of peasants filling what appeared to be large baskets with earth. Another group was planting live shrubs in the baskets.

"They are the Dan Cong," Noy explained after observing them briefly. The Dan Cong were the labor detachment of the Viet Minh, composed of ordinary peasants compelled to work as slaves a certain number of days every month for the cause of "liberation." The shrubs in the basket were a clever camouflage against air observation. Simply by moving the baskets onto the trail, the enemy could blot out the road and consequently the evidence of Viet Minh presence in the area.

Schulze, who had been watching the enemy for some time, suddenly turned toward me. "Look at that, Hans!" He handed me his field glasses excitedly. "Do you see what I see?"

"Dammit!" I swore in genuine astonishment. The scene which we observed was a most extraordinary and rather terrifying one. Down at the river, in plain sight, moved a small convoy of field howitzers. For the first time in Indochina we encountered Viet Minh artillery. I edged toward the precipice to have a better look.

Shouting and gesturing, a group of guerrillas entered the river and pulled ropes toward the opposite bank. "Look at it!" Erich exulted. "They even have a bridge there, a whole goddamned underwater bridge. We have got them dead center. This is not the shuttle service but a Viet Minh highway."

Indeed, the enemy appeared to be moving, or rather wading, across the river as if the water were only ten inches deep. They certainly *had* a bridge there, built to remain underwater. Otherwise the reconnaissance planes would have spotted it long ago. Hitched to teams of water buffalo, six small howitzers rolled down the grassy slope of the far bank and onto the bridge. The foremost terrorists had reached our bank and tightened the ropes on either side of the bridge to mark the way. Milling around the guns, pushing and pulling at the wheels, another Viet Minh group was assisting the animals. The enemy artillery caused considerable excitement among my troops.

"It seems that Giap is up to some big business somewhere in the not too distant future," Schulze remarked, lowering his field glasses. "I wonder where the howitzers are going?"

"I am kind of curious myself," Karl remarked.

I turned to Riedl. "Where is Xuey?"

"He went farther west with Krebitz and *Gruppe Drei.*"

"Where in the hell farther west? There is the river!"

He shrugged. "A river won't stop Krebitz. . . ."

"Send word to Eisner. He should move farther up, closer to the bridge, but no one is to fire before we open up here."

"Understood!"

I pointed toward the forest line where the trail entered the woods. "Karl! You should deploy on either side of the trail, keeping low. Riedl will join you."

Shouldering their submachine guns, Karl and Helmut rose. "Wait a moment," Noy spoke, lifting her kit. "I am coming with you."

I pulled her back in a not very gentle manner. "I have the feeling that you are not going anywhere. You are staying right here."

"But I only –"

"Noy! You just do as I say."

She sat down.

"Where are Chi and Thi?"

"With Sergeant Zeisl, I think," Suoi replied hesitantly.

"I asked you to keep them in sight, Suoi. Zeisl won't have time to look out for them."

"I am sorry. . . ."

I sent a trooper to fetch the girls.

The guns were coming across the bridge. A short, stocky guerrilla waded forward. Gesturing and hollering toward the peasants, he called to them; the peasants dropped their tools and rushed to help the guerrillas hauling the howitzers. On the other side of the river more Viet Minh emerged from the woods. Suspended from long poles which four men were carrying on their shoulders hung crates and sacks. Still others were pushing bikes laden with bags and boxes.

"A nice party," Erich commented. "The air force would love to join it. Shouldn't we call them, Hans?"

"Some other time, Erich. I want to get hold of those howitzers – undamaged."

He looked at me sharply. "The heck you want them. We cannot haul artillery pieces."

"You will be surprised. We are going to haul them right up here and prepare a reception party for some others."

"Are you planning to hold this hill?"

"This is a busy trail, Erich, with plenty of targets coming our way."

For a moment he looked startled; then he shrugged. "I guess we could camp out here," he said. "We have a good platform for the MGs, ample cover, and a good view of the river."

"Exactly!"

"Sergeant Krebitz is calling," Corporal Altreiter reported, holding the earphones for me.

"Krebitz.... Where the hell are *you?*"

"Across the river – watching the show."

"How did you get there?"

"We forded a mile upstream. No one has spotted us yet."

"How far are you from the bridge?"

"How far?" he repeated my question. "Can you see that tall peasant just moving down the trail toward the river? He is wearing a straw hat with a net hanging from it. The one with the bike ... tin cans all over it...."

I picked up my field glasses.

"Right now, he is passing a bare tree."

"I can see him."

Krebitz chuckled. "If I stretch my leg a bit I can kick him in the ass."

"Keep an eye on the group."

"How about keeping a couple of MGs on them?"

"Don't shoot until we open up here."

"Understood!"

The six howitzers were rolling along the trail and had almost reached the woods – where, if all went well, Karl and Helmut should be ready for them. A group of about fifty Viet Minh were still on the bridge; another party was between the bridge and the forest. The rest of the enemy detachment, I thought, was covered by *Gruppe Drei*.

"*Achtung!*" I warned my gunners, who tensed; eyes focused, trigger fingers tightened, gun barrels traversed slowly from left to right, then back again as the men tested the pivots.

"Fire!"

The muffled MGs caused little noise but their effect was shattering. We carried a large number of automatic weapons and, although as the attack progressed we gradually phased out a number of guns to save ammunition, our initial assault was always delivered with everything we had. The weapons were muffled to confuse the enemy at least for a few minutes. Afterwards the mufflers had to be removed to prevent the guns from overheating.

Between the river and the woods a section of the trail ran unprotected. The enemy was exposed to our fire from all sides. Within minutes the majority of the guerrilla company lay dead or wounded in the shrubbery along the trail. With our superior position resistance was futile. The surviving terrorists bolted for the forest only to run into Karl's favorite toy – the flamethrower.

Belching eighty-foot flames, Pfirstenhammer's group advanced on the river, burning the bewildered escapees as they went. Riedl took possession of the howitzers along with discarded crates and bags which littered the trail. The detachment caught on the bridge had been wiped out. Our six sharpshooters were busy picking off the swimmers and the few men who had managed to reach the far bank. On our side of the river, the enemy rout was complete. On the far side, Sergeant Krebitz and *Gruppe Drei* fared not so well. After the initial surprise the Viet Minh commander had managed to gather his battered company and they now began to fight back. The sharp staccato of the enemy MGs could be heard distinctly. Soon a dozen or more Viet Minh machine guns were chattering above the rapidly increasing volume of rifle fire.

Suddenly I realized that there must have been considerably more enemy troops on the far side of the river than Krebitz had previously observed. Since Krebitz had only about forty men with him, I began to worry for their safety. My fears seemed justified when a few minutes later mortar shells began to explode on and around the hill which Krebitz occupied. We later learned that a full Viet Minh battalion was only a mile from the river when the shooting started. Rushing forward, they joined the battle and the sudden reinforcement was now threatening to swamp Krebitz.

I called him on the wireless. "Tell Krebitz that he should have his eyes examined," Schulze yelled. "He sees a platoon where there is a whole goddamned brigade."

"Krebitz! How are things over there?"

"Shitty!" he replied flatly. "Is the way to the river free, Hans?"

"For the moment at least. Evacuate immediately and cross the river if you can manage it. Dammit, Rudolf – we cannot afford to lose you."

"Thanks for your concern about me, Hans."

"I am concerned about *Gruppe Drei*, you idiot!"

"Just have a few clean underpants ready for us," he cracked, "we might need them."

"We are giving you cover. Move out!"

I sent a message to Eisner to advance on the bridge and provide covering fire for *Gruppe Drei*. My gunners concentrated on the narrow strip of shrubbery that stretched between Krebitz and the Viet Minh MGs. The mortar fire was intense, and shells began to burst around our own positions. Five of them exploded below the hill but others were creeping upward, seeking our machine guns. We were heading for a major battle with a large enemy force, probably two battalions, and our immediate future did not seem too bright.

I watched Krebitz and his men as they came dashing from cover to cover between the shrubs. Bullets threw dust and dirt all around them. Every one of our weapons was now covering *Gruppe Drei* but even so, a couple of the men fell, never to rise again.

"They already got four of them!" Schulze yelled and swore. The next instant I heard a swift "whoooz" and we ducked instinctively. Three mortar shells screamed in and exploded in rapid succession. Whoever was directing the enemy mortars must have been an expert, for shells now began to fall everywhere; on the hill, in the river, along the trail. I saw that Eisner's company was getting its fair share, too.

"They are firing from over there!" Schulze yelled, pointing at a wooded hill about a mile from us on the far side of the river. Focusing my field glasses, I could just make out a group of Viet Minh working a dozen mortars. We managed to pin down the enemy MGs and riflemen while Krebitz was crossing the river. They couldn't use the coverless bridge, so *Gruppe Drei* had to wade and swim for the shrubby sanctuary on our side. None of our machine guns could effectively reach the enemy mortars, though some of Erich's gunners tried to jam them by firing at extreme angles.

"It's a waste of slugs," I told him. "At sixteen hundred yards they will only scratch the place where they hit."

"Never mind," Schulze replied. "We still have a faint chance of getting some of them in the eye."

I had to refrain from using our mortars. We had to preserve the limited amount of shells we had, for valuable targets such as Viet Minh camps, ammunition depots, and the like. To use them in an open battle only to silence a couple of enemy mortars and kill a dozen men would have been "extravagant", a luxury that we couldn't afford. The enemy could shell us at leisure. Only Pfirstenhammer's group appeared to be spared by the mortars, so, I decided after all, to send the girls to him.

"Say, Hans!" Schulze turned to me suddenly. "Shouldn't we ask Karl if he has any shells for those howitzers?"

"The howitzers!" In my excitement I had completely forgotten about the guns. It took only seconds to get Karl on the set. "Karl!" I called him excitedly. "We are having trouble with the mortars. Our MGs can't reach them. . . ."

"I gather that . . . do you want me to use the howitzers?"

"Have you got shells?"

"Some. . . ." Karl was obviously amusing himself.

"Then get moving. Karl. If the Viets keep firing at the rate they are blasting away at us now –"

"All right, all right . . . you can tell your sob story later, Hans," he cut in with a chuckle. "The guns are ready. I was about to call you myself. Just give me the elevations."

"I am sending the girls over to you."

"Nice of you, Hans. Start talking!"

With Schulze observing the enemy positions, I began to radio the trajectories. The first salvo was a hundred yards short. The second and third volley struck home, blasting men and mortars.

"How was it?" Karl asked; firing over a patch of woods he could not possibly observe the explosions.

"You are hitting them squarely, Karl. Keep firing!"

The rest was only routine.

The Viet Minh mortars ceased firing. The enemy commander thought it prudent to change location. While they were moving, Karl pumped a dozen shells into the shrubbery where the guerrilla machine gunners were deployed. Shortly afterwards the mortars fired again, though only a couple of rounds, and stopped before we could seek them out with the howitzers. Their shells scattered about the hill, blasting a few trees, chipping the rocks, a long way off target. Nevertheless, reports on casualties began to flow. *Gruppe Drei* reported eleven dead. More had been wounded by shell fragments. I ordered Krebitz to carry the wounded over to Karl's section where the nurses could safely attend to them. I was calling Eisner when a salvo of around twenty mortar rounds screamed in and plastered the foothills where Bernard was deploying in the shrubbery. The moment the shells exploded, I felt a grip at my throat. The wireless cut out. Schulze dropped his field glasses and buried his face in his hands.

"Eisner has had it!" Corporal Altreiter cried.

I rushed to the radio set.

"Adler . . . Adler calling Stella . . . Adler report in . . . report in. . . ." Altreiter kept calling, then lowered his earphones and shook his head.

"There's no reply."

I dispatched two men to look for survivors.

Moments later we spotted two large enemy detachments moving toward the river with the obvious intention of crossing above and below our positions and probably delivering a two-pronged attack at dusk. Since a third enemy unit was still occupying the shrubbery and woods on the far side of the river, I realized that we had grossly underestimated the strength of the enemy. Schulze thought that there was at least a Viet Minh brigade in the vicinity of the river. More and more mortars came into play and we learned that the six howitzers which we had captured were *not* the only ones the enemy possessed. Soon our howitzers were engaged in a vicious duel with four similar guns on the opposite hills. I began to dislike the situation.

One of our machine gunners called from the ridge overlooking the river. Rushing over to him, we saw a macabre drama on the enemy-occupied bank. Pursued by a group of terrorists, a comrade from *Gruppe Drei* was staggering toward the river. The trooper was obviously injured. He must have lain unconscious in the shrubbery for some time only to come to with enemy troops surging all around. The Viet Minh did not fire. They wanted the man alive.

Reaching the water, the trooper fell. He rose and waded a few more steps. An instant later the guerrillas swarmed over him. We could do nothing to save him. The terrorists were dragging him back toward the woods.

I ordered three machine guns to open fire on the struggling group. A young trooper at the nearest gun closed his eyes, swallowed hard, then grabbed the fire lever. He knew only too well what would be waiting for our comrade in the hands of the Viet Minh.

The group was caught in the murderous crossfire of the three MGs. In a few seconds it was all over. For our wounded comrade it was indeed a mercy killing. The Viet Minh would have skinned him alive. It had happened before.

The troopers whom I had sent to look for Eisner returned. They looked pale and shaken, trying to catch their breath. "Eisner is dead," one of them reported. "Sixteen others received direct hits. . . . Nothing's left of them but bits of flesh and clothes."

"Sergeant Zeisl and nurse Thi are tending the wounded," the second trooper added. "Nine men were hit, some of them badly."

The rate of the enemy fire was still on the increase. Defying our machine guns, more and more guerrillas deployed on the far side of the river, but no crossing was yet attempted. Karl must have silenced some of the Viet Minh howitzers but a few shells were still coming in to blast the trail and the hillside. Seven more of our comrades were killed. The mortars sent salvo after salvo. I could see projectiles bursting around the small patch of shrubbery where Karl had deployed. He was already moving the howitzers to a safer place.

All of a sudden Erich swore and rushed to the wireless.

"What's the matter?" I yelled after him.

"The girls!" he shouted and for a moment my breath failed me. "Look at them!" Schulze waved in the general direction of Karl's position. The next instant he was calling Pfirstenhammer.

Grabbing my field glasses I scanned the trail along the woods and understood Erich's consternation. I spotted Suoi and Noy kneeling beside a wounded comrade, ducking whenever a shell screamed overhead. Mortar shells exploded all around them.

"Karl!" I heard Schulze shout, "get the girls out of there and be quick about it."

"They are with a badly wounded man, Erich."

"I don't care if they are with Jesus Christ. . . . Get them out of there."

"I'm sorry, Erich," I heard Karl replying. "I have to attend to the guns. We have a battle going here, if you haven't noticed it."

"Karl, if anything happens to Suoi. . . ."

"I love Noy as much as you love Suoi, Erich."

I was much too preoccupied to listen to the rest of their conversation. I had to improvise a plan for tackling the situation and I had to do it very quickly. It was evident that as soon as darkness fell the enemy would cross the river. It was also very likely that they could wipe us out before sunrise through a series of human-wave assaults. I decided to call for reinforcements and aerial support.

"Hans, let me go over to the girls," Schulze spoke with a miserable look on his face.

Still preoccupied with my own thoughts I replied mechanically, "Go!" I knew he would be of little use to me if I refused.

Unable to do anything but sit tight, I sent word to our widely dispersed troops to ease up on the ammunition. The machine guns were gradually phased out, but the riflemen went on firing at individual targets when the target was clear enough to give a fair chance of scoring. Since we were self-supporting and independent from supplies and reinforcements, prolonged engagements with the enemy could cause us serious setbacks. We simply could not afford to fire off ammo at a rate of two to three thousand rounds per minute.

Our lower rate of fire only increased the guerrilla endeavors. One Viet Minh company crept right up to the river and made preparations for an early assault across the bridge. Our sharpshooters were picking off the boldest ones as fast as they could fire, reload, and fire again, yet the fearful toll did not seem to lessen the guerrillas' determination. They were pressing closer and closer to the possible crossing places.

In the nick of time two squadrons of fighter bombers dived out of the clouds. The moment the planes appeared, the enemy ceased firing on us and sprang for cover. The planes began to hammer away at the guerrillas, scores of whom had no time to reach the woods. Cannon shells, fragmentation bombs, rockets, and napalm rained from above. It was a great spectacle to watch – and needless to say, a welcome spectacle. Taking the mike, I settled down at the radio to send corrections to the squadron leader.

"How long has it been going on?" he asked me from somewhere above.

"Since morning!" I informed him.

He whistled. "You're lucky to be alive, man – you stepped into a real anthill. They are swarming all over the place."

"It's *your* game now, squadron leader. Make the best of it."

Again the planes screamed in over the treetops. The Viet Minh advance parties were plastered with steel and fire; explosions rumbled along the riverside and thick, oily smoke rose where the napalm bombs had been at work. The squadron leader came back on the line.

"They say you have enlisted a couple of cuties in your outfit just to keep up spirit," he called.

"We need lots of spirit," I replied. "There's no five-o'clock tea in the jungle, squadron leader."

"Just clear the trail of those guns. When the party is over we might decide to land, *cher ami.*"

"At the rate you are moving you'd burrow a tunnel through the hill."

I heard him chuckle. "Roger . . . Roger. . . . There is a whole bunch of them down below ready for the frying pan."

"*Très bien,* Charles, Roger, *zéro-cent-dix-sept – zéro-huit.*"

"*Attaquez!*"

Three of the planes banked, came down over a patch of forest and rained napalm. At four o'clock the transport planes arrived. The Paratroops began to descend, twelve hundred of them. Air ambulances settled at the foot of the hill. Their arrival signaled that for once we could deliver our wounded comrades to a hospital.

The battle came to a sudden end. The Viet Minh ranks eddied and then fled. On the far side of the river the trail was covered with hundreds of shattered bikes, wagons, boxes, crates, bales – and corpses; in the woods a hundred fires burned and the Paras were busy shooting down the panicked oxen and water buffalo that milled along the riverside. Not even beasts could be spared, for they were the principal means of Viet Minh transport.

That evening we gave a last salute to sixty-five of our fallen comrades. Among them were Sergeant Schenk and Bernard Eisner.

16

The Little Traitors

I FOUND the muffler-equipped machine guns which we used on so many occasions extremely effective, so long as no prolonged firing was necessary. With mufflers the barrels would quickly overheat. Another shortcoming was that mufflers blotted out the gunsights and tracers had to be used to zero in on the target. After several months of experimenting, Sergeant Krebitz discovered that fairly good silencers could be made from sections of hollow bamboo, padded with wet clay and wrapped in layers of cloth. The result was a clumsy contraption which nevertheless worked.

The soundless death coming from the "nowhere" always shattered the guerrilla morale. The initial shock and the ensuing panic usually prevented the enemy from executing necessary defensive measures. By the time their leaders decided what to do, it was too late for them to do anything but flee or perish. So whenever given a chance we killed in silence.

Scouting the Phu Loi mountains, *Gruppe Drei* spotted twelve terrorists as they were moving across a narrow footbridge suspended eighty feet above a deep gorge. Our sharpshooters went into action with their telescopic, silencer-equipped rifles. Within seconds the twelve Viet Minh were dead; their bodies fell into the abyss to be swept away by the swift current. The footpath leading to the bridge circled a cluster of rocks. Subsequent groups coming toward the crossing could not see the bridge and consequently were unaware of the fate of their comrades. Thinking that the group ahead of them had already crossed and entered the woods, the enemy detachments kept coming in groups of twelve at hundred-yard intervals. They were in turn shot off the bridge quietly but efficiently. Our sharpshooters exterminated three groups before one mortally wounded guerrilla entangled himself in the supporting ropes and remained hanging over the precipice in plain sight. Even then we managed to kill seven more Viet Minh who rushed forward to help what they thought was a comrade in distress. The rest of the enemy then dispersed among the rocks and we refrained from any further activity. The enemy could do nothing but watch our side of the gorge. Hours went by while the opposing parties waited in tense expectation; then we spotted a couple of guerrillas crawling toward the bridge. The sharpshooters allowed them to proceed until they showed their heads; alas, that was the last guerrilla endeavor to reach the bridge. Our sharpshooters were quite capable of hitting a man in the head from five hundred yards.

At another time we encountered a small Viet Minh detachment as it moved single file down a trail. Our sharpshooters went into action. They began by shooting the last man in the file. With a bullet in the brain, one does not make much noise. The rearmost terrorist dropped and those ahead of him marched on unaware of the mishap. A dozen terrorists could be liquidated before their comrades realized that they were under attack.

In such attacks the survivors would disperse and take cover, not knowing where to turn, where to shoot. The sudden realization that the jungle was no longer their ally, that it harbored an invisible adversary who killed in silence, the thought that they might be sitting in the center of a deadly trap, demoralized the enemy. In my opinion all troops engaged in antiguerrilla warfare should be issued rifle silencers. It was the kind of opposition the Viet Minh dreaded: the unknown, the unseen, the unheard death. One should remember that the majority of their troops were primitive men, naïve and superstitious. When fighting against primitives, every psychological "trick" that one could think up should be exploited; the fact that the Viet Minh had discarded their spears and bows and, thanks to the benevolent Soviet supplies, now brandished rifles and automatic weapons did not cancel out the fact that they were still primitives. Except for a few of their higher leaders, the average intelligence and general mentality of the Viet Minh fighter was that of the Stone-Age man, educated only in the art of killing.

With my battalion at large in their jungle sanctuaries, the guerrillas could no longer set up camps in the hills or in the villages. Only at the constant risk of severe punishment could they light open fires, play music, chatter aloud, laugh or sing. When they ignored the new rules of the game, death came to them swiftly and unexpectedly. By the end of our fifth week in the Communist rear, the Viet Minh High Command had mobilized about five thousand men to trap and exterminate us. Their equipment had been seized from the French or was the very best that their Soviet and Chinese patrons could offer.

But we moved too fast for their liking and slowed down only to trap a posse that came too close for comfort. We annihilated one large Viet Minh detachment and decimated two others. Inestimable casualties were caused by the mines and booby traps which Sergeant Krebitz planted in their path. Once, when a Viet Minh company followed us for over a week, Riedl and Schulze lured it into a depression and blasted a sixty-foot cliff over the lot. Another posse marched headlong into Karl's flamethrowers and was burned up before it had a chance to utter a death cry. But regardless of their losess the enemy kept pressing us. We, too, suffered casualties; two men here, five men there – something we could not afford.

Having established our presence in the Phu Loi mountain area for the benefit of our pursuers, we quit the district quietly and cut back to the Nam Ou river, so as not to reveal ourselves on the way, we refrained from bothering enemy-held localities, which we bypassed. Camping down near the bank we spotted a number of barges floating downstream, loaded with guerrilla supplies. Xuey suggested that we should allow them to proceed undisturbed. During a reconnaissance trip, Xuey had discovered a major Viet Minh depot in a village some eight miles from where we were, "We should not spoil the big catch by destroying a small convoy," he said and I agreed with him. The barges were coming from China and were heading for that depot anyway.

Moving through the dark field the battalion deployed swiftly. By dawn the village was completely surrounded. We moved in shortly after sunrise and encountered no resistance. No one in the settlement professed to know anything about weapons, or the Viet Minh, though in the huts we discovered a quantity of Communist propaganda material. From a pole hung the flag of the Liberators.

"The guerrillas put it there two weeks ago, when they were passing through our village," I was told. "The Viet Minh commander said that if we removed the flag, they would burn our village." No, there were no terrorists in the locality.

But we knew that a large number of terrorists were around. We had kept the place under observation since the day before and had seen many armed guerrillas who could not have departed during the night. Schulze and Riedl had covered every exit – the road, the footpaths, and even the river. Sergeant Krebitz and Xuey had counted at least fifty terrorists coming and going in the village, unaware of our presence in the nearby woods. Then they must have spotted us and scurried to safety. Now everything appeared quiet and peaceful.

Why did the enemy decide not to resist? Either because they found us too strong, or because something in or about the place was much too important to be revealed.

The Viet Minh had resorted to one of its favorite tricks of camouflage: guerrillas dispersed among the dwellings, posing as members of the various families, or, submerged among the peasants, engaged in some peaceful activity in the fields. Some could have also withdrawn into secret tunnels or cellars to "sweat it out" until we departed.

We rounded up the male population, save for men of advanced age, and separated them from the women and children. While Pfirstenhammer and Suoi questioned the women about the men, Xuey, Schulze, and I concentrated on the men. Among them we discovered a few individuals who could have been local or visiting terrorists but we never executed anyone on mere suspicion. I employed a simple but effective method for weeding out terrorists: I requested the women to name and describe their male relatives who lived under the same roof. The identity of husbands, sons, brothers, and other genuine relatives was quickly established. Answers and descriptions given by the men had to match those given by the women. When the mutual replies showed discrepancies, the "adopted relatives" could be flushed out in no time.

Occasionally the nonresident guerrillas prepared cover stories in advance. A woman, for instance, could name and accurately describe a "brother" or an "uncle" who, in fact, was a total stranger – and vice versa. Assumed identities, however, could never pass additional questions related to more intimate particulars. Naturally, when alleged brothers and sisters disagreed about the features of "their" deceased fathers – for example, whether or not he had a scar on the right cheek – the questioning ended then and there and the shooting started.

Small children would often reveal a terrorist who was trying to pose as a close relative. Our system functioned brilliantly against the nonresident guerrillas and could also be used to uncover the local Viet Minh. Children between three and five years of age were remarkably useful. Before we questioned a child we separated him or her from the parents and gained the child's confidence with candy or small toys. Tribal children seldom receive either candy or toys. Sometimes it was enough to take a small boy or girl, show them a pistol or a machine gun, and ask them, between bites of chocolate, if they ever had seen anything similar. The innocent reply would come: "Uncle Han has many in his cellar."

Once our conversation with a five-year-old boy ran somewhat like this:

"Whose little boy are you, Xui?"

"Mother's and father's."

"And where is your father now?"

"He is away hunting. We need food."

"Does he hunt often?"

"Oh, yes. . . ."

"Then he has a gun, eh?"

"Yes, a big gun, and many little ones. The soldiers gave them to him."

"What soldiers, Xui?"

"Father Ho's soldiers."

By questioning people individually, we managed to uncover a dozen or more nonresident guerrillas, who were taken into the woods and executed. The troops proceeded to search the huts. In one of the shacks we spotted a small, clever-looking boy about five years of age. He did not look frightened but walked up to Schulze and boldly asked him if he was a French soldier.

"No, we are German soldiers, not French," Erich replied jokingly. His answer seemed to satisfy the boy, who then asked: "Do German soldiers shoot French soldiers?"

"Sometimes they do indeed," Erich replied and we all laughed. After all, Erich *was* telling the truth.

"Then you are good soldiers," the boy stated. "French soldiers shoot people, Father Ho says."

His mother tried to hush him up. I ordered her to be taken out. She wouldn't leave but threw herself on the floor screaming, imploring us to leave the boy alone.

"We are not going to hurt him," Xuey told her, but to no avail. The woman continued to scream and outside the civilians began to join in.

"Take her out of here," I ordered the troopers. "The others may think we are torturing or raping her."

Sergeant Krebitz needed four companions to drag the struggling woman outside. The boy began to cry and wanted to run after her. Schulze caught him and placed a small toy tank on the ground.

"We only wanted to give you a present," Xuey explained smiling. "We did not want your mother to see it."

The moment the tank began to move, with its turret shooting sparks, the boy stopped weeping; eyes wide in astonishment, he sprang after the toy and grabbed it.

"It is yours, you see," Xuey said. He explained to the boy how to wind the spring mechanism. "What is your name?" he asked.

"Nuo," came the reply, without the boy even looking at us. He lowered himself to the floor and followed the tank with fascinated dark eyes. I signaled to my companions and we sat down on the ground to run the tank between us and the boy, talking to hold his attention.

I placed my rifle on the mat and Nuo clapped his hands as the tank clambered over its stock. "Do you know what this is, Nuo?" I asked him.

"Yes, I know – a tank! The soldiers say the French have many tanks, real big ones. When we have tanks, we will shoot many many French soldiers."

"What soldiers say that, Nuo?"

"Father Ho's partisan soldiers."

"Do Father Ho's soldiers visit your village?" Xuey asked winding the tank.

"They always come to tell us how many Frenchmen they shot." He looked up sharply. "You said you were not French soldiers."

"Do I look French to you?" Xuey smiled.

"Not you – but *you*." Nuo pointed toward us.

"We are Germans, Nuo. I've already told you that."

"Where is your home?"

"Many weeks' walk from here," Schulze obliged. "Where you see the sun going down – there we live."

"Your village is big?"

"Very big, Nuo. Do you know where Father Ho's soldiers are now?"

"In the tunnel," he said matter-of-factly, playing with the tank. "But they will come out soon."

We exchanged glances and Xuey signaled me to let him do the talking now. He wrinkled the mat in such fashion that the tank could clamber up and down the ridges.

"Why did Father Ho's soldiers go into the tunnel, Nuo?" Xuey asked quietly. "We are friends."

"They thought you were Frenchmen. When they see that you are not French, they will come out."

"Is it a big tunnel?"

"Very big. Many men sleep there."

Nuo carried a blanket to the cot and let the tank run on it. We helped him to arrange the folds in various patterns of "hills" and "valleys".

"Do you know where the door of the tunnel is?" Xuey asked the crucial question casually. "Is it here in your house?"

"No," he shook his head. "One door is under Bo's house but there are many others too. The soldiers use the door in the well."

"Which well?"

"The well behind Xuong's house."

Ten minutes later we knew everything. The tunnel had several exists but the guerrillas used an opening placed halfway down in a well. There was also an underwater exit into the river for emergency use.

The boy glanced up. "Can I go and show the tank to the boys?"

"Sure – show them, Nuo." Erich nodded.

Xuey led the child gently toward the door. "Don't tell anyone that you spoke about the tunnel and Father Ho's soldiers. . . . Not even to your mother."

"Why not?"

"Because it is a secret. They will beat you and take your tank away."

"Then I won't tell," he said determinedly.

"Good boy!"

I sent a trooper to take Nuo to his mother, who, with the rest of the civilians, had been removed from the village. We could not detect where the underwater exit was, so I lined the riverbank with fifty men at twenty-yard intervals. Then we went to examine the well.

It was about forty feet deep. Our searchlight revealed no opening in its walls, which appeared to be smooth earth, covered with planks here and there. Riedl hauled up the wooden bucket. It was bone dry. "They aren't using this well to get water, that's for sure," he commented.

Pfirstenhammer examined the rope. He cut away the bucket and began to wind the loose end about his waist. "Give me a lamp," he said, "I'm going down."

"All right, but be careful."

He flung his legs over the ledge and started to descend. Schulze and I were playing out the rope slowly. Karl suddenly yelled, "Hans!" His voice sounded hollow as it echoed from the well. "It is right here – facing the house. . . . It is covered with a stone slab. . . . Oaaaaah!" We heard his cry of agony; his voice trailed off and his lamp fell, shone for a moment than went out.

"Karl!" I cried. "Are you all right?" There was no answer but his weight on the rope seemed to have increased.

"Let's get him out of there!" Schulze shouted. Bracing ourselves we hauled on the rope like a pair of madmen. I could hear a strange grating sound as Karl came up.

"*Gott im Himmel!*" Riedl cried, his face ashen.

We lifted Karl to the ground. Blood was oozing from his breast and he was breathing his last. A four-foot spear with a two-inch-wide blade had been driven into his chest. His eyes were open but he could not speak. Moments later he was dead.

"*Sauhunde!*" Erich swore. He sprang to the well, his face distorted. Tearing a grenade from his belt he threw it into the well, then staggered away as the blast erupted from down below. He grabbed the spear in Karl's breast and pulled it free.

"Keep this!" He handed it to Krebitz, who had just arrived panting at Karl's body. "I will put the blood of a hundred terrorists on this blade," he cried. "By God, I will!"

Taking his kerchief, Riedl wiped the blood from Karl's face. He was sobbing openly. "We are going, we are all going . . . Eisner, Schenk, now Karl . . . we are too few and we are all damned. . . ."

"Shut up, Helmut!"

As the news spread, small groups of troopers gathered around us in silence. Sergeant Zeisl and the girls came. Realizing what had happened, Noy uttered a faint cry and collapsed beside Karl. Riedl lifted her and led her away. With his eyes narrowed and his lips set in a savage thin line, Schulze walked back to the well. He flashed his light into the depths, then turned toward me.

"What do you intend to do about it, Hans?"

"We are going to blast them, Erich."

"Shall I go down to see what we can do?"

"Like hell you will!" I snapped. "We have had enough climbing for today."

"Now we know what to expect."

"Not on your life."

Sergeant Zeisl and the medics laid Karl on an improvised stretcher and covered him with a blanket.

"We will take him into the hills and bury him decently," I said slowly, then turned to Riedl. "Deploy around every hut, every barn, and every object that might conceal an exit from the tunnel. Open those which the boy spoke of and fill the holes with earth and rubble. No one is to enter any cellar or tunnel. Understood?"

"Understood!"

"Take Noy with you," I added after a moment. "Take care of her."

"I will do that, Hans."

I spoke to Krebitz. "Do you think we can blast the way open from the well?"

"I should first see where to put the charge."

"That's out of question. You cannot go down."

He pursed his lips. "Then it's going to be difficult, Hans. To blast the entrance we would have to suspend a charge down below, approximately opposite the opening, then cover up the well to force the blast to work horizontally instead of escaping upward into the open."

"You may have the whole village to work for you."

He shook his head. "It is not a question of workmen. The terrorists would cut the rope and drop the charge long before we could cover up the well and prepare for the blasting."

"What do you suggest then?"

"I can blast a hole *down* to the tunnel from above."

"From where?"

"From here – where we are standing. Karl said that the entrance appeared to face the house." He walked slowly in the direction of the tunnel, then stopped. "From here!"

"How long will it take?" Schulze queried.

"Who cares?" I said. "We are going to stay right here until we have got all those bastards."

"I should say ninety minutes. It depends on the ground," Krebitz said.

"Do it then."

Sergeant Krebitz collected his men and they set to work, digging a shaft. Ten minutes later Krebitz yelled: "Take cover!"

An explosion rocked the village; at the well a twisting pillar of smoke spiraled skyward. I went to see the crater. It was about six feet deep and ten feet wide. When the dust settled, the men clambered down to bore another shaft for the subsequent blasting.

With the fourth charge, Krebitz blasted into the tunnel. At the bottom of the now twenty-foot-deep crater we saw a wide jagged hole. Krebitz flung four grenades into the opening, then descended. Keeping clear of the hole, the men of *Gruppe Drei* set up a flamethrower with its muzzle pointing down into the hole at an angle. Soon a cloud of thick smoke emerged from the crater. Holding on to the ropes, Sergeant Krebitz ascended, coughing and spitting. "Now let's get out of here just in case the thing is blazing away at an ammo crate," he yelled.

With hand grenades we demolished every hut that concealed a tunnel exit, then, accompanied by Schulze, I went down to the river. "Now they will either roast alive or swim for it," Schulze said bitterly.

Back at the hole Sergeant Krebitz installed the second flamethrower that was soon followed by a third one. Suddenly a pair of hands popped to the surface, eighty yards downstream from where we stood. They submerged instantly.

"There they go!" a trooper yelled and cut loose with his submachine gun.

The hunt was on!

More hands appeared, singly or in clusters of threes and fours – a couple of heads broke the surface, but stayed in sight for only a fraction of a second. As the guns sprayed the water, Schulze yelled, "Use hand grenades, men! The grenades will bring them up or send them down for good."

Many of the swimmers escaped the bullets but none survived the subsurface explosions. The grenades were deadly. As the river erupted in a dozen muddy funnels of water the swimmers popped to the surface, many of them dead. Others who suffered internal injuries from the concussions thrashed aimlessly until the machine guns silenced them forever. Twenty yards from where we stood a pair of hands rose from the subsiding waves of a blast; the fingers moved, twisting and grasping like a disembodied pair of ghastly limbs trying to signal. The nearest trooper pivoted his light machine gun toward the easy target. A hail of slugs hit the hands and tore them away at the wrist. The bleeding stumps shook crazily, then sank out of sight. A wounded guerrilla emerged and stood waist-deep in the water with blood oozing from his ears and nostrils; raising his arms he staggered toward the bank; he fell, rose again, crying: "Mercy . . . mercy." An instant later the slugs knocked him back into the water.

One after another the guerrillas surfaced – dazed, shocked, exhausted, unable to swim the corridor of death. A few of them tried to crawl ashore, others just stood in the shallow water dumbfounded or blinded, until the bullets spun them back into their murky graves.

Suddenly there were no more guerrillas in sight. The river flowed peacefully as if nothing had happened.

When the smoke cleared, Sergeant Krebitz surveyed the tunnels, altogether two hundred yards long. It was a well-built complex with several large chambers for stores and sleeping quarters. Krebitz counted three hundred bunks.

Three of the chambers were loaded to capacity with weapons and ammunition. Sergeant Krebitz selected what we could use, then the tunnels were blown up with delayed-action charges. The explosion tore a thirty-foot-wide and twenty-foot-deep trench across the village; the ensuing air pressure flattened every hut within a radius of five hundred steps in either direction.

None of the villagers had been hurt, except by the sad fact that they had no village to return to, but, alas, *c'est la guerre!* If one plays with fire, one can burn oneself.

We buried Karl Pfirstenhammer on a hill and placed a heavy boulder over his improvised grave. I sat there for a long time with Noy, telling her of my meeting with Karl on the Danube in 1945; the wine we drank, the fried fish we ate, his clay pipe . . . his little sister Erika, who was now a young lady, studying to become a doctor. In my kit I had Karl's wallet with her picture, and it was my gloomy task to write her a letter – the last letter she would receive from Indochina.

Sergeant Krebitz erected a small wooden cross. On it we nailed Karl's French beret and his Wehrmacht belt inscribed: "*Gott mit uns*" – "God be with us" – that he always wore.

We stood in attention, then sang in a low tune:

Heil dir im Siegeskranz,
Heil dir im Siegeskranz. . . .

A last salute – then tears were wiped away and guns flung over the shoulders.

Forward!

17

The Red Highway (Operation "Deluge")

THE battalion was camped for the fifth day, but the downpour did not seem to lessen. It was raining without a break; the hours of daylight shortened and deep in the jungle between the thickly forested hills the hours of darkness stretched to almost eleven hours. A wicked wind blew from the southeast, tearing at our flimsy lean-to shelters and driving the heavy drops through our fatigues and underwear.

Cooking was out of question and our tobacco turned into a soggy mess that could not be lit. Since the rain started our diet had consisted of dried fish, biscuits, and vitamin pills. The only fire which we were able to light was burning inside a shallow crevice, barely large enough to accommodate the girls. There we prepared boiled sweet potatoes, rice with curried fish, and occasionally a cup of tea for the girls and for Xuey, who was down with fever and abdominal pain.

Sergeant Zeisl suspected appendicitis, a condition which in the circumstances was a death sentence. Our faithful little Indochinese companion knew it too and he accepted the inevitable with a faint ironic smile saying: "We all have to go one day. Just let me go without much pain." I sat beside him for a long time under the tarpaulin sheet which the men had rigged up between the trees to make a primitive tent.

"You have reached your objective," Xuey said, giving my hand a feeble squeeze, "but you will have to be very careful from now on. A hundred times more careful than ever before. Those down there are professionals." He turned his face slightly toward the steaming valley. "They overlook nothing." Even now he only thought of our welfare. Then he asked for some sleeping pills and Zeisl obliged.

The densely wooded plateau where we had established ourselves, for better or worse, was the only place where the streams, now swollen to rivers, wouldn't flood us. Throughout the night we heard the crashings of uprooted trees and the distant thud of tumbling rocks and earth. During the day, the entire world seemed to be moving downward, along the slopes, into the valley.

Barely two miles away, in a narrow valley, was an important terrorist supply base, "a king's ransom" as Schulze put it. A twelve-foot-wide jungle road ran through the enemy camp and into it entered a network of smaller paths. We had arrived at the long-sought "Red Highway", the main terrorist supply route between China and the southern provinces. No troops of the Foreign Legion had ever before come closer to it than a hundred kilometres. Its existence had been suspected but never proven. Only airplanes were able to penetrate so far into the Communist rear; they had done so on many occasions but had observed nothing but unbroken jungles. Like all the important Viet Minh establishments in the hills, the Red Highway was a masterpiece of camouflage. It had been cut through the jungle without allowing as much as ten yards of it to be exposed to the skies. At a few less densely wooded sections, hundreds of trees had been roped together and drawn closer to one another with the aid of pulley-like contraptions. Then they had been fastened in such a way that their crowns intertwined over the road. In the open ravines networks of strong wire had been stretched between the slopes to support creepers, which had soon blotted out the road beneath.

The jungle road included permanent bridges, twelve to fifteen feet wide, most of them constructed a few inches underwater to fool aerial observation. Difficult or swampy sections of the road had been "paved" either with stones or with logs leveled with gravel. Along the Red Highway were checkpoints where guerrilla MPs controlled transport or troop movements. Rest-houses and service stations where carts and bicycles could be repaired also were located on that incredible network of trails. Its very existence was ridiculed by some leading French statesmen. It was simply too incredible to believe. Yet it was there!

Here the enemy was no longer taking chances. While trying to approach the camp to have a better look, Xuey and Sergeant Krebitz had had to stop short of concealed machine gun positions at eight different points. The emplacements were not easily observable, though they were not hastily dug foxholes but what one may rightly call permanent fortifications. Small blockhouses, constructed of heavy logs, covered with earth in which shrubs had then been planted, commanded all the approaches to the Viet Minh base. Along the relatively short section of the jungle road which Xuey had been able to investigate, he spotted two Viet Minh observation platforms. Rigged up high on the hilltop trees, the platforms offered a perfect view of the neighborhood. The guerrilla lookouts could spot not only airplanes but also any overland intruders who imprudently proceeded across the nearby ridges.

The base must have been only one of many similar bases established along the Red Highway. It included permanent huts where the arriving troops or coolies could rest for a while before resuming their long walk south.

Despite the difficult approach, Krebitz had identified nine storage shelters which contained hundreds of bulky bales, jute bags, and wooden crates. He had also observed brisk traffic in the area. Viet Minh units arrived or departed at about six-hour intervals, even at nighttime. Among them were armed troops and coolies who drove heavily laden bullock carts or pushed bikes. Still others transported crates suspended from long poles shouldered by four or six men.

Xuey had wanted to infiltrate the base alone. There were so many strangers in and about the place that he thought he would be in no danger while mingling with the enemy. Then the downpour had started and Xuey had come down with fever and the pain in his abdomen.

Sergeant Zeisl was sure of his diagnosis of appendicitis. "I don't think I am mistaken," he said.

"What are his chances?" Schulze wanted to know, much depressed by the unexpected calamity.

Zeisl shook his head slowly. "Without an operation – none at all, Erich. The antibiotic will slow down the infection but Xuey should be on the operating table very soon."

"How soon?"

"Within twenty-four hours at the most."

Xuey dozed off into a restless sleep and we huddled under the narrow burlap, trying to decide what to do.

"We are certainly having it all right," Riedl fumed. "And it had to happen right now. . . . What do you want to do about Xuey, Hans?" He was looking at me as though fearing my answer in advance.

"What do *you* want me to do, Helmut?" I asked him in turn.

He flicked away his cigarette butt and ran a nervous hand through his dripping hair. "We just can't watch the poor devil die."

"We should call for a copter," Schulze suggested.

"Call a copter?" Sergeant Krebitz chuckled. "Sharks might fly in this downpour but nothing on wings, Erich."

"Copters have no wings," he sulked. "Xuey is too good a buddy to let him die like this."

"Besides we might need him in the future," Riedl added gloomily.

I was already considering that possibility. Whether the army would be willing to risk craft and crew on such a mission remained to be seen. Besides could the pilot find us in the pouring rain with visibility amost zero?

"We are very close to the enemy base. They will hear the copter coming in," Krebitz remarked.

"No, not in this rain," Erich insisted. "You wouldn't hear a thirty-two-centimeter shell exploding two hundred yards from here."

"The rain might stop at any time."

"We could move Xuey a few miles from here and guide the copter to a safer place."

"That we might try," Krebitz agreed.

"If they will send a copter at all," I remarked.

"Colonel Houssong will send one," said Riedl. "He would never let us down."

I turned to Corporal Altreiter. "Will the radio work, Horst?"

He shrugged. "One can always try."

"Try it then. . . ."

And so we decided to do something for Xuey that we had seldom done for our own kind. . . .

Twenty minutes later our signals were answered and my message went through. A copter was to take off within an hour and we could expect it to arrive in three hours. I chose to transport Xuey to a barren ridge four miles away. It was a devilish undertaking in the pouring rain. The stretcher bearers had to ford swollen streams and climb slippery elevations where every instant landslides or tumbling trees threatened to wipe out the group. Eight men of *Gruppe Drei* volunteered for the perilous trip, and they had to start immediately if they were to reach the ridge before dark.

We agreed to transmit a steady radio beam which the copter could "ride" to within a few miles of our camp, then Sergeant Krebitz was to take over with walkie-talkies.

I wrote a short but informative report to Colonel Houssong, in German. The colonel did not understand German, but neither did the Viet Minh. If my report, written in French, fell into enemy hands the consequences would be immediate. The German text would always provide us with time to do whatever there was to be done. The guerrilla commanders had no immediate means of learning the implications of a message in German.

In this respect, however, I underestimated the Viet Minh. A few months later we learned that for over six months three German nationals from the Soviet Zone had been attached to the Viet Minh High Command. Their principal task was to keep track of our communications and to evaluate our activities in general. The three German Communists had often been to the field, sometimes quite close to places which we had actually attacked and badly mauled. Knowing us well, the Viet Minh had been extremely careful not to allow them into any dangerous areas but since our movements were, in most cases, unknown to the enemy, their precautionary measures had been quite useless. It was only sheer luck that prevented our treacherous "compatriots" from falling into our hands on two occasions. From the interrogation of prisoners we learned that we had missed by only three miles the turncoat camp at Muong Bo. On another occasion, they had been among the thirty-four survivors who escaped Pfirstenhammer's flamethrower attack on a small Viet Minh camp south of Cao Bang, an action in which over a hundred terrorists had perished. It would have given us immense pleasure to entertain those envoys of Walter Ulbricht. Erich nicknamed them "the ratpack of Pankow" and we loathed them even more than we hated the Viet Minh.

We had bad luck with our Communist counterparts but we did manage to capture a Soviet instructor in 1950; according to his papers he was Major Senganov. His interrogation led to the capture of one more Russian "adviser" and two high-ranking Chinese officers in a tunnel system two miles away. After questioning, the Chinese were shot out of hand. I was about to call for a copter to ferry our illustrious Russian guests back to Hanoi when Erich quietly remarked that we should not place Colonel Houssong and his superiors in an impossible position.

"Not even Paris," he reasoned, "can hold the Ivans and at a word from Stalin they will be given a first-class air ticket back to Moscow." Indeed, with the Berlin blockade still fresh in the postwar history, the incident could easily trigger another crisis with unforeseen consequences. "The moment the French High Command knows about the Russians, their hands will be bound by Paris and in the end we are going to pay for it," he explained. I accepted his reasoning.

We executed the Russians in a cave which Sergeant Krebitz then blasted shut. Seven months later, when we passed the place again, the fallen boulders and earth were already overgrown with vegetation, erasing all traces of the secret tomb. When told of the incident, Colonel Houssong's only comment was a relieved "*Dieu merci.*"

"You cannot imagine what would have happened if you had brought them in," he said and requested us to erase the place from our maps – even the footpath that led to the one-time cave.

The men of *Gruppe Drei* improvised a stretcher and lay the

dozing Xuey on it. Schulze covered him with a burlap, which he then fastened to the primitive contraption with a couple of belts. "The sedative will keep him asleep for a while," Sergeant Zeisl told me. "Let's hope he gets to Hanoi all right."

We shook hands with Sergeant Krebitz. "The hills are going to be slippery. Take care!"

"Don't worry," he replied, wiping the rain from his face. "If we cannot climb, we are going to swim them. There is enough water in the hills to float a raft between the peaks."

The party departed and we sank back under the burlap. Suoi and the girls prepared some biscuits with jam. Noy poured five cups of hot tea – a very tempting delicacy which we gently declined to accept.

"You drink it," Schulze urged the girls, nodding toward a dozen of our comrades who were sitting miserably soaked beneath the dripping trees. We never accepted a privilege that was denied to our comrades. It was rule number one of our jungle code of companionship.

"So much for Xuey's reconnaissance trip," Riedl remarked quietly, as Sergeant Krebitz and his small group disappeared into the woods. I, too, was thinking of our fat prize so temptingly close yet now so far out of reach.

Then all of a sudden Noy stood before me. "I go there, commander," she announced resolutely. "I can do what Xuey wanted to do. . . . See camp. Thi comes with me."

"I come," Thi nodded. The two must have discussed the matter already.

Riedl protested. "That's ridiculous, Hans," he began, but he stopped short of saying anything else. He, too, realized the importance of Noy's mission. We desperately needed information. Someone had to go and only a native Indochinese could penetrate the base.

"There are many, many women in the camp," Noy insisted. "They come and go."

"Nobody will know us not belong there," Thi added in her broken French. "We see camp and come back."

"What do you think of it, Erich?" I asked Schulze.

"I think it is quite feasible."

I turned to Noy and reached for her hand. "Do you think you will be all right, Noy?"

"*Jawohl*, commander," she replied in German and smiled. "We go there, see all and come back. Then you can attack."

"It is very important for us that you *do* come back, Noy. Not only because of the information you might bring back but because we all like you very much and we think you belong to the battalion."

She blushed slightly, lowered her head, and said quietly, "I am doing it for Karl." She looked up and smiled. "Don't worry."

"If you overstay, I shall go and bring you back myself," Riedl stated. "Be careful."

Noy and Thi had been away for three days, and we could do nothing but hope for the best and wait for their return. The day after their departure the rain finally stopped but the sky remained overcast, and we had to keep our sodden clothes on until they dried from our own body heat. Sergeant Krebitz and his party returned muddy to the ears and dead tired – but also successful. Xuey was safely on his way to Hanoi. Schulze, who somehow always managed to keep his tobacco dry, lit a cigarette for Krebitz. "How was your trip?"

"*Merde!*" Krebitz grunted, puffing contentedly. "Twice we slipped into a river, performed a ski slalom with stretcher, provisions, and all down a hundred-foot slope, missed a falling boulder by inches, and almost guided the copter into a cliff. The pilot finally managed to land the thing with its left gear hanging over a precipice. The crew dumped some crates, we pushed the stretcher through the hatch; a guy grabbed your report and off they went. And just as well, because half a minute later the whole precipice began to crumble. I guess the vibration had done it. The whole works went to hell, and we barely managed to jump clear."

"A magnificent venture," Schulze grinned; reaching into his rucksack he withdrew a canteen. "You deserve an extra rum, Rudolf."

"You should see what's in the crates big daddy sent us."

Krebitz gulped some rum, wiped the canteen, and handed it over to one of his troopers. "Toss it around and don't be shy – it's on the house."

Colonel Houssong had been thoughtful enough to send us everything we were short of. The crates contained, among other items, tea, coffee, cigarettes, tobacco, jam, insect repellent, saccharin, matches, drugs, and letters. Among them were two for me, from my parents and from Lin. There is nothing more heartening than to receive letters in the jungle – "a hundred miles beyond God's back," as Karl used to say. Letters from Europe, from people who lived (incredibly enough) in nice homes with beds, electric light, and bathrooms.

"Yesterday we spent a magnificent day at Bexhill-on-the-Sea," Lin wrote. "My uncle has a small plot and a trailer there. After lunch we went to the movies and saw a terrific French picture with Yves Montand, 'The Wages of Fear'; in the evening we had a garden party with barbecue. I truly hope you will visit us here one day. . . ."

Cities, highways, bars, cinemas – people changing their shirts twice daily, people at beach parties . . . *Europe*. . . . I read the letters as if they brought news from another planet.

"I hope you are not living too dangerously," Lin wrote. "The news about Indochina is quite fearful. Please don't risk your own well being for a transient advantage that is going to be lost anyway. The newspapers here are writing that whatever you may do (or for that matter, whatever the British Tommies may achieve in the British dependencies) the future of the colonies will be decided here in Europe, or maybe in America. Don't risk your life in chasing the shadow of a victory that cannot be yours, Hans."

How right she was. . . .

"Life is improving here," my father wrote. "There is much talk about a peace treaty which would restore Germany to her own people. Personally I believe it is only twaddle. I doubt if Stalin will ever conclude a peace treaty with us. Eighty percent of whatever Russia now has, from photo cameras to printing machines, is coming from the zone that the Russians are busy milking round the clock. Stalin will never give up his German 'cow.' Here in the west we now have enough provisions. Most of the industries have been rebuilt, also the cities and villages. Everything was financed by the Americans! Naturally not because they began to 'like' us, but for the simple reason that they need a strong buffer state between the Reds and the rest of Europe. The prosecution of the so-called 'Nazi criminals' continues. It will probably go on forever. The only change is that it is no longer the Allied Military Tribunal but German courts who prosecute and condemn. Alas, son – Germans versus Germans. Those who were slimy enough to escape prosecution themselves now prosecute the less fortunate ones. There are so many 'anti-Nazis' and 'resistance fighters' here that one should indeed wonder how Hitler ever managed to gain control of the Reich."

The letter bore a Swiss postal stamp. There was still strict censorship in Germany. Most of the letters I received from home had been mailed in Switzerland. The return address was also a Swiss post office box.

But our own world now centered on an area two miles downhill – in a Viet Minh camp. We gathered to discuss our coming operation against the guerrilla establishment, and, in general, our possible undertakings along the jungle road. Much depended on the girls. Although their loyalty could not be questioned, I ordered the customary precautions immediately after their departure. The defense perimeter of our camp was drastically altered. Sentries changed positions, machine guns and flamethrowers were removed and placed elsewhere. Our supplies were moved farther uphill. I also dispatched two hundred and fifty troops to deploy higher up in the woods. Our original establishment became a ghost camp. Whatever Noy and Thi may have seen was of no consequence now. A surprise Viet Minh attack would hit only the vacant woods.

Riedl at first took my arrangement as a "personal insult," and seemed annoyed as he commented, "Noy will never betray us, Hans." I explained to him that the girls could be captured and tortured into making admissions. They could be placed under surveillance, permitted to move about the camp, only to be shadowed on the way back to us. In our position we could not take chances. Not even if those chances were one in a million.

Although we did not dare approach too close to the jungle road, my prolonged efforts to gather intelligence had not been without results. We had spent considerable time in surveying the surrounding country, and Schulze had drawn a map of the area about five miles on either side of the Red Highway. Curiously enough it was the only accurate map ever made of the district. It was truly amazing to see how the uniform landscape, indicated on the regular maps only as forested hill-tracts, resolved itself into individual hills, valleys, ravines, and streams, revealing the vital details without which it would have been very difficult to plan an attack.

Even without Noy's report we soon agreed that a direct assault on the base should not be attempted. There were too many hidden machine guns along the road and at the foot of the hills. The eight emplacements which had been spotted by Xuey and Krebitz were likely to be only a fraction of the total number of guns deployed near the Viet Minh lifeline.

The base, however, did have its Achilles' heel. Like most of the other terrorist bases in the jungle, this one, designed to accommodate several hundred people, had been constructed at a permanent water source. A small river, about twelve feet wide, ran through the compound and this became the focal point of our attention.

Erich, who had surveyed the hills farther westward, boldly suggested that we should cut the flow of the river by blasting a dam across a deep ravine further up, about a mile and a half from our jungle hideout.

"The moment the river begins to ebb the base commander will send a party to investigate. It is the only logical thing for him to do," Erich reasoned. "Finding the river blocked with debris, the enemy will think it was due to a landslide."

"You can't blast the ravine in silence," Riedl remarked, pointing out that the distance between the enemy base and Schulze's proposed blasting site was far too short.

"We considered that," Sergeant Krebitz interposed. "What we can do is to rig the site now and then do the actual blasting during a thunderstorm. Look at the skies. . . . I think we won't be lacking storms in the coming week."

It was an ingenious idea. Fortunately my men were never short of ideas. "Time the blast for right after a close bolt of lightning and during the thunder. That way the guerrillas won't know the difference," Schulze concluded with a chuckle. He turned toward me with his brows raised. "What do you think of it, Hans?"

"I was wondering if we will have enough explosive to blast a block across the river," I said, glancing at Krebitz although I knew what his answer would be.

"I am afraid we are a bit short," he conceded. "To block the ravine we will need at least three hundred kilograms of explosives."

"How much do we have, Rudolf?"

From his hip pocket Sergeant Krebitz extracted a small wrinkled notebook. He consulted his notes briefly, then replied: "We have about eighty-six kilograms of paxite and thirty-one-point-five kilogram packs of gelignite."

"*Voilà.*" I shrugged. "We also have our problem number one."

Riedl suggested that we should try to "requisition" some explosives from the enemy. I reminded him that we wanted to avoid action in the area, especially before the river was blasted.

"Who said that we should raid them here?" Riedl exclaimed. "There are hundreds of coolies moving along the road and every one of them is carrying something. We could ambush a convoy twenty miles from here."

"Make it thirty miles," I suggested mildly. "It has to be far away from this place, Helmut."

"And make it without leaving witnesses," Schulze added. "Let one of them escape and he will spread the news. If the base is alerted, we might as well move on without doing anything."

"Are you willing to give it a try?" I asked Riedl.

"Sure, Hans." He grinned. "It will be a welcome diversion. I am kind of bored just sitting up here."

"If you hit a convoy, do a clean job. The corpses must be removed from the road."

He nodded in assent.

"How many men do you want to take?"

He glanced at Krebitz. "At least twelve from *Gruppe Drei* and the *Abwehrmannschaft*. Lots of MGs and flamethrowers," he added after a short pause.

"Flamethrowers?" Erich cut in. "You will blow up the stuff you want to loot, man."

"Don't worry. We will aim at their little toes," Riedl wisecracked, then added seriously, "it has got to be done fast and quietly. If we can fry them first, they won't be shooting back."

I suggested that he should leave early in the morning, but Riedl preferred to wait until after Noy and Thi returned. "The girls might bring important information. They might know what kind of ammo the Dan Congs are ferrying south."

"Besides you will need Noy as your interpreter," Schulze remarked.

"Could be," Riedl agreed but he cast an inquisitive glance at Erich as though not quite certain whether Schulze's remark was serious or if he was only teasing.

"With whom do you intend to converse?" Erich laughed. "You aren't supposed to take prisoners."

"All right. Let's go back to the river," I suggested. "Provided that Helmut returns with explosive and that we do manage to block the river." I turned to Schulze. "You said the guerrillas are going to send a surveying party. It is likely, for they need plenty of water. What then?"

"Hell, man, they will send hundreds of people to clear the rubble. The base will be empty, Hans."

"And then we attack it!" Riedl cut in.

"Like hell we do." Schulze chuckled. "We will permit the enemy to march into the ravine, then . . . trrrrr," he imitated the clatter of a submachine gun.

"And how about the bunkers around the base?"

"The water will take care of them."

"What water?"

From his map case, Schulze extracted a diagram and unfolded it on the ground between us. "You know that I would never insist on doing something based only on guesswork," he said. "I surveyed the ravine with Krebitz, calculating as accurately as possible without the proper instruments. We agreed that the blast should bring down enough rubble to form a block in the ravine from fourteen to sixteen meters high." He glanced up. "That is the size of a five-story building, Hans."

"Carry on."

"I believe a temporary reservoir is going to form right here." He ran his pencil across a section of his diagram. "It will be six hundred meters long and twelve meters wide. When full, the ravine could hold one hundred and twenty thousand tons of water."

"Do you think your barrage can stand the pressure?"

"I can't say that," Erich admitted, "but that's unimportant. When the pressure reaches the critical level the rubble is going to burst." He looked at me triumphantly. "Now what do you think will happen when all that water rushes downhill? It will swamp the entire rat-hole."

"And a long section of the road as well," Krebitz added.

"The water in the ravine flows at a rate of approximately seven tons per minute, Hans," Schulze continued. "Our reservoir should fill up within thirty-six hours. Since we intend to blast during a thunderstorm, the downpour will probably cut that time by half."

"How did you calculate that rate of seven tons per minute, Erich?" I asked, casually examining his diagram.

"It was very simple," he replied with a grin. "We built a one-meter by one-meter crate with a sliding door opening upward, sank it in the river, opened the door, and measured the seconds it took to fill."

"You did that, eh?"

"Sure, Hans. A one-by-one crate holds exactly one ton of water," he went on explanatorily. "The crate filled to capacity in six seconds. The width of the ravine could accommodate twelve similar crates – which would come to one hundred and twenty tons per minute or seven thousand and two hundred tons of water per hour and so on."

"And so on," I nodded, quite overwhelmed by Erich's rapid display of mathematics.

"What do you think of it?" he asked me.

I was actually thinking that one could not lose a war with companions like Erich Schulze. But I reserved final judgment until after I had seen the site myself.

Leaving the camp to Riedl and taking only twenty men along with Schulze and Krebitz, I set out for the hills. Schulze and his party had already cut a path to the ravine, so we traveled light. Even so it took us almost four hours to cover the five miles between the camp and the ravine.

The jungle appeared so peaceful it was hard to believe that it belonged to a ravaged country, where men had endeavored to exterminate their fellow men for over a decade, with still no peace in sight. Now with the terrain wide open before us, Erich explained his plan again in detail. I found it plausible. Although Sergeant Krebitz hastened to emphasize that it might be some time before Schulze's plan could be realized, we remained enthusiastic about the idea. Riedl's expedition, Sergeant Krebitz reminded us, might take a week or ten days. The mining of the ravine would also require three days of hard work and when all was ready we would have to wait until a thunderstorm came.

How long that waiting would be, no one could foretell. Our dependence on the caprice of Mother Nature was the only kink in Erich's ingenious scheme. But then, we had been searching for the Red Highway for many months. And as long as our supplies lasted, we never lacked patience. I would prefer to strike a month later and preserve the lives of my men than embark on a premature attack only to suffer casualties.

Every day small three-man patrols kept the jungle road under observation. Their reports invariably said that Viet Minh units were on the move – armed guerrillas and Dang Cong coolies. Then to our immense relief the girls returned and from their excited account I deduced that the base was indeed a major one. Apart from tons of ammunition and weapons, foodstuffs enough to sustain several regiments and five hundred bicycles had also been stored there. Bicycles were the principal transport vehicles of the Viet Minh. The quantity of material which the terrorists could load onto bicycles and transport for hundreds of miles bordered on the incredible. A three-hundred-pound load on a flimsy bike was quite common for the coolies to manage. Of course they had to walk, guiding the bike by an extra long handlebar.

There were consistently five to six hundred people in the base, Noy said. Around the compound were trenches with machine guns. "You cannot get close," the little nurse insisted. "Every path is covered and the forest is mined."

For two days the girls had worked with a group of women carrying ammunition boxes into underground shelters. "We go down seventeen wooden steps into a cellar," Thi explained. "Twelve cellars full to ceiling."

I asked them about the crates and bales which we had previously observed in stored open sheds. "Many sheds have rice, salted fish in them. Others store bullets and bicycle tires," Noy stated.

The next morning Riedl and his men departed. Noy went along with Helmut. Sergeant Krebitz and fifty troops moved to the ravine and began to prepare the blasting site. Schulze, Suoi, Corporal Altreiter, and a platoon went to prepare the site where we intended to ambush the terrorist working party. Erich selected over fifty concealed positions where machine guns and flamethrowers could be deployed to our advantage, covering not only the ravine but also the escape routes.

"We are not going to wait for the pressure to burst the barrage. It would be too chancey," Sergeant Krebitz informed me two days later. Using watertight containers, *Gruppe Drei* planted fifty pounds of high explosive in the ravine. "The charges will be buried under the rubble," Krebitz said, "ready to blast the barrage at the right moment."

Our sojourn in the woods soon became a trial. To be on the move is relaxing but to hide in the woods so close to the enemy, keeping quiet, doing nothing but watching and waiting is exasperating. The men were terribly bored. Their activities were severely restricted. There was no loud talking, no laughing, no unnecessary walking about, for even the crackling of the dry branches could have alerted a terrorist outpost, the closest of which had been detected by Krebitz barely a mile from where we camped. Fires were naturally out and our spirit cubes were insufficient for cooking a decent meal of sweet potatoes, rice, and meat. Small hunting and fishing parties, however, were constantly making forays farther west, where the silencer-equipped rifles could be used. Game was plentiful in the area. In eight days our hunting parties bagged five boars, two deer, and over a hundred jungle fowl. We weren't choosy about our meals and consumed practically everything that moved and had flesh. Hedgehogs, monkeys, snakes, and monitor lizards also belonged to our regular diet. Reptiles, as a matter of fact, taste very good and their flesh is quite tender.

Since we could light no fires in our camp, the meals had to be prepared by the hunting parties and brought back neatly portioned and roasted. One day Sergeant Krebitz suggested that we could solve our rice and potato problems, too, by carrying the stuff two miles into the woods for cooking. Thi and Chi decided that they could be of better use if they joined the hunting parties, especially when it came to the question of preparing the meals. Thereafter we enjoyed a marked improvement in the quality of our meals – the female magic touch. The girls collected sacks of wild vegetables, which proved delicious either cooked or prepared as salad with salt and spices.

Ten days went by before Riedl and his party returned upset and decidedly empty-handed. Helmut had not only failed to get explosives from the enemy but had not been able to approach the jungle road at any favorable point without severe risk. The Red Highway was expertly protected from interference on the ground.

"By God, Hans," Helmut swore, "there are at least two thousand armed Viets with nothing else to do but sit along a twenty-mile stretch on guard duty. Whenever we found a suitable place for setting an ambush we bumped into bunkers and foxholes that covered the entire area with MGs."

It was a bitter blow but I couldn't blame Riedl for the failure. The enemy was becoming wiser. Our activities behind their lines had had their effect. Unable to track us down and eliminate us for good, the Viet Minh decided to play it safe along their vital lifeline from China. We learned a few months later that Giap had deployed over sixty thousand guerrillas along the six-hundred-mile-long Red Highway with nothing else to do but protect it.

Riedl had acted wisely when he decided not to rush an attack that could alert the enemy and fail in the process. We all looked to Sergeant Krebitz for a solution.

"Well, Rudolf, it is all up to you now," Schulze said hopefully. "We have come a long way to do a great job. It would be a pity to turn back now."

"I cannot shit gelignite, Erich," he replied crudely.

"Can't we do something with what we have?" I asked.

Krebitz screwed up his lips and gave a low chuckle. "With what we have? We have already buried most of it in the ravine."

"Any other solution?"

"Request an air drop."

"We can't have planes coming here, and to embark on another thirty-mile expedition. . . ."

"Then I can see no other way but to strip the battalion, Hans."

"Strip it of what? Revolver bullets?"

"Hand grenades."

"Why, hell!" Erich exclaimed. "That is the solution. Everybody still carries grenades."

"Sure, but it's me who will have to rig them up piece by piece," Krebitz grunted.

"Do you think it will work, Rudolf?"

"One can always try!"

Soon Krebitz had a neat pile of over seventeen hundred grenades. "Here you are, Rudolf," Riedl exclaimed with great enthusiasm. "You have all the explosives on earth. If you need any help just say so."

"You're most welcome," said Krebitz, slapping Helmut on the shoulder. "Now all you have to do is to get your can opener, cut the shells, and scrape the candy into a rucksack. But don't blow yourself up in the process."

Three days later the ravine was set for blasting. All we needed was a thunderstorm. One finally came eleven days later and marked our thirty-third day in the woods, "sitting it out" only two miles from the Red Highway. The moment the first thunder cracked the troops began to move out to take their positions along the ravine. It did not start to rain until well in the afternoon when lightning bolt after lightning bolt illuminated the rolling clouds. Soon it sounded as though the skies were about to split apart. Synchronized with a savage thunderbolt, Krebitz plunged the detonator lever. The roaring thunder obliterated the explosions and had we not seen the flames we would have thought the charges had misfired. The rocky precipices tumbled down, triggering a landslide which filled the river up to fifty feet high. On the far side of the barricade the water began to rise rapidly.

The following noon a scouting party of twelve guerrillas was spotted wading upstream in the now barely trickling river. It was still raining but our dam held firm. We permitted the Viet Minh party to proceed right up to the dam and then to return to base without being molested. Just as Schulze had predicted, a large working party of about four hundred men arrived the day after, carrying demolition tools and satchels of explosive. Luckily it was still raining. The downpour deadened the sound of the machine guns. Confined in the ravine the enemy had no chance of fighting back. Most of them carried no weapons, only picks and spades. When they turned to flee, Riedl and his gunners were ready for them a mile downstream.

In twenty minutes the battle was over. The afternoon went by with no signs of another Viet Minh sortie from the base. At nine P.M. our dam sprang more leaks and looked ready to collapse. To prevent an ineffective partial burst, Sergeant Krebitz decided to blast the reservoir free. Carrying tons of rocks and broken timber, the torrent rushed downhill. Still swollen fifteen feet high when it reached the jungle road, the flood hit the guerrilla base with the force of a tidal wave. It was already dark so our observers witnessed little of the actual impact of the flood, but when we focused our binoculars the next morning on the enclosure I saw nothing but piles of debris amidst a shimmering swamp.

18

The Last Battle (Operation "Firefly")

We left the area immediately, refraining from harassing the enemy along the road. We ignored half a dozen smaller transit camps, guerrilla checkpoints, and convoys in order to deny the Viet Minh a chance to determine our direction and our next target. A week's trekking over very difficult terrain put a good forty miles between the swamped enemy base and ourselves. Our route took us up and down across a chain of steep ridges, some of which we had to climb to the summit, past the three-thousand-foot mark. We blazed our own trails most of the time, since that was the only way to avoid a few primitive tribal settlements whose inhabitants were alien even to our girls, and whose language none of us could understand. No one knew where the loyalty of the tribesmen might lie. I thought it prudent to avoid them altogether. Had we used their comfortable hunting trails, we could have made a faster journey but we would also have met with tribal hunters whom we would have had to kill in order to remain undetected in the area. News in the jungle can travel almost as fast as a teletype message.

The battalion stuck to the unbroken woods. Hampered by thorny thickets of wiry bracken and stingy shrubs which flourished with incredible vitality, we made our way. That ten days of trekking was probably more trying than a two-hundred-mile march on an open road. Yet even in the unbroken woods we came upon a small clearing with a primitive hovel, where a young tribal woman was looking after five naked children, all ridden with festering sores. Our sudden appearance terrified her, and she burst out in a torrent of high-pitched words which not even Noy could understand. Gathering her children, she was ready to flee into the woods when the sight of our girl companions quieted her fears. With some effort and by using at least as many signs as words, Noy succeeded in making contact with a female human being from the Stone Age. Her husband had been away hunting in the woods for five days. The family lived entirely on what the forest provided. They grew nothing themselves and had not seen money for years. The woman had no idea of a war going on in the country. Occasionally she saw armed people moving along the path down in the valley, sometimes as many as ten times ten armed bandits (she explained by showing ten times her opened palms). They were neither white-faced nor as tall as we were. To her all armed men were bandits (including ourselves) and the words Viet Minh, Ho Chi Minh, Hanoi, French, Foreign Legion, army, terrorists, etc., had no meaning at all.

When we arrived, the woman had been frying a jungle fowl in the green sauce of a variety of wild vegetables. She offered us a portion of the meal which we gently refused, pointing out that there were enough mouths for her to feed. Schulze presented her with a small bag of salt – something very valuable in the jungle – and a pack of tobacco for her husband.

Suoi and the nurses treated the sores of the children, the eldest of whom was only about seven years old. They cleaned their festering ulcers, and Noy gave a jar of antibiotic ointment to the woman, explaining to her that she should repeat the treatment every day for at least a week. Sergeant Zeisl donated a box of vitamin pills. It took some time until the woman understood that only one pill per child per day should be used, and that she should hide the container from the children.

She wanted to return our kindness. She led us to a narrow concealed path. Motioning for the girls and me to follow her, she descended about a hundred yards to where a small creek formed a large deep pool. It teemed with fish and the woman gestured that we should take as many as we wanted. We spent the better part of the day spearing and netting fish, for I did not want to spoil their pond by using explosive charges – our customary and much faster way of fishing. We had a splendid meal of rice with curried fish. From Krebitz's rucksack came a few small toys; each child received something. We departed as good friends. Our hostess agreed that we were not "bandits," although it was quite obvious that she could place us in no other category of manhood. The words "army" and "soldier" had no meaning for her.

The husband had not returned before we left but the woman was not worried about him. Tribal hunters would often undertake long trips which lasted for days. In a way, I was sorry for his prolonged absence, for even by using sign language we could have obtained valuable intelligence from the man, who traveled a great deal in the area. But as the date of his return was uncertain, I decided to push on.

After three more days of tortuous going, during which we drew a distorted semicircle through the hills, we closed in once again on the Viet Minh lifeline. It ran close to the town of Muong Ham, and from there it turned sharply eastward to skirt Paksane along the Khong River. Krebitz and twelve men from *Gruppe Drei* discovered another large guerrilla base which, apart from regular supplies, also harbored twenty to thirty large river barges. Everything was covered with green and well hidden from air reconnaissance. Closer observation revealed that the camp was not a depot for storing barges but rather a manufacturing complex to produce them. So it was another valuable target!

Like the other base, this, too, had been erected in a spacious depression between a chain of forested hills, but here we found no river that crossed the camp, and any thought of repeating our previous coup could be discarded. A direct attack might have been successful, but it would have also been costly. Such large guerrilla establishments accommodated several hundred terrorists and the approaches were properly defended.

We spent a couple of days surveying the neighborhood. The lower hills, immediately around the base, were all occupied by Viet Minh lookouts. The higher elevations, five to six hundred yards from the camp, were vacant. Without wasting time we occupied those with sharp platoons. I was already nursing the idea of trying there an as yet unexploited ruse: A night raid by fighter bombers. I told Erich about my idea. His only comment was: "Are you having a sunstroke or something, Hans?"

Indeed the idea sounded like a crazy one – a night attack by planes against a target that was invisible beneath the thick foliage even during the daytime. I reminded Schulze that when he came to me with his flooding scheme, I gave him a chance to convince me. He wouldn't agree with my comparison. "I came to you with all the details worked out," he protested.

"What makes you think that I haven't worked out my own details, Erich?"

"Because I think that there aren't any details to be worked out, Hans. The planes can never find the base, not even if we guide them by radio," Erich insisted.

"I have something better to guide them with than radios," I replied, inviting him to sit down. He dropped to a tree stump.

"Can you bring the planes to the target?"

"On the bull's-eye, Erich."

It was very simple. We would place heavy MGs on the dominant hills, six hundred yards around the base, and mark the target area within the convergence of tracers. To illustrate my idea, I drew a crude sketch and soon both Schulze and Krebitz agreed that it could be done. Henceforth we referred to similar actions only as "boxing in" the target. It turned out to be an entirely new concept of cooperation between a ground force and the air force – at night.

I sent a long coded report to Colonel Houssong, giving more details about the Red Highway and explaining my plan for a bombing raid. Three days later I received the go-ahead with the instructions: "Mission No. 1 of Operation Firefly will commence on Wednesday at 0200 hours."

I knew that everything would depend on the effectiveness of the on-the-spot guidance. Our only long-range transmitter would have to be set up on a hilltop twelve miles from the target area, to transmit a steady beam on which the planes could ride home. This would bring them in close enough to receive the final coordinates on the spot. It would be imprudent to use a transmitter any closer to our target.

On D-Day, Sergeant Altreiter and twenty men departed for "Hill 811" to establish the radio beam. We deployed on Hills

"1022" and "1023" before sunset; Schulze and forty troops occupied the former, and I with fifty troops the latter elevation. Riedl and the rest of the men remained in the camp.

Early in the afternoon the clouds began to thicken and by five P.M. the sky was overcast. To our great relief it did not rain and although the moon remained hidden, the raid still had a fair chance of success. The enemy base lay perfectly still and concealed beneath the jungle foliage – a dark shape that expanded into infinity. Our MGs had been sighted during the day and were now locked firmly in position. When fired, the lines of tracers would converge to "box in" the enemy camp.

The hours dragged by in tense expectation until shortly after one-thirty A.M., when we heard a faint drone which gradually resolved into the roar of approaching planes. The squadron was coming.

A few steps from where I stood our machine gunners tensed. Others were holding their signal pistols ready. Moments later the foremost planes were within range of our walkie-talkies.

"*Oiseaux – Oiseaux* . . . firefly on yellow very lights. Waterfall within quadrangle . . . waterfall within quadrangle."

"*Septeuil – Septeuil* . . . message received. Signal time 0146. Coming in."

The very lights shot skyward, drawing lazy semicircles over the jungle.

"Fire!"

The MGs erupted with a vicious clatter, spitting a hail of tracers over the treetops – taut lines of fire, as though burning wires were stretched between the hills. An instant later Schulze opened up from Hill 1022. His tracers converged with ours. The gunners under Krebitz joined the display. Even from our position, we could clearly see the quadrangle of steel which now enclosed the invisible Viet Minh base. It was a magnificent sight.

With engines howling at high pitch, the fighter bombers screamed over the hills. Another set of MGs took over the marking and the jungle erupted in a multitude of explosions. The first salvo of bombs went home. Demolition bombs, rockets, and napalm rained from the skies. In a few minutes the forest was an inferno.

"*Septeuil – Septeuil*," the squadron leader called. "Cut out the markers. It is bright enough now."

We stopped firing.

The planes came in one after another. More bombs, more rockets, more napalm. Secondary explosions began to rock the hills. Hundred-foot flames and grey smoke rose from the valley. The forest that had hidden the Viet Minh base so conveniently now became a sea of flames. Where we stood at six hundred yards away, we could read the engraved serial numbers on our guns.

The raid lasted for only twenty minutes. When the planes departed the base no longer existed. "Just give the French a chance and they will do a magnificent job," one of my gunners remarked appraisingly. "Look at that valley . . . none of their bombs went off target."

I called Schulze and Krebitz and told them to move closer to the target. Our descent was easy, as the entire hillside was now bathed in light. Along the edge of the inferno we spotted small groups of running shapes: the survivors. We approached the jungle road as close as the heat permitted us, then began to pour bullets into everything that still appeared to move, not quite knowing if our targets were fleeing terrorists, panicked animals, or only some crazily waving bushes illuminated by the fire.

We moved on, skirting the Red Highway, dealing death and destruction as we went, not knowing that those were our last weeks of glory in Indochina.

For our last battle we lost.

It was not Viet Minh guns that ended the saga of the Headhunters . . . just as it was not the Red Army of Stalin which defeated the German Wehrmacht. The Wehrmacht had been defeated in the Hinterlands. We were defeated in Paris – in the Chamber of Deputies.

Having realized that they couldn't beat us in the hills, the enemy embarked on a last desperate offensive. Not only the Viet Minh but the entire Communist world joined forces to win that final and decisive battle. It was not to be fought with machine guns but with printing presses, radios, and loudspeakers – and not in the jungles of Indochina but in the capitals of the world.

"SS marauders in the French Foreign Legion massacre innocent civilians," the Communist press screamed.

"Hitler's scum at large in Indochina."

"How long will the French government tolerate?"

"Outrage! Outrage!"

And what the regiments of Ho Chi Minh could not achieve in five years the international Communist fifth column accomplished in five weeks.

We were ordered to return to Hanoi.

The consternation among the international Communist parties could be well understood. "The SS marauders" had arrived at the principal Viet Minh highway between China and Saigon. Six vital guerrilla bases had already been destroyed. In manpower and material, the Viet Minh losses were enormous. The fate of the whole "liberation" movement in the south was at stake. They had to stop us – at any price.

So the battalion was disbanded. The ranks, with time to serve, were incorporated into the various mixed units of the Foreign Legion. Those who had already "worked overtime" could choose between transfer or resignation. We resigned. We were free to leave and the world suddenly seemed wide open. Only then did it occur to us that we were French citizens, officers and honorable reservists of the Army of the Republic. *Vive la République!*

When Erich Schulze married Suoi in a civilian ceremony, he no longer needed a *permis* from the forces. Nor did Helmut Riedl need one to hear the happy "I do" from the little Indochinese nurse Noy.

A few weeks after our departure, Colonel Simon Houssong handed in his own resignation. Not because he was a Nazi or because his former SS marauders were embarrassing him now. The colonel was a true patriot, and we regarded him a great soldier who did not feel like becoming a member of a team which might be compelled to sign the articles of surrender. "For whatever they may call it, it will be surrender," I remember him saying. The colonel thought that France had signed enough articles of surrender – on the wrong side of the table.

The "Battalion of the Damned" had ceased to exist. It lived exactly 1,243 days, during which it destroyed 7,466 guerrillas by body count, 221 Viet Minh bases, supply dumps, and camps; it liberated three hundred and eleven military and civilian prisoners from terrorist captivity and covered roughly 11,000 kilometers on foot.

We lost 515 men – for us a very heavy loss indeed.

Once again the guns of Nguyen Giap could roll freely. The jungle trails became highways and the forts of the Foreign Legion turned into graveyards. The French soldiers could fight bravely and go down gloriously. They were not permitted to win. They had been stabbed in the back again, as they had been so many times in the past, by their own superiors, by their own government.

Seven hundred days later came Dien Bien Phu, but the Indochina war did not end there. It did not end with the fall of Hanoi and the loss of the northern territories either.

It went on. . . . It is still going on. . . . It will go on for a long time to come. . . .

NEL BESTSELLERS

Crime

T031 306	THE UNPLEASANTNESS AT THE BELLONA CLUB	*Dorothy L. Sayers*	85p
T031 373	STRONG POISON	*Dorothy L. Sayers*	80p
T032 884	FIVE RED HERRINGS	*Dorothy L. Sayers*	75p

Fiction

T034 879	CRUSADER'S TOMB	*A. J. Cronin*	£1.00
T034 925	HATTER'S CASTLE	*A. J. Cronin*	£1.50
T027 228	THE SPANISH GARDNER	*A. J. Cronin*	45p
T013 936	THE JUDAS TREE	*A. J. Cronin*	50p
T015 386	THE NORTHERN LIGHT	*A. J. Cronin*	50p
T034 755	THE CITADEL	*A. J. Cronin*	£1.10
T027 112	BEYOND THIS PLACE	*A. J. Cronin*	60p
T016 609	KEYS OF THE KINGDOM	*A. J. Cronin*	60p
T029 158	THE STARS LOOK DOWN	*A. J. Cronin*	£1.00
T034 852	THREE LOVES	*A. J. Cronin*	£1.25
T031 594	THE LONELY LADY	*Harold Robbins*	£1.25
T038 114	THE DREAM MERCHANTS	*Harold Robbins*	£1.50
T031 705	THE PIRATE	*Harold Robbins*	£1.00
T033 791	THE CARPETBAGGERS	*Harold Robbins*	£1.25
T035 239	WHERE LOVE HAS GONE	*Harold Robbins*	£1.25
T032 647	THE ADVENTURERS	*Harold Robbins*	£1.25
T038 130	THE INHERITORS	*Harold Robbins*	£1.25
T035 427	STILETTO	*Harold Robbins*	£1.00
T038 092	NEVER LEAVE ME	*Harold Robbins*	£1.00
T032 698	NEVER LOVE A STRANGER	*Harold Robbins*	95p
T032 531	A STONE FOR DANNY FISHER	*Harold Robbins*	90p
T037 053	79 PARK AVENUE	*Harold Robbins*	£1.25
T038 084	THE BETSY	*Harold Robbins*	£1.25
T035 689	RICH MAN, POOR MAN	*Irwin Shaw*	£1.50
T034 720	EVENING IN BYZANTIUM	*Irwin Shaw*	85p
T031 330	THE MAN	*Irving Wallace*	£1.50
T034 283	THE PRIZE	*Irving Wallace*	£1.50
T033 376	THE PLOT	*Irving Wallace*	£1.25
T030 253	THE THREE SIRENS	*Irving Wallace*	£1.25
T033 171	SEVEN MINUTES	*Irving Wallace*	£1.25

Historical

T022 250	THE LADY FOR A RANSOM	*Alfred Duggan*	50p
T017 958	FOUNDING FATHERS	*Alfred Duggan*	50p
T035 050	LEOPARDS AND LILIES	*Alfred Duggan*	90p
T035 131	LORD GEOFFREY'S FANCY	*Alfred Duggan*	75p
T024 903	THE KING OF ATHELNEY	*Alfred Duggan*	60p
T032 817	FOX 1: PRESS GANG	*Adam Hardy*	50p
T032 825	FOX 2: PRIZE MONEY	*Adam Hardy*	50p
T032 833	FOX 3: SIEGE	*Adam Hardy*	50p
T032 841	FOX 4: TREASURE	*Adam Hardy*	50p
T028 092	FOX 14: CLOSE QUARTERS	*Adam Hardy*	50p

Science Fiction

T027 724	SCIENCE FICTION ART	*Brian Aldiss*	£2.95
T030 245	TIME ENOUGH FOR LOVE	*Robert Heinlein*	£1.25
T034 674	STRANGER IN A STRANGE LAND	*Robert Heinlein*	£1.20
T037 045	I WILL FEAR NO EVIL	*Robert Heinlein*	£1.20
T030 467	STARMAN JONES	*Robert Heinlein*	75p
T026 817	THE HEAVEN MAKERS	*Frank Herbert*	35p
T035 697	DUNE	*Frank Herbert*	£1.25

T032 663	DUNE MESSIAH	*Frank Herbert*	75p
T023 974	THE GREEN BRAIN	*Frank Herbert*	35p
T023 265	EMPIRE OF THE ATOM	*A. E. Van Vogt*	40p
T027 473	THE FAR OUT WORLD OF A. E. VAN VOGT	*A. E. Van Vogt*	50p
War			
T027 066	COLDITZ: THE GERMAN STORY	*Reinhold Eggers*	50p
T020 827	COLDITZ RECAPTURED	*Reinhold Eggers*	50p
T012 999	PQ 17 - CONVOY TO HELL	*Lund & Ludlam*	30p
T026 299	TRAWLERS GO TO WAR	*Lund & Ludlam*	50p
T025 438	LILIPUT FLEET	*A. Cecil Hampshire*	50p
Western			
T017 892	EDGE 12: THE BIGGEST BOUNTY	*George Gilman*	30p
T023 931	EDGE 13: A TOWN CALLED HATE	*George Gilman*	35p
T033 945	EDGE 14: THE BIG GOLD	*George Gilman*	60p
T022 706	EDGE 16: THE FINAL SHOT	*George Gilman*	35p
T024 881	EDGE 17: VENGEANCE VALLEY	*George Gilman*	40p
T026 604	EDGE 18: TEN TOMBSTONES TO TEXAS	*George Gilman*	40p
T028 135	EDGE 19: ASHES AND DUST	*George Gilman*	40p
T029 042	EDGE 20: SULLIVAN'S LAW	*George Gilman*	45p
T029 387	EDGE 21: RHAPSODY IN RED	*George Gilman*	50p
T030 350	EDGE 22: SLAUGHTER ROAD	*George Gilman*	50p
General			
T020 592	SLAVE REBELLION	*Norman Davids*	35p
T033 155	SEX MANNERS FOR MEN	*Robert Chartham*	60p
T023 206	THE BOOK OF LOVE	*Dr David Delvin*	90p
T028 828	THE LONG BANANA SKIN	*Michael Bentine*	90p
Mad			
N862 185	DAVE BERG LOOKS AT LIVING		70p
N861 812	MAD BOOK OF WORLD POWER		70p
N766 895	MORE MAD ABOUT SPORTS		70p

NEL P.O. BOX 11, FALMOUTH TR10 9EN, CORNWALL:

For U.K.: Customers should include to cover postage, 19p for the first book plus 9p per copy for each additional book ordered up to a maximum charge of 73p.

For B.F.P.O. and Eire: Customers should include to cover postage, 19p for the first book plus 9p per copy for the next 6 and thereafter 3p per book.

For Overseas: Customers should include to cover postage, 20p for the first book plus 10p per copy for each additional book.

Name ....

Address ....

....

Title ....
(Sept)

While every effort is made to keep prices low, it is sometimes necessary to increase prices at short notice. New English Library reserves the right to show on covers and charge new retail prices which may differ from those advertised in the text or elsewhere.